A CATHOLIC HISTORY

OF

ALABAMA AND THE
FLORIDAS

A CATHOLIC HISTORY

OF

ALABAMA AND THE FLORIDAS

BY

MOTHER MARY A. CARROLL,
A MEMBER OF THE ORDER OF MERCY

BOOKS FOR LIBRARIES PRESS
FREEPORT, NEW YORK

First Published 1908
Reprinted 1970

STANDARD BOOK NUMBER:
8369-5417-3

LIBRARY OF CONGRESS CATALOG CARD NUMBER:
70-124228

PRINTED IN THE UNITED STATES OF AMERICA

CONTENTS.

3

4

CONTENTS.

CHAPTER III.

PAGE

CHAPTER IV.

CHAPTER V.

CHAPTER VI.

CONTENTS. 5

CONTENTS.

CONTENTS.

CONTENTS. 15

CHAPTER XLIV.

CHAPTER XLV.

CHAPTER XLVI.

CHAPTER XLVII.

CONTENTS. 17

2

CHAPTER LIII.

CHAPTER LIV.

DEDICATION

TO

THE MEMBERS
OF THE
CATHOLIC HIERARCHY AND CLERGY
THE SUCCESSORS
OF THE
HUMBLE, SAINTLY APOSTOLIC MEN
WHO, IN THE PAST
LABORED SO ZEALOUSLY AND FAITHFULLY
AMID PRIVATIONS AND HARDSHIPS
INNUMERABLE
EVEN TO THE SHEDDING OF THEIR BLOOD
TO PROPAGATE THEIR FAITH
IN ALABAMA AND THE FLORIDAS
THIS WORK
COMMEMORATING THE GLORIOUS DEEDS
OF THESE
NOBLE PIONEERS OF CATHOLICITY
IS
MOST REVERENTLY INSCRIBED
IN THE HOPE
THAT THEIR SUCCESSORS
MAY BRING BACK TO THE FOLD OF CHRIST
THE STRAYED SHEEP
LIVING IN THE REGIONS
SANCTIFIED BY THEIR PRAYERS
AND LABORS

PREFACE.

———

This history is due chiefly to the inspiration of the eminent Bishop of Mobile, Right Rev. Dr. Allen, who has taken a deep interest in the work, and placed at our disposal the Registers of the ancient Parish of Mobile, and his valuable library. Despite his numerous avocations, he has always found leisure to encourage the writer, and aid her with many judicious Apostolic suggestions.

His Excellency, Most Rev. Archbishop Chapelle, Apostolic Delegate, gave the writer much encouragement to undertake this work. His illustrious successor, Most Rev. James Hubert Blenk, made interest with his clergy to procure us special assistance. From this source we obtained information not otherwise procurable, especially from Right Rev. Monsignor Laval V.G. and Rev. Father Chambone. Right Rev. Bishop Heslin, who has long honored us with his friendship, kindly allowed us access to many valuable letters and diaries connected with the important diocese of Natchez.

To John W. Fairfax, Esq., we owe many privileges as, admission to public records and files of old papers in New Orleans. This gentleman has taken a steady interest in our work, and given us valuable aid in many ways.

23

Very Rev. Father Girardey, C.SS.R., to whom we are indebted in ways innumerable, found time to read our manuscript. Despite his almost incessant toil, he gave us useful suggestions from his wide experience as a writer and publisher of excellent works.

We have sought information wherever it could be found, though, in the interest of conciseness, authorities are frequently mentioned as they occur in the text.

Among the works consulted are: Shea's Histories, Colonial Mobile, The Colonization of the South, and The Anglo-Saxon Border, by Peter Joseph Hamilton, Esq., of Mobile, Crétineau Joly, (especially Vol. 2.), Gayarré's works, and many works on Alabama and Florida by Pickens, Campbell, etc.

We are deeply indebted to the Ursulines of New Orleans and the Visitandines of Mobile, for information not to be found elsewhere.

It is a pleasure to us to mention Mr. T. P. Thompson, of New Orleans, who placed his unique private library at our disposal; and Mr. Hamilton of Mobile, who did us a similar favor. Also, the Public Libraries, as the Howard, etc., in which we were received with unvarying courtesy by the officials.

Though unable from want of space to mention all from whom we have received favors, we shall ever cherish the memory of their kindness. Nor should we omit from our benefactors the name of that sterling Catholic gentleman, Thomas Fitzwilliam, Esq., of New Orleans.

A CATHOLIC HISTORY

OF,

ALABAMA AND THE FLORIDAS.

CHAPTER I.

THE history of Alabama goes back further than the histories of most other States of what is now the American Union. Not to speak of the aborigines who, though often powerful, and skilled in savage warfare, kept no records, this history begins with the invasion of its broad plains by the renowned Spanish Cavalier, (1540) Hernando de Soto, a native of Xeres. This Hidalgo had already had his baptism of fire in the New World. He had been the companion of Pizarro in the conquest of the incas in Peru, and was celebrated on two continents for his extraordinary valor.

It was thus, according to a cherished tradition, that Alabama received its name. A band of Indians who quitted Mexico during the upheavals consequent on the arrival of the famous ship-burner, Cortez, wander-inging eastward in search of a new home, reached the noble river now known as the Alabama. Their chieftain, charmed with the wondrous beauty of the forest scenery, gave the signal to halt, and drawing up under the shade of a magnificent oak, struck his spear in the ground, and exclaimed, with enthusiasm:

" Alabama ! " which being interpreted, means : " Here we rest ! "

The motto on the great Seal of the State of Alabama is : " Alabama ! " " Here we rest ! "

It is also said that this State takes its name from the tribe of Alibamons : " Soft is thy name, Alabama ; and sweet is thy flower-laden gale."

Alabama, said by an Indian scholar to mean " vegetation gatherers," was applied to those who cleared the forest for crops.

From successful fighting in South America, De Soto had returned to his native land, a man of high renown, as a soldier of fortune, and of fabulous wealth. After tasting of all the honor and glory Spain could bestow on her distinguished son, De Soto, athirst for greater fame, besought the powerful Emperor, Charles V. to allow him to seek fresh laurels in the lands beyond the sea, and to fight, at his own expense, for the opulent cities and splendid empires which his vivid imagination saw scattered over the arid plains and mountain fastnesses of the New Continent.

The Emperor, full of admiration for the brave soldier, willingly granted his request and showered honors and dignities upon him. He created him a Knight of the Military Order of St. Iago, and made him Captain-General of Cuba, and perpetual Adelentado of Florida. The Emperor, indeed, made it a chief condition of his grant that " De Soto should carry and bear with him the Religious and priests who shall be appointed by us for the instruction of the natives in our holy Catholic Faith."

De Soto's army was one of the most splendid that ever set out by the Water Gate of Seville. It included more than two hundred horses, animals which the Indians had never yet seen. His star had long been in the ascendant, and now reached its zenith.

He was accompanied by his newly married wife, Isabella de Bobadilla. They set sail, April 6, 1538, and stopped for fresh provisions at the Canary Islands. In due time the expedition reached the harbor of Santiago de Cuba.

The young couple having had to leave Spain hurriedly, celebrated their nuptials in Havana, with balls, tournaments, banquets, and games. By spring all was ready for the voyage to Florida. He installed Doña Isabella, Gouvernante of Cuba, bade her a tender farewell, and, embarking in his flag ship, sailed out into the bright waters of the Mexican Gulf. Messages were exchanged, as opportunity offered, between De Soto and Isabella.

After a voyage full of variety and adventure, the Adelentado found himself, with one thousand picked soldiers, and all the munitions of war within the limits of the State of Alabama.

Mobile,[1] the oldest and most historic of Alabama's towns has a name which sounds strangely in European ears, and seems to suggest a shifting city. It is not, however, derived from anything connected with mobility, but from a tribe of Indians whose lands stretched from the coast far into the interior. Near a bluff on the Alabama, stood their most important town, Mauvila, the strongly fortified residence of their

---

[1] The Chatats, a small tribe residing near Mobile, later embraced the Catholic religion, as did also the Thornez. They, with the remnant who survived the invasion of De Soto, were called by the French, to whom they were devoted, " Mobile Indians." They worshipped the true God. —Du Pratz's *Louisiana.*

Emperor, Tuskaloosa, the black warrior. From this powerful cacique, who made a desperate stand against the invaders, and perished, while defending his ancestral domains, a former capital of Alabama, Tuskaloosa, (The Druid City) is named. Mauvila was fortified with block houses and palisades.

The historian, Garcilasso de las Vegas, says that the Mauvilians lost, in the conflict, nearly 11,000 warriors. Their name is perpetuated in the Gulf City, a name suggestive of martial daring and heroic deeds. It became Maubila in the mouth of the Spaniards, who sounded *v* as *b,* a pronunciation lately condemned by the Spanish Academy. From the French we have Mobile.

The awful battle between the ferocious soldiers of the proud and cunning giant King, Tuskaloosa, and the pale-faced strangers, raged all day, October 18, 1539, fire being added to its horrors. The city became a smoking ruin. So dreadful was the slaughter that Bancroft writes: " I know not if a more bloody Indian fight ever occurred on the soil of the United States."

Eighteen Spaniards were killed, and one hundred and fifty wounded, while thousands of natives were left dead on the field. Several lesser fights followed, for the Indians were implacably hostile. The Spaniards required some time to recuperate. But, as an ancient King of Epirus said of a triumph that cost him much: " One more such victory, and I am undone," the Captain-General might have said when he looked at the broken ranks of his once magnificent army, all but annihilated by various causes, some time later.

The site of De Soto's great battle has not yet been

accurately located. It is commonly thought to have been fought near Choctaw Bluff, on the Alabama, though some place it on the Tombigbee, and even on the Mobile River.

In an interesting pamphlet, Mrs. Henry C. Semple, who is well acquainted with the topography of these regions says, p. 21.

"A late historian locates the old Indian city of thirty or forty thousand, within three miles of our house on the Alabama River, at "Frenche's Landing," the same that was destroyed by De Soto, leaving few to tell the tale. A Spanish settlement was made in Clarke County, one hundred years before the Pilgrims landed on Plymouth Rock."

Mrs. Semple was one of the first Catholics in Clarke County. She writes: "I was baptized, received Holy Communion, and was confirmed, by Bishop Portier of Mobile, 1851, for which I have thanked God ever since. I was married, November 22, 1848, by Father Rampon, a Catholic priest. Mr. Semple was received into the Church one year before our marriage." "Nowhere are there more beautiful watercourses than in Clarke County."

"On one of our fishing excursions we saw men in their beaded costumes, spearing the fish when the water was so clear, that shoals of them could be seen near the surface. The banks were lined with wild flowers that came out early in spring. Indian mounds abounded." [1]

1 Reminiscences of my Early Life.

Mrs. Semple says, incidentally, that there was a Spanish Settlement in this place, (Clarke Co.) one hundred years before the Pilgrim Fathers landed on Plymouth Rock, the traditional Blarney Stone of New England.

CHAPTER II.

Towards the opening of spring 1541, the Spaniards resumed their march until they came to the Mississippi, which they crossed, May 5. After traversing the country during the summer, they wintered on the banks of the Wachita, and passed down that river to the Mississippi. Certain it is that De Soto's men did not follow up their advantages. They wandered far from the scene of their glory and disaster. Their wanderings have never been accurately described. Wearied by their toilsome marches through the wilderness, the splendid army reduced to a mere handful, the Captain paused at the great river, below the mouth of the Arkansas, little knowing how tragically his last journey was to end for himself.

His health had sunk entirely under the conflict of emotions. His spirits were broken, and a malignant fever, which never left him, threatened to cut him off in the vigor of his manhood. The prostrate warrior knew that this meant death. As a soldier and as a Christian, he began to prepare for the dread hour which was soon to place him before the judgment-seat of his God and Creator. What follows seems like a passage from the Lives of the Saints.

He confessed his sins with lively sorrow and humble hope of forgiveness, through the merits of Christ. He summoned the officers of his council, and the chief men of his army. He gazed lovingly on them as they surrounded his poor bed, and told them he was going to give an account, in the presence of God, of all his past life. He thanked his gracious Saviour for calling him to himself. He expressed gratitude for their love and their loyalty to him, and said he had intended to reward them when it should please God to give him rest and prosperity. He begged them all to pray for him to God that, in his mercy, He would forgive his sins and receive him into eternal glory. He asked pardon for any wrong he might have done them, or others, as their Captain or fellow soldier.

He had many things to say to them, but above all he charged them *to prosecute the conversion of the natives to the Catholic Faith.* This was the chief ambition of the great men of these times who would compass sea and land, to make a proselyte. And he prayed them most tenderly, to live in peace and love with one another. As for the restitution which, under other circumstances, he might have been obliged to make, if he had not done so already, no doubt his confessor reassured and consoled him, for he was now as poor as the poorest.

Next day, May 21, 1542, the seventh of his illness, he died, grieving for his sins, but full of confidence in the merits of Christ and his mercy. "And thus," concludes the chronicler, "departed out of this life, the valorous, chivalrous, and most noble Captain, Don Hernando de Soto, Governor of Cuba, and Adelentado of Florida, whom fortune raised, as it had done many others, only that he might have the higher fall. The danger of his followers perishing without him in that country was clear before their eyes, and they grieved that they had borne ill will to him, or that they had not held him in the esteem they ought to have done.

And now as they wept over their great chief, they recalled his courteous, engaging manners, his humane and merciful treatment of them, his bravery and high courage, his patience in every toil and hardship, his deeds of daring—how he had fought five hours standing in his stirrup at Mauvila, and one hour in a loose saddle at Chickasaw. They might have added his patience in grievous illness, his resignation when everything went against him—his fortune gone, swallowed up in this ill-fated enterprise—his fame, his hope of family, and the great estate he was to found—all had vanished as the dream of a dream, and only shadows were left behind.

The new Captain, Luis Muscoso, chosen in deference to the wish of the fallen Adelentado, decided to conceal his death from the Indians. He ordered that the corpse be kept hidden in the house for three days. At midnight, the priests, officers, and cavaliers, carried the dead commander, to an open space outside the village, and laid him in a deep pit which they filled with earth.

But the Spaniards were uneasy. The Indians were watching their movements, and the Spaniards knew that if the watchers suspected the burial of a body among their pits, they would, if necessary, dig up the whole plain with their hands, and never rest until they had found it. And should they find the conqueror of their great chief, Tuskaloosa, they would wreak upon him dead, the vengeance they dare not think of in his presence, living.

Then came the inspiration to bury the Captain-General in the great river which he had discovered,

where alone, in these wilds, his remains would be safe
from savage insult. They found in the channel a
depth of many fathoms, and there they resolved to
make his grave. As there were no stones with which
to weight the body, they caused an enormous oak to
be felled. In the trunk of this they hollowed out a
cavity, about the size of a man's body.

The next night the Adelentado was disinterred with
all possible secrecy, and placed in the oak, as in a
coffin, amid the tears and prayers of his bereaved followers. "They steadfastly gazed on the face of the
dead," and reverently closed the opening. Priests and
cavaliers carried all to mid-stream, and recommending
to God with all possible fervor the soul of their great
Captain, with the touching prayers of the Church he
had loved so well, they dropped their precious burden
overboard, and watched it sinking into the wonderful
waters he had discovered. "He fell in the wilderness," says McGee, "and the sorrowing Mississippi
took him, in pity, to her breast." He died beneath
the shadow of the cross he had planted on its banks.
His body, wrapped in his poor mantle, was consigned
to its depths. "He had crossed a large portion of
the continent," says Bancroft, "and found nothing so
remarkable as his burial place."

The first *Requiems* sung above the eddies of the
great river were for the eternal repose of the valiant
De Soto. And who can look into the depths of that
grave, even in spirit, without thinking of the loyal
Catholic Knight who found rest beneath its turgid
waters, and repeating the simple, holy words of the
sublime liturgy of the Church of ages: "Grant him,
O Lord, eternal rest. And let perpetual light shine on
him! May he rest in peace!

The bravery of De Soto and his followers became a fountain of poetry and legend for future generations. His chivalrous hosts were always accompanied by priests, in brown, or white, or black, who, besides attending to the spiritual wants of their countrymen, no doubt converted numerous Indians. Some must have stayed behind when the hero swept, comet-like, through the western wilderness in search of other lands to conquer. Benign shades of gracious priests sometimes appear in Indian legend. Students of legendary lore will recall the priest mentioned as going out in a frail barque, at twelve of the clock, on Christmas night, lured by the mystic music of the Pascagoula, in the vicinity of Mobile, and many another phantom priest.

Traditions of a picturesque Spanish column that marched through these regions in their burnished breast-plates and shining helmets, were long rife among the aborigines. Indeed, rapiers of old Toledo, steel, fitted with carved silver handles, ancient brass helmets of a pattern worn by European infantry in remote times and hardly seen since the early days of the great Louis—rusty war-knives, tomahawks, human bones in the sand dunes, coarse pottery, and many other relics of a day that is done, have been turned up by the spade of the laborer, on these ancient battle-fields, around which the Indians of many a tribe lived, and warred, and ruled in barbaric glory, long before the English Pilgrim Fathers touched the shores of America.

After weary wanderings and awful sufferings, a wretched remnant of De Soto's once brilliant hosts escaped into Mexico.

Meanwhile, no herald had as yet published the death

of De Soto. But in many lands expedition after expedition sought him and his followers, in vain. In October, 1543, however, one of the old soldiers learned, at Vera Cruz, that the Captain-General was no more, and that the few who survived of his once magnificent army, had lately escaped into Mexico.

When the faithful Isabella, after years of grief and anxiety, learned of the failure of De Soto's expedition, the loss of their fortunes, the ruin of their house, and, above all, the death of her beloved husband, whose body lay buried in the fatal river he had discovered, she could not survive under such a weight of misery. After three days of conscious widowhood, the first vice-queen of Havana died of a broken heart.

Of the remnant of the adventurous men that sailed on De Soto's expedition with such high hopes and such noble aspirations, some returned to Spain with only memories for their companions, but from bitter experience they would now rather be poor at home than rich in the New World. Several entered religious houses, especially of their favorite Order of St. Francis. De Soto's gallant successor married a wealthy lady of Mexico. And a few went to Peru, where they gained fame and fortune.

Practically, the Spaniards in North America were confined to Mexico and Florida, the English-speaking to the Atlantic seaboard, and the French to Canada and the gulf coast.

CHAPTER III.

The speech and sentiments of De Soto and the followers who consoled his sorrowful last moments, as they have come down to us in the Chronicles, remind us of the piety of many of the secular population of Spain at that epoch.

The family life of the great Queen, Isabella, was marked by every virtue. Her daughters were instructed by the best of tutors, under her own supervision. Greater care, if possible, was bestowed on her son, Juan, a youth of the brightest promise, whose death in his twentieth year, was the sorest trial of her chequered career. She improved the religious and intellectual life of her whole Kingdom, and, like King Alfred, she made learning an indispensable condition of ecclesiastical preferment. Her daughters emulated, in other courts, her noble example, but they enjoyed little of her prosperity. Her eldest, Isabella, Queen of Portugal, died with her first-born. The picturesque insanity of Juana, widow of the dashing Philip of Flanders, lasted till her death in old age. Catalina went to England, where she became the persecuted but glorious Katharine of Aragon, the most venerated Queen in English history.

Queen Isabella, deservedly styled " the Catholic," proclaimed herself the mother and protectress of the

Indians whom she called her children. Not even Las Casas himself was more anxious to bring them, one and all, into the true Church.

All those immediately connected with the discovery of America appear to have been Catholics of the highest type. Columbus had led a holy life from childhood; and his deathbed eloquently teaches the nothingness of human glory. He was an extraordinary genius, but above all he was a great Catholic. " The finger of the historian," says Prescott, " will find it difficult to point to a single blemish in his moral character. . . . . It was in perfect harmony with the grandeur of his plans and their results, more stupendous than those which heaven has permitted any other mortal to achieve."

When Columbus discovered a new region he knelt, and kneeling uttered the following short, but beautiful, prayer, which all other Catholic discoverers were wont to repeat after him:

" O Lord God, Eternal and Omnipotent, who by Thy divine word hast created the heavens, the earth, and the sea! Blessed and glorified be Thy Name, and praised Thy Majesty, who hast deigned by me, Thy humble Servant, to have that Sacred Name made known and preached in this part of the world! "

The discovery of America was a pre-eminently Catholic enterprise. Columbus undertook his voyages that he might carry the gospel to pagan lands, and raise funds to free the Holy Sepulchre from the infidels, for the age of Christian chivalry never ceased for him. No sooner was a new land found, than the discoverers felt obliged to begin the conversion of the natives or cause it to be begun, by some priest of the ship.

Columbus was intensely pious. Religion mingled with the whole course of his thoughts and shone forth in all his private and most unstudied writings. The voice of prayer and praise arose from his ships, as they beheld the New World, and his first action on landing was to prostrate himself on the earth, and render thanks to God. Every evening the *Salve Regina* and the *Ave Maris Stella* were sung by his crew, and all his enterprises were undertaken in the Name of the Holy Trinity.

Columbus died the death of a Saint in Valadolid in the seventieth year of his age, in 1506. In his will he thought of the Indians and said, among other things: " Schools of theology are to be established for the instruction of those who will devote themselves to the conversion of the Indians." [1]

Pope Alexander VI. issued a bull, (May 9, 1493) in which he made it obligatory on the Catholic Sovereigns, Ferdinand and Isabella, to send to the newly found lands " tried men who fear God, learned and skilful and expert, to instruct the inhabitants in the Catholic Faith, and teach them good morals."

Navigators from other lands showed the zeal and piety which we laud in Columbus. Thus Champlain, the first projector of the Panama Canal, was wont to say: " The salvation of a single soul is worth more than the conquest of an empire."

When we look at the homes of Spain, from which so many of the heroes of these times came forth, we are not surprised at their piety and high principles. See the family of St. Francis Borgia, Duke of Gandia,

---

[1] Columbus said he felt he had been chosen by God to be His messenger to these people in new lands beyond the seas, and to bring them to Christ.

while living as a grandee of Spain. Think of St. Teresa's father, at Avila, "the city of Knights." Her brother who had seen the New World, and helped to build her convents; her uncles, versed in the higher secrets of sublime prayer. Her friend, Francesco Salcedo, afterwards a priest, to whom she opened her whole soul in the earlier stages of her spiritual life, and who, having given her excellent instruction on that abstruse subject, the discernment of spirits, introduced her to the Jesuits who had just come into Spain. They calmed her perturbed soul and taught her to bless God for his gifts though extraordinary.

In that favored age piety seems to have dwelt in every walk of life from the patient, industrious mother of Venerable Luis of Granada, to the powerful emperor of Spain and the Netherlands, who had renounced crowns and sceptres to prepare for death in the monastery of St. Just.

Luis of Granada was a distinguished preacher and one of the ablest ascetic writers of his day. Once, when preaching, he saw his mother, a poor washerwoman, at the church door, eager to hear her beloved son. " I pray you, Señores," said he, to the gentlemen who crowded about the church door, " to make a little room for my poor mother, who is anxious to hear the Sermon." Needless to say the best place in the church was instantly vacated for the venerable mother of such a son.

Another saintly poor creature, John Yepez, born in Old Castile, 1542, led in the world a life of heroic sanctity, dividing his time between study in college and labors in the hospital. Never was he without crosses. St. Teresa, a kindred spirit, chose him to reform the Carmelite Brethren. His enemies were literally those of his own household, and his persecution ceased only with his life. When asked to choose between a convent ruled by a holy Friar, his friend, at Baëza, and a convent whose Superior had denounced him as " an apostate, and a companion of devils," at Ubeda, he chose Ubeda! (Life of St. John of the Cross.)

The family of Alonzo Sanchez de Cepeda, father of St. Teresa, were singularly connected with America. His son, Fernando, was a friend of Pizarro. Teresa's favorite brother, Rodrigo, who as a child went with her in search of martyrdom, and was drowned later in the Indies, leaving her heir to all his wealth,—her brother, Lorenzo, whom she converted to great piety after his return from America, Antonio, a Dominican, who died young, Pedro, who went to the Indies and returned with Lorenzo, Jeronimo who died at Peru, " like a Saint," as Teresa says, Augustine, a distinguished Captain, victorious in seventeen battles against the inhabitants of Chili, but, being eager for glory and ambition, received a supernatural warning from his sister that his salvation would be in danger if he accepted fresh commissions,—he forgot her words and went out again; but when he reached Lima he was struck by a mortal illness, and, strengthened by the invisible presence of his blessed sister, he accepted his death with resignation, as the penalty for his sins, This is attested by Father Luis de Valdivia, S. J.— who confessed Augustine in his last illness,—in his deposition at the canonization of St. Teresa.

St. Teresa dearly loved her native city, Avila.[1] In a

[1] In Avila is the ancient Church of San Pedro. In front of its beautiful rose window is a pedestal, on which stands the statue of St. Teresa, in her Carmelite robes. On the sides of the pedestal are in-

letter to her brother, Lorenzo, who had just returned from the Indies, she says: " I have forgotten to tell you what facilities you will find in Avila for giving your sons a good education. The Fathers of the Society of Jesus have a college, where they teach children their grammar; they confess them regularly, and train them so well in the paths of virtue, that it is truly a matter for which to thank God. They have likewise a course of philosophy. For theology, the people to go to the convent of Santo Tomas,[1] so that you can find all that you need, both in knowledge and piety, without going outside Avila. The town is so virtuous that every one who comes to it from other parts, is impressed by it. The people are much addicted to the practice of prayer and of confession, and even those in the world lead perfect lives."

Speaking of her family St. Teresa says: " We were three sisters and nine brothers; and all, through the goodness of God, were like our parents in being virtuous, except myself." [2]

We may imagine the good which youths so piously brought up were able to do in the new country, and of what assistance they were to the missionaries.

It is pleasant to be able to add that Avila preserves into our own days its reputation for piety. In 1868,

scribed the names of warriors by land and sea, of authors, poets, wise men, and saints, born in Avila. Here may be found the honored name of Pedro Melendez. St. Teresa is regarded as the queen of all these great ones.

[1] The convent of St. Tomas still exists, occupied by Dominicans who teach many novices there. They show the gratings at which St. Teresa used to confess.

[2] Life of Saint Teresa. By Henri Joly. 1906. With the imprimatur of H. E. Cardinal Vaughan, Archbishop of Westminster, March 19, 1903.

at the time of the disturbance, after the fall of Queen Isabella II., the convents were threatened once more, and the Carmelite Convent, especially, was thought to be in danger. The women of Avila thereupon protested most vigorously to Marshal Serrano. They invoked both the memory of their great compatriot, and the promises of liberty made in the name of revolution. " Yea, your excellency, we beseech you with one voice, and with streaming eyes, in the name of the principle of association, proclaimed by the Revolution, to leave these good souls in their Convents; ease our troubled minds, and you will thus powerfully contribute to the upholding of the principles of liberty." [1]

[1] *La Liberdad christiana de Madrid.* Dec. 4, 1868.

CHAPTER IV.

And for further consideration of the piety of these Spaniards, we will turn again to De Soto and others. See in what a Christian spirit Balthasar Gallegos comforts him, in the names of the other warriors when death drew nigh. He emphasized for the dying Captain-General, the shortness of life in this weary, miserable world, adding that God shows a singular favor to those whom he calls out of it soonest. And though his death, under such circumstances, would surely grieve his loyal followers, yet they, as well as he, must learn to conform themselves to the holy will of God.

When an Indian chief besought De Soto to beg his God to send rain on the parched corn after a prolonged drought, he said: "Though I, and my soldiers, are sinners, we will pray to our Lord God to shew favor to us, and grant our petitions." He then commanded a carpenter to make a colossal cross of the finest pine in the forest. A solemn procession was ordered for the next day. It was led by the priests, chanting the Litany of the Saints, which the rest devoutly answered. The chief walked beside De Soto; the warriors were in line with the cavaliers. Falling on their knees they all prayed aloud to the great God. Then rising, two by two, they approached the cross and venerated it. The procession returned

chanting the *Te Deum*. And, just before midnight,
the same day, the floodgates of heaven were opened,
and the rain fell in torrents for two days, to the great
joy of the Indians whose crops were saved.

Later, the chieftain bringing two blind men to the
Captain-General, asked him to have his God open their
eyes. De Soto gave him a lucid explanation of the
Christian Religion, and taught him for what we should
pray, and how, concluding:

" Pray to God who is in heaven, only for what you
need."

Among other pious navigators was Alonzo de
Ojeda,[1] " the bravest of the brave," called " the Don
Quixote of Navigators," who settled the Isthmus of
Darien in 1510. He accompanied Columbus in his
second voyage, and was noted, for his practical Faith
and fervent piety. Ojeda was greatly devoted to the
Blessed Virgin Mary, and called himself her Knight.
He finally abandoned the world, and became a Franciscan Monk at San Domingo, dying soon after. His
last words were: " Lay my body at the portals of
the monastery that, in humble expiation of my past
pride every one who enters may tread upon my grave."

Among the successors of Columbus there were those
who came with fire and sword, for gold and lands.
But men of self-sacrifice came too, and brought the
Gospel and the sacraments. Nor can it ever be com-
puted how many souls were attracted to the good God
by the new Apostles. Chief among them was the
heroic Las Casas, who labored for sixty years with
untiring energy, for the welfare of the Indians. He
was entirely and enthusiastically devoted to them, and
gloried in being styled " the Protector of the Indians."
That he might be able to give confirmation and Holy

[1] The history of the Spanish Main began with the voyage of Ojeda.

Orders, he was consecrated Bishop of Chiapa, having refused the mitre of the rich city of Cuscos, which is so beautiful, that it was called, " a piece out of heaven."

In 1528, Right Rev. John Juarez, a Spanish Franciscan, was appointed by the Holy See, Bishop of Rio de las Palmas, in Florida. He underwent great hardships in laboring for souls, and with a brother missioner, John de Palos, perished by hunger or at the hands of the Indians, 1528.

In 1559, Tristan de Luna tried to plant a colony of Spaniards in Alabama, but the attempt was soon abandoned. Yet in one sense, these Catholic colonizers deemed it eminently successful. Many babes and adults were baptized by the priests who accompanied the expedition.

Most accounts of the Spanish conquests in the New World were written by the enemies of Spain, and, unhappily, the evils were exaggerated and the good minimized. But no one is more severe on his countrymen who failed in mercy and kindness to the Indians, than the Seville Bishop, Las Casas, especially in his " General History of the Indians," graphically translated from the Spanish by the late Rev. Luigi Dutto, of the Diocese of Natchez, and published in St. Louis, 1902.

It cannot be denied that many explorers were filled with zeal to convert the pagans of the New World. And, surely, hundreds, nay thousands, were gathered into the One Fold, of whom history takes but little cognizance.

The piety of the Spanish people at this epoch may be gathered incidentally from the Foundations of St. Teresa, and similar works, and from the Lives of many Saints of that nation. Non-Catholic writers have not always hidden the name and the fame of the Apostolic men who strove to draw honey from the rock and oil from the flinty stone. " The Catholic priest," says Washington Irving, " went even before the soldier and the trader; from lake to lake, from river to river: the missionaries pressed on, unresisting, and with a power which no other Christians have exhibited, won to the Faith the warlike Miamis, and the luxurious Illinois."

" Not a river was entered, nor a cape turned," says Bancroft, " but a Jesuit led the way."

St. Francis Xavier writes to the gentle Father, Simon Rodriguez, who was confessor to John III., King of Portugal: " You should see, my dear Brother, that the King fulfils his duties well, and that he sends all the necessary help to the Indies for the growth of the Faith."

In 1581, three Franciscans who had attempted a mission in New Mexico, met there a martyr's crown. Others succeeded, and long before the English had made any permanent settlement on American shores, whole tribes on the Rio Grande had been converted and civilized, and many a red man of the forest had even learned to read and write. In 1583, Espego, a Spanish nobleman, with soldiers and missionaries, founded Santa Fé, the second oldest city in the United States.

CHAPTER V.

MELENDEZ, the greatest Admiral of his day, was
sent from Spain, 1565, to colonize Florida. He had
lately lost his only son, who was believed to have been
wrecked on the Florida coast. He clung to the hope
of finding him with the French pirates, or among the
Indians. The thought that he might be able to rescue
him induced this great man to accept the commission
of colonizing Florida, and it is sad to have to record
that he never found any trace of this well-beloved
son.

Melendez was one of the brightest ornaments of the
golden age of Spain, as the reign of Charles V. was
often styled. " To him," says an admirer, " Spain
owes a monument, history a volume, and the muses
an epic." It is related that in early youth, Melendez
saved the life of the great Charles V. He was one of
the splendid retinue that accompanied Philip II. to
England, and commanded the vessel in which the
Prince [1] sailed, to marry Queen Mary Tudor, a marriage so inauspicious for the bride and her Island-King-
dom. When King Philip, arrayed in robes, of velvet,

---

[1] Philip was not yet publicly declared King. It was after the marriage ceremony, July 25, 1554, that Bishop Gardiner announced, while
still in his own Cathedral, Winchester, that the Emperor, Charles V.,
to make, his son who as yet was only Prince of Spain, a more equal
match for the bride, a Queen-Regnant, had resigned to him the King-
doms of Naples and Jerusalem (1554). No mention is made of the
American possessions.

with diamond collar, stood up to plight his troth, Melendez was in attendance between his royal master and the maiden majesty of England. The royal pair were married by Mary's friend, Stephen Gardiner, Bishop of Winchester, England. The chair in which the Queen sat is still shown in the old Cathedral. No doubt so pious a Catholic as Melendez offered many a fervent prayer for the full restoration of England to the true faith.

A few years later when Queen Mary, had learned, the nothingness of earthly grandeur, and died in her poor Franciscan habit, her eyes ecstatically fixed on the sacred host elevated at the mass, offered for her happy translation from the miseries of earth to the glories of heaven, no doubt our great Admiral was in spirit present at this truly heavenly death-bed, and followed the daughter of Katherine of Aragon to the cloisters of Westminster Abbey, where her holy remains were laid to rest with such pomp and ceremony.

In 1565, St. Augustine, the oldest town in the United States, was founded by Melendez and named from the Saint on whose Feast he sailed into its harbor, August 28. Many missionaries accompanied him. Soon after, the Pope, St. Pius V., issued a brief to Melendez to excite his zeal for the conversion of the Indians, 1569. Like St. Teresa and many other holy personages, Pedro Melendez was born at Avila. He had had a stirring career before he became the colonizer of Florida. Under Philip II., he rose to the highest rank in the Spanish navy, then the finest in Europe. He brought out twelve Franciscans, and four Jesuits, to work for the conversion of the Indians. In the very year in which Melendez laid the foundations of St. Augustine, St. Francis Borgia, General of the Society of Jesus, sent out Fathers Martinez and Roger, and Brother Villa Real, to labor on the Florida mission. They were all men of high sanctity.

On the eve of departure, Father Martinez said to a holy friend of his: " O Father, how I long to shed my blood for the Faith at the hands of the savages, and battle for it along the shores of Florida." His holy ambition was gratified; on reaching Florida, he landed to explore the shore. He had scarcely done so, when a gale arose and drove the vessel out to sea. He was quickly surrounded by the Indians and put to death. He was noted for his rare abilities and personal holiness, as indeed were many of the earlier missionaries. The scientific knowledge of Columbus often stood him in good stead with his wayward children, the Indians. He obtained astonishing command over them on one occasion, by predicting an eclipse of the moon. Father Martinez was the first Jesuit that entered the territory now known as the United States.

The sonorous Spanish was the first European tongue spoken on the American Continent and the adjacent islands. The new Apostles came in robes of brown, or white, or black, or grey, with hood or cowl, or bare-headed. They were with the explorers, or they went before them. The achievements of these daring pioneers to-day seem fabulous. They penetrated forests and surmounted innumerable obstacles, crossed rivers, climbed mountains—without streams, roads, or guides,—bore cold and heat, thirst and hunger—and all in the hope of saving the souls, often of their enemies. Columbus said he felt he had been chosen by God to be his messenger to these people in new lands beyond the sea, to bring them to Christ, and so felt the holy men who followed in his wake.

4

The Spaniards were the first to evangelize the Indians, and bring them under the civilizing influence of the Gospel. We need but name the saintly Las Casas, but hundreds followed him. And no other motive was recognized as one which could lure the great men of Spain's glorious past from their stately homes, their beloved kindred, their cherished literary and scientific occupations, than an unconquerable desire to draw souls to Christ.

The Emperor Charles V. ordered Lucas Vasquez De Ayllon who fitted out an expedition at his own cost, to carry missioners with him at the expense of the crown: The Emperor wrote: " Our principal interest in the discovery of new lands is that the inhabitants and natives thereof, who are without the light of the knowledge of Faith, may be brought to understand the truths of our holy Catholic Faith. And this is the chief motive you are to hold in this affair. And to this end it is proper that Religious persons should accompany every expedition." So that ships prepared for the transatlantic voyage, looked as if they had been made ready for a great missionary enterprise.

The brilliant career of Columbus and his well known zeal to bring souls to God, induced many daring men to brave the dangers of the deep to obey the divine command: " Go, teach ye all nations—" inspired the Catholic Cabots (Gabotas), Italians in the service of Henry VII. to share in the great work of saving souls. These enlightened navigators discovered the North American Continent.

Father Tolosa and other disciples of Las Casas visited Florida to convert the barbarians but found a speedy death. The first Jesuit martyr, Father du Poisson, while *en route* for New Orleans stopped to celebrate mass at Natchez. While carrying the Blessed Sacrament to a sick person, he was struck dead with an Indian tomahawk; and a general massacre followed. Father Doutreleau, while offering mass on the banks of the Mississippi, was assailed with a volley of arrows, but escaped almost miraculously. A seminary priest, Father Gaston, was martyred. Many died victims of the wasting climate, and the total lack of care and nourishment. In 1736, Father Senat, S.J. was burnt at the stake, on Palm Sunday. Such were the dangers from the Indians many had to carry their guns to mass. Arms were stacked before the church and sentinels paced up and down while mass was celebrated. And yet a certain writer, styles a ship carrying missioners as well as other passengers:

"The roving expedition of gallant freebooters in quest of a fortune."

The wise and upright Don Antonio de Mendoza, directed Father Mark, an illustrious Franciscan from Nice, to penetrate into the interior, and to assure all the nations he encountered that the Viceroy had put an effectual stop to the enslavement of the Indians, and sought only their good. "The service of the Lord," said he, "and the good of the people of the Land, is the aim of the pacification of whatever is discovered.

Father Mark became Provincial of his Order in 1531, being the earliest of priestly explorers. Unarmed and afoot, he penetrated into the heart of the country in advance of all other European—"a bare-footed Friar effecting more," as Viceroy Mendoza wrote, "than well armed Spaniards had been able to accomplish."

Lay Brothers and Brothers of the Third Order often

helped the priests. On one occasion a Negro and an Indian received the habit. These zealous souls not being ordained to priestly functions, determined to set up the CROSS in all the neighboring villages, instruct the people in the articles of Faith, baptize dying children. In this way, no doubt, thousands of souls were saved of whom history seems to have made but little record.

Melendez governed Florida for ten years and used every effort to restore the colony to comfort and safety. He was indefatigable in conciliating the natives and in winning them to the Catholic Faith. At his request, missioners were sent from Spain, chiefly Franciscans. They visited the remotest tribes, and by their address, the mildness of their manners, and the simplicity of their lives, devoted to teaching the arts of civilization, obtained an entire ascendancy over the savages.

In 1584, many missions and convents wers founded in Middle Florida. Their ruins now excite the investigation of the curious. Here was a great religious Province, chartered by the see of Rome, under the Franciscan Order, known as Santa Elena, whose representative government was fixed at St. Augustine. The Catholic religion was acknowledged by most of the tribes north of the Gulf of Mexico and east of the Mississippi, (*Monette,* from Williams' *Florida.*)

The Jesuits invited to help the Franciscans in the glorious work of teaching, penetrated the Indian towns, lived with the savages, bore unparalleled hardships, ministered to the wretched, instilled the teachings of Christianity into the minds of any who would give them a hearing, and thought no danger or sacrifice great enough to deter them from carrying on their work. The Indian world was their parish. Wherever they went they made keen observations of all they saw, and reported to their superior in France, in a remarkable series of letters called the Jesuit Relations.— THORPE'S *History of the American people*.

Father Pareja translated many religious books into native dialects which were very useful in instructing the Indians.

CHAPTER VI.

IN every way Melendez was untiring in his efforts for the prosperity of Florida. He was often recalled to Spain, always to the detriment of his colony. His relations with the natives were very friendly. If they showed any disposition to embrace the Catholic Faith, he sent the most fervent missionary to their aid. His last recorded wishes were that he might return to Florida, and spend whatever remained to him of life in saving the souls of the poor Indians. He was recalled to Europe to command the famous Spanish Armada, but died before it sailed. Had the great Admiral lived to command the Invincible Armada, history might have a different tale to tell of the results. He closed his remarkable career in the fear and love of God, at Santander, on the feast of the stigmata of his beloved St. Francis, September 17, 1574. But we must mention matters which occurred before his death.

Spain claimed Florida by right of the discovery of Columbus and Ponce de Leon's exploration. But the Huguenots [1] having taken possession, Melendez was

[1] The invasions of the Huguenots were not the least bloody scenes. They were pirates. They gave no quarter to priests, especially of Orders. I find no case where the Calvinists in Spanish waters gave quarter to Catholics, except in the hope of a large ransom.

A most atrocious case was that of Ignatius Azevedo, who was captured on his way to Brazil, with thirty-nine missionaries, all of whom were put to death, in 1570.

Jacques de Sorie (1551), after pledging his word to spare the Span-

sent by the King, Philip II., to drive them out.
Melendez built a fort which in honor of the day he
called St. Augustine. Just as Ribaut's ships were at-
tacking the Spaniards, a hurricane scattered his squadron. Melendez meanwhile captured Fort Caroline, on
the St. John's River, in Florida. Every man in the
garrison was put to death.

To revenge his countrymen, a Frenchman, named
De Gourgas, fitted out three vessels. Sailing for
Florida, he surprised the garrison that guarded the
Spanish Fort, and hanged every man within it.

" Whether in his treatment of the French Huguenots, he regarded them as pirates, or as parties perhaps in the death of his son, or acted in obedience to
the orders of Philip II. or to his own persecuting spirit,
can never be known, but in no point of view can his
conduct be justified." SHEA.

After the death of Pedro Melendez, the prosperity
of Florida declined. But the great leader had set his
work on the place and on the people, and it soon became more prosperous than before, by following his
counsels and example. But we must go back to its
earlier days.

The beautiful peninsula in which the gallant Juan
Ponce de Leon sought the fountain of youth, and to
which he gave the sweet-sounding name Florida—

---

iards who surrendered, put them and his Portuguese prisoners to death.
Negroes he hanged and shot while alive.

The Huguenots crossed to Havana, burned the town and church.
The inhabitants were put to death—many fled to the mountains. Melendez knew all this. He sent a vessel and men from his fleet to restore
the place.

They made their Protestantism a pretext for their plunders.

Pascua Florida—the Spanish name for Easter—the day he discovered it—contains as to its history, besides a not inconsiderable martyrology—all the elements of poetry and romance. But it is not the design of this work to enlarge upon the story of the valiant Christian Knight who won and consecrated its soil to the great God; who sought a wonderful spring to restore youth to the aged that they might continue to labor for Christ. I shall have much to say of the zealous missionaries who led the way for the conquerors, or followed in their steps, to draw new peoples to Christ.

We have seen the mysterious "Everglades," with floating islets of lilies moving over their shallow lakes, and the hunters and trappers that seem to lose themselves in their mighty swamps. And drowsy St. Augustine, with its gray walls and time-eaten doorways, transfigured by the amber sunlight or the white moonbeams, into a city more entrancing than the Tadmor of the desert. And the wilderness of bloom and beauty watered by the limpid St. John, whose banks are carpeted by red and gold blossoms, and delicate azaleas, and shaded by palm and cypress, robed in moss and mistletoe. And the orange-orchards that grow grateful refreshments for races in far-away lands, where mere existence is not always a pleasure, as it often is under the bright skies, and in the salubrious atmosphere of Florida.

Yet charming as these natural beauties are, our eyes were not satisfied with feasting on them. We followed in spirit, and, when possible, in reality, the blood-stained traces of the Apostles and martyrs who came in such numbers to convert the barbarian hordes, or die for Christ.

Father Luis Cancer, one of the many friends of

Las Casas, and, like him, a Dominican, visited Florida
to convert the natives, and was, with two other priests,
scalped by the savages.   Father Padilla and Brother
John of the Cross taught the doctrine of Christ till
they were slain by the infuriated pagans.   Many bands
of Franciscans reached Florida, 1573-1593, and
brighter days appeared.   By degrees the heathens were
gathered into the One Fold, and Florida became an
Eden of peace.

Father Pareja, a Franciscan, drew up in the
Yemassee tongue, an abridgment of the Christian
doctrine, the first Catechism ever published in any
Indian dialect.

The missionaries who accompanied Pedro Melendez
assembled in the Franciscan Monastery, Santa Elena,
and from that favored spot the benign light of Christianity shed its pure rays over the Floridian peninsula.

In 1597, Father Corpa was slain at the foot of the
altar by the dissolute companions of a young chieftain,
whom, with apostolic liberty, he had reproved for his
vices.   The spot sanctified by his death is now venerated in the Catholic Cemetery of the ancient city.   The
mild climate and the refreshing breezes from the surrounding waters make St. Augustine a winter paradise
for invalids and the weakly.   But, at least, Catholics
among them should think of the soldiers of the cross,
who, in this place, gave up their lives for the Name
of Christ, with superhuman love and divine generosity.

The first European to see the Mississippi was
Alvarez de Piñeda who discovered its mouth and spent
six weeks cruising upon it.   He named it Rio de
Espiritu Santo (River of the Holy Ghost).

We should like to think that the sparkling waters of
the Fountain of Youth gave true life to many savages

when poured on their heads as baptismal waters, by the holy missionaries.

The Silver Spring which tradition asserts to be the Fountain of Youth, is forty feet deep, and transparent to the bottom. A beautiful Carib maiden, Aleida, made its existence known to Ponce de Leon, and accompanied him on his peaceful, romantic mission in search of the elixir which was to restore strength to his tottering limbs, and the light of youth to his faded eyes. In the legendary lore of these days you will learn that an angel came daily to drink of the waters of life, and the dew-drops, falling from his glittering wings, gave to the spring its wonderful virtue to restore, or to beautify, as the pilgrims believed.

The natives of Florida whom the early invaders met for the first time, were of splendid physique, all appearing youthful and handsome. This may have given rise to the myth, the fountain of eternal youth, Bimini ! the land where none grow old—the fountain which he thought he saw pictured in its luminous atmosphere on that radiant Easter Sunday. It is said that many of the early Indians of Florida were hydropathists. To bathe in the clear waters and quench their thirst at the crystal springs, were their universal remedies for the evils that flesh is heir to. In health and symmetry, many Indians equalled the classic Greeks.[1] To this day, springs abound in Florida and Alabama,[2] and are sites for water cure establishments more or less crowded.

It is not so much in legend, as in hard fact, that

[1] Yet the Indians were not all of this classic formation. In Apalache a chief is mentioned who was so fat that he was compelled to move about his house on his hands and knees.—Albert James Pickett.

[2] Thus Stafford Springs, Vosburg, are called in the Indian dialect, " Boga Hama," water of life, and are much frequented.

we see the wonderful zeal of the priests who were
willing to give their lives for the conversion of the
barbarians of the New World. " It is impossible," says
Mr. Hamilton, " to read the story of the Fathers who
accompanied the colonists and devoted their lives to
the conversion of the natives, without a feeling of
admiration. They abandoned everything dear to man,
with the aim and hope of doing good to the ignorant,
often cruel, natives of the New World. While priests
always accompanied the soldiers, soldiers did not always go along with the priests. In the outlying districts near every fort, there would gradually be built
chapels for the natives; and these were centres not of
religious work alone. The Fathers would teach the
Indians whom they influenced how to cultivate the soil,
and the simple forms of handiwork and manufacture,
for their method was the same in Florida as in Texas,
or in California.[1]

The Indians of the coast were not entirely nomadic.
They lived by agriculture and the chase. The men
hunted, the women cultivated their fields and gardens.
They supplemented the game brought home by their
braves, with maize, peas, squash, which have remained
staples to this day. Everyone, however remotely connected with an Indian settlement, has heard of their
sweet herbs and sassafras, and tisanes, in which only
the creoles rivaled them.

A few scattered wigwams, here and there, are all
that now remain of their once populous villages or
pueblos. Their roads were mere bridle paths. It was
said somewhat reproachfully, that the Spaniards
thought that the New World was made only for them-

[1] Peter Joseph Hamilton: The Colonization of the South: George
Barrie and Sons: Philadelphia: 1904.

selves.   But it is probable that as much could be said
of every European nation that descended on the
picturesque haunts of the Red men, or sought to rifle
the treasure-galleons that sped over the high seas with
their precious freight of yellow bars and ingots.

Franciscan missionaries came with Columbus to the
New World.   From time to time their numbers in-
creased until they had preached the Gospel from
Florida to the Pacific, and from Colorado to Patagonia.
In the Antilles, in our Southwest, in Mexico, Peru,
Chili, Paraguay and Argentina, their monasteries were
the centres whence civilization and religion flowed to
the native tribes."   At this time practically, the entire
Christian world was in communion with the See of
Rome, and all the great discoverers were Catholics.

In 1513, a Spanish navigator, Balboa, while exploring the Isthmus of Panama, was told by an Indian
chief of a great sea beyond the mountains.   He pushed
eagerly forward, and, on July 25, 1513, saw before
him the greatest of the oceans.   Both he and his men
knelt down and thanked God.   On reaching the shore,
they waded into the sea, and took possession of the
Pacific Ocean and the lands bordering thereon, for
Leon and Castile.[1]

---

[1] The discovery of the Pacific was the greatest single exploit since the
discovery by Columbus.   Balboa beheld a great stretch of water—the
great South Sea.   He marched into the rolling surf and took formal
possession for Leon and Castile :

> ——— " the first that ever burst
> Into the silent sea ! "

CHAPTER VII.

If the blood of the martyrs is the seed of the Church, Christians should be numerous in many parts of the South, for the soil has been soaked again and again by martyrs' blood. In 1704, the English and some apostate Indians, destroyed St. Marks, of the Apalachee mission. Apalachee was considered the granary of Florida. Three Franciscans were martyred on this spot with all the horrors of Indian cruelty. Eight hundred Indians, all Christians, were massacred, and fourteen hundred taken into slavery by the leader of these outrages, Governor Moore,[1] of South Carolina.

Two hundred Christians, including a Jesuit, and a Franciscan, were massacred by the Natchez Indians, in 1729. They spared the children, many of whom formed the nucleus of the first Orphan Asylum in what is now the United States, under the Ursulines, who had recently established the first Convent in the same territory. A French force destroyed the Natchez as a nation, in the same year, 1729.

Father Segura, with ten other Jesuits, and a large number of converts, were massacred in 1570, by Indians, led by a perfidious chief, who had apostatized. Father Segura and his companions had been specially chosen for Florida by St. Francis Borgia, (1568) who

---

[1] " When Moore raided this country, he found it well inhabited and civilized. Part of his glory consisted in destroying churches, and carrying off the plate," etc.—" The Anglo-Saxon Border." Hamilton, p. 279.

was keenly interested in the American mission, and had sent many zealous laborers to that thorny field. Father Rogers, a zealous Jesuit, who had long labored in the interior of Florida, was chosen to accompany Melendez, in his search for the murderers of Segura. They captured eight. Father Rogers anxiously endeavored to obtain their pardon, as their crime had been prompted by the apostate chief, Don Louis. He failed, but procured a respite, and had the happiness of converting and baptizing the criminals. They died perfectly resigned to their fate, and with sentiments of the deepest contrition for their sins, blessing God for His mercies in saving their souls.

Peninsular Florida, the part lying east of the Apalachicola River, was called East Florida, with its capital at St. Augustine. West of the Apalachicola, towards the Mississippi, was a separate province, called West Florida, with Pensacola for its capital.

Pensacola has been a shifting city. It began where Fort Barrancas now stands. Here, the first Spanish Governor erected a church, in 1719; within a short period this region changed masters three times, but was restored to Spain, 1722. Meanwhile, Pensacola was removed to Santa Rosa, on the site of the present Fort Pickens. Floods and storms drove the settlement back to the Continent, 1754, and a town was begun on the unrivaled site now occupied by Pensacola.[1] Narvaez who discovered the Bay four centuries ago, called it St. Mary's Bay. But it has long since resumed the name by which it was known to the Indians.

In 1521, Ponce de Leon of Florida, informs his

[1] Pensacola in 1777 contained several hundred habitations. The governor's palace, a large stone building, was ornamented with a tower. —Bartram's Travels.

august master, "that he returns to that country that
the Name of Christ may be praised there." It was no
longer a region of perpetual youth, where the aged
might drink of the magic fountain, and where the
young should never grow old, but a land that called
for the toil of holy men and their earnest prayers to
draw the natives to praise the Name of Christ. Cardinal Borgia writing to Bishop Carroll, June 26, 1802,
asking information as to erecting new episcopal sees—
inquires whence priests could be obtained to labor
among the Indians, "whose conversion should be an
object of solicitude."

Bishop Durango, of Santiago, whose diocese embraced Florida, asked Philip II. to plant colonies there.
The Provincial of the Dominicans in Mexico was commanded to send Religious with the expedition. The
head of the missioners, Father Peter Feria, went
forth in the most fervent dispositions, saying that
he did not intend that the Indians should be
reached by conquest, but "by good example,
with good works, and with presents, to bring the
Indians to a knowledge of our holy Faith and of
Catholic truth." It may be said that there were missioners almost everywhere. "Before the fire of the
trapper's gun struck down his woodland game, before
the edge of the exile's axe had caught a ray of western
sunshine, a mild and steady light is perceptible in the
primitive forest; and by its friendly aid we discover
the Indian kneeling before the pine tree cross, while
the Blackrobe pours on his humbled head, the waters
of regeneration."

The Spaniards were the first exploring pioneers in
the valley of the Mississippi, and the French were the
first permanent settlers on its banks. It is difficult to

speak too highly of the splendid actions of the Spaniards in early days. Religious zeal was the life and soul
of all maritime enterprise. It was the great motive of
Columbus, and the darling scheme of his patroness,
Queen Isabella," one of the purest and most beautiful
characters on the pages of history," says Irving.

CHAPTER VIII.

DR. ANDREW TURNBULL, of infamous memory, was commissioned by an association in England to establish manufactures and plantations in Florida. For this purpose he brought out fourteen hundred Minorcans and Greeks, in eight vessels. They landed in Florida, June 26, 1768.[1] Dr. Camps, Missionary Apostolic, and Father Casas Novas, a Franciscan from Minorca, were appointed to attend to the spiritual welfare of these and other immigrants in a new Parish, formed about seventy miles south of St. Augustine, at New Smyrna, by the Bishop of Santiago de Cuba: Dr. Camps had special faculties from Rome to confer the Sacrament of Confirmation for twenty years.

These settlers were most cruelly treated by Dr. Turnbull. Nine hundred of them perished in nine years, though the baptisms show a natural increase.

Father Casas Novas, for his courage in remonstrat-

---

[1] Dr. Turnbull sailed for the Peloponnesus and for £400, got leave of Governor Modon to convey to Florida a large number of Greek families from Corsica and Minorca. He augmented his settlers to 1500. He made many promises but never complied with any.

It was found impossible to advance settlements into the wilderness without the spirit of meekness and benevolence which had characterized the early missioners.

5

ing against the cruelties perpetrated on his flock, was seized and sent back to Europe. Dr. Camps in order not to deprive the poor people of his ministry, labored on in silence.

In 1786, Dr. Camps had been sixteen years on the mission without salary, and had kept his flock safe from loss by heresy. In 1769, the poor Minorcans rose against their cruel oppressor. But Turnbull was a member of the Colonial Council, and the governor, Grant, took sides with him. Five of the leaders were taken to St. Augustine, tried, convicted, and sentenced to death. Two were actually hanged, one of their friends being compelled to act as hangman. Turnbull fulfilled none of his stipulations, with the unfortunate Minorcans. And by their unsuccessful revolt their condition was rendered worse than before. Finally, they abandoned New Smyrna, and set out for St. Augustine, led by the brave carpenter, Andrew Pellicer. The old men, women and children were in the centre of the sad procession, the able-bodied men kept guard, armed with sharp poles. They numbered about six hundred, including two hundred children born in Florida. Governor Moultrie examined the case, and the survivors were declared free from a contract of which Turnbull had failed to observe his side. The tyrant rode many miles after them and overtook them before they reached St. Augustine. But his entreaties to induce them to return were unavailing. He could show no cause for their detention, and they were set at liberty.

The Minorcans did not wish to return to a place where they had endured such hardships; a part of the city of St. Augustine was assigned them, where their descendants remain to this day, faithful to the Catholic religion. They had no redress for the wrongs they had endured, no restitution for the wages of which they had been defrauded. " Such," says Monette, History of the Valley of the Mississippi, " have been the tender mercies of the English in all their conquests."

Two of the descendants of the brave Pellicer have worn, respectively, the mitres of Mobile and San Antonio, and are still reverently and lovingly remembered in these cities. As the earlier churches of St. Augustine were destroyed by the English, Dr. Camps, being without means to erect a chapel for his flock, said mass for them at a house in Carrera, near the city gate.

Pensacola, which had been ceded to the English in 1764, surrendered to Galvez, May 8, 1781, and Count Arthur O'Neil was appointed the first Spanish Governor. The Catholic King provided for the future of the Church in this ancient province. He selected Rev. Thomas Hassett and Rev. Michael O'Reilly, as parish priest and curate of Pensacola, desiring them to obtain faculties and proper installation from the Bishop of Santiago de Cuba.

The first colonists of St. Augustine came from Spain, 1656, many a decade before the Pilgrim Fathers landed at Plymouth Rock. Even at that early period the church was fully organized. It had a complete set of records, in perfect preservation. For safe keeping they were carried to Havana, when Florida passed under English rule. When Count Arthur O'Neil took charge of Pensacola, the Catholic service was immediately restored there, under the Capuchin, Father de Velez.

St. Augustine when restored to Spain was in a

miserable condition. The few Catholics were mainly Minorcans, with some scattered Indians, remnants of native prosperous missions. There were few English-speaking Catholics—no church. Tolomato and Nuestra Señora de la Leché were in ruins.

The Franciscan Convent was a barracks. The chapel of the Fort was unrecognizable, as to its original purpose. In our own day, the chapel of Nuestra Señora de la Leche was dug out and restored. A statue of the Virgin Mother was erected on the spot.[1] Spanish and English-speaking priests were needed. The Catholic King sent out from Spanish Colleges, Fathers McCafferty and Crosby, '84-'91. Father Trocerius of the strict observance, came to teach the school, Father Juan, as chaplain of the Fort, and Father Font to aid the pastor.

Some of the early explorers came to the New World as to a land flowing with milk and honey, a land of mystery, where gold and gems might be had for the gathering, where the air was leaden with perfume, and fountains sparkled that gave perpetual youth:

> " Where the rivers wander o'er sands of gold,
> Where the burning rays of the ruby shine
> And the diamond lights up the secret mine,
> And the pearls gleam forth from the coral strand."

But whatever were their hopes or cravings, it was put before them as their first and chief business, to reclaim the children of the forest from paganism. The sovereigns of Spain certainly deserved in their colonies the noble title " Catholic." The same missionary

---

[1] Bishop Verot built a church at Tampa in honor of St. Luis, Father Luis Cancer, martyred off that coast, three hundred years ago.

college, Salamanca, which prepared priests for Ireland where Catholic education was proscribed, was often called on by the King of Spain to send laborers into his harvests in America, and never failed to respond, as history shows.

Heroic men planted the faith in these southern regions, and watered it with their blood. Most of the priests who accompanied De Soto in his straggling marches through so many trackless deserts, perished, and no religious chronicles give details of their later hours. They met Indians with their frightful war-paint, gaudy feathers, wampum, scalping knives, and other hideous accoutrements of their savage warfare. But we should like to think that the missioners, " beseeching them with the mildness and benignity of Christ," were able sometimes to attract them to God, to enlighten their ignorance, to pour on their heads, the saving waters of baptism. But of this, history makes little mention.

When Florida, by the treaty of 1763, ceased to be part of the dominious of his Catholic majesty, it was thought that the Spanish population could remain Catholic under their new masters. But they were compelled to migrate almost in a body. Bishop Morel, of Santiago de Cuba, ordered that an inventory be made of all the movable property of the church and confraternities of St. Augustine, and had these articles conveyed to Havana. In direct violation of the treaty, the Catholic population was subjected to all manner of vexations. The Bishop's house was seized for the use of the Church of England, the Franciscan Convent for the British troops. Of the suburbs of the city nothing was left. The church in the Indian town was converted into a hospital.[1] The parish church became a heap of ruins.

The most obvious result of this invasion was the destruction of the Catholic religion wherever the English ruled. Yet groups of Catholics, European and Indian, sometimes assembled, by stealth, to be present at a nautical or dry mass, a form of worship which gave such consolation to the survivors of many of De Soto's brilliant army.

Where wine and wheaten bread cannot be procured, and neither consecration nor consumption of the elements takes place, the mass is said to be a dry mass. In celebrating a Dry Mass the sacred vessels were allowed. But inasmuch as no consecration took place, the use of the chalice was unnecessary. The sacred vestments were worn. The Introit, Kyrie Eleison, Gloria, Credo, Gospel, and Preface were read. To make the Dry Mass as solemn as possible, deacon and subdeacon were present. Nautical was sometimes applied to the Dry Mass from the fact of its being chiefly confined to sea voyages where the difficulty of celebrating ordinary mass would be great on account of the rolling of the vessel, and other causes. Such masses are no longer celebrated by sea or land.

The Spanish were always anxious to provide for the hearing of mass, even when only temporarily in the country, as in the case of the Spanish minister in Philadelphia, in 1786, who could not hear mass even on Sundays and holidays. He applied to his Government for a chaplain and a chapel. The King of Spain

---

[1] The Council of Nice ordered that a hospital be built in every city. Needless to say that it was not in obedience to the merciful injunction that the enemies of religion stole the Indians' church and changed it into a hospital.

readily granted his request, and Father John O'Connell, of the Hospital of the Irish Dominicans at Bilboa, on the coast of Biscay, was selected for the office, and reached Philadelphia, May 17, 1786. Requisites were bought for a private chapel, for six hundred and nine dollars and one real. No doubt many Catholics of Philadelphia, English-speaking and Spanish, availed themselves of Father O'Connell's ministry. The Catholic King as usual assumed all the expenses.

We find, too, many evidences that priests and people were anxious for the sacrament of Confirmation. Thus the missionaries of Philadelphia applied to the Bishop of Santiago de Cuba for the Holy Oils, and they were supplied to them, with the consent of the King of Spain. Regarding other parts of the country we read: "Unable to obtain the Holy Oils as usual from England, and intercourse with Canada being impracticable, the Holy Oils were supplied from the same source, 1779." Don Jose de Galvez' reply, July 17, to Don Juan de Miralles, May 16, 1779.

In our own day, Father Salvador di Pietro, S. J. of British Honduras was empowered by Pope Pius IX. to give confirmation in Central America. He was afterwards consecrated Bishop.

When the missionary priests of the Thirteen States besought the Pope to give them a Superior, they lamented that " no one in these regions can bless the Holy Oils, chalices, or altar-stones, no one administer the sacrament of Confirmation . . . . . to empower a priest to perform these offices in the present necessity . . . . . that the people may no longer be deprived of confirmation, or die without extreme unction."

This power was given in 1784, to Father Carroll,

afterwards Archbishop of Baltimore. Bishop Challoner of pious memory, Vicar Apostolic of the London District, was anxious for the appointment of a Bishop in the colonies. He wrote to Rev. Dr. Stonor, 1766: "There be many thousands here (in America) that live and die without Confirmation." And elsewhere: "It is a lamentable thing that such a multitude have to live and die, always deprived of the Sacrament of Confirmation."

Early in the history of the colonies appeared the negro. He was instructed, converted when possible, and baptized. It was the English, for the most part, who brought slaves to America, nor was there ever in those days the slightest scruple in connection with slavery. Hawkins, the pirate, told Queen Elizabeth that in bringing negroes from their savage homes to a Christian country he was doing them a positive benefit."

They were used in the fields, for domestic service, and in the church. But a negro consigned to the clergy was held to have a pleasant sinecure: "A priest's negro," was a proverbial expression for a slave who could, to a great extent, do much as he pleased. Mr. Hamilton says that the slaves, as a rule, seem to have been docile, happy, and well treated. "Indeed, Governor Perier said that the negroes made better soldiers than the refuse sent from France in his time, who usually fled at the first flash of an Indian's gun. But negroes were too valuable to be used as such."

There was little disturbance regarding slavery. People seemed satisfied with things as they were. They thought slavery was a rather venerable institution. St. Paul made the runaway slave, Onesimus, return to his master, and Onesimus is revered as a Saint of the

Catholic Church. The same St. Paul instructed the masters: "Masters, do to your servants that which is just and equal, knowing that you, also, have a master in heaven." The Church had always befriended the slaves. For them Sunday Schools were established, and the masters were fined if the servants failed to attend. The Catholic Church admitted them to all her privileges.

I shall now give, the first time any information of the kind has been published, some notes on the manner in which slaves were treated in a typical religious house, the oldest in the United States, the Ursuline Convent of New Orleans. That I can do so is due to the kindness of some ancient and cultured ladies in that venerable Convent.

"Disguise thyself as thou wilt, Slavery," says old Stern, "still thou art a bitter draught, and though many have been compelled to drink of thee in all ages, thou art not, on that account, the less bitter." Let us see how the Convent slaves were treated by one of the earlier mothers and her colleagues in ante-bellum days.

About half way between the Convent and the place known as the negro quarters, is a comfortable brick building of four large rooms and a spacious attic, having dormer windows. Well, this still retains the name of Hospital, because it was long used as such by the slaves who required medical treatment, which was given with as much charity to them as to members of the community. At some distance is a frame building called "the Carpenters' Shop" which, on festive occasions as marriages, served as a banquet hall, wherein the inhabitants of the quarters, carpenters, masons, smiths, gardeners, cooks, house-maids, seamstresses, old and young were allowed to enjoy innocent pleasures, to their hearts content."

Should a negro or negress prefer to choose a life-partner elsewhere, the steward was authorized to purchase such partner. Two apartments were fitted up for the new couple, whose marriage took place at a nuptial mass. The groom was dressed in French fashion; the bride wore a snow-white robe, a tulle veil, and a wreath of orange blossoms. Of course, each had prepared for the sacrament of matrimony by a good confession and Holy Communion. After the ceremony, they were accompanied by their friends, in processional order, to their own apartments, where a delicious breakfast was served. In the evening, old and young, in the quarters, all dressed in holiday attire, accompanied the newly wedded pair to "the Carpenter's Shop," now transformed into a bower of roses, where all remained feasting, singing, playing, dancing, till near midnight, when they quietly retired to rest, "happier, perhaps," said one who had frequently mingled in these scenes "than the richest and freest in the land."

The children usually received the names of the Saints on whose feasts they were born, or baptized. To the baptismal name was occasionally added another, indicating some trade or peculiarity. Thus one was called "Louis l'avocat;" "Louis the lawyer" because of the tact with which he settled differences, etc.

At Easter each family received a supply of summer clothing; and at Christmas a supply for winter. Every adult in good health was required to work a certain number of hours daily. Those who wished to labor beyond the prescribed time, received remuneration for the extra work done. Attached to each cabin was a small garden which the owners could cultivate for their own use during their leisure hours.   They were also permitted to raise poultry.

Thus a system was created whereby an industrious negro could secure his freedom by saving the amount of his first cost to his master.

They were assembled daily for morning and night prayers, also, for religious instruction; on Sunday afternoons, when the chaplain gave them religious instruction, after which they recited the Rosary, sang a hymn, and were present at Benediction of the Blessed Sacrament.   One of the Sisters taught them the Christian Doctrine and prepared them for the worthy reception of the Sacraments.

They were wont to testify their appreciation of the maternal interest taken in their welfare, by coming in a crowd on New Year's Day, and on the eve of the Mother's feast, to offer their best wishes and some token of gratitude, such as fruit, pralines, etc.[1]   On these occasions they assembled on the gallery in front of the Sister-Treasurer's office, and one addressed the Superior in the name of all.   The Mother having thanked them and expressed satisfaction, gave each twenty-five cents.   After they had played some tunes, and sung some favorite songs, she dismissed them with kind and encouraging words.   Towards the close of the war, however, many of the colored inmates of the monastery, elated with the bright prospects held forth to them, left to seek their fortunes elsewhere.   They did not always find in liberty a primrose path.   But when troubles assailed them, they were welcome to their first home, not as slaves, now, but as hired servants.   The faithful old Louis de Gonzague said to his

---

[1] Pralines—Cakes made of cocoa-nut and sugar.

wife, Constance, when freedom was proclaimed: "You may go if you wish, but I am determined to remain." Of course she was too good a Christian to leave her husband, " and," says my informant, " I venture to add, that each enjoyed a happier life and died a holier death than if they had left in quest of liberty." This ancient pair lived to pass the century mark. Constance was the head cook of the establishment till death called her home. The young people who aided her regarded her as a Saint. Her only fault was that, not uncommon in her profession, irritability. But when she yielded to temper in the morning she was always missed in the afternoon. She could not rest until she went to confession. Her confessor, Father Roussillon, was well known in New Orleans at that epoch, and had a very high opinion of the virtue of his ancient penitent.

The deceased slaves were buried in the front yard of the old Convent, on the left of the flagged court. Their remains were not disturbed when the nuns removed to their new Convent, 1824. But the buried nuns were reverently removed to the cemetery of their new home.

In 1817, Spain prohibited the importation of African slaves into her colonies.

There is nothing new to be said on slavery in the South. There was little if any ill-treatment of slaves in Cuba, *Querida Cuba*.[1] Ballou, Abbott, and other American travelers say, there was none.

The claim has been made that slaves were kindly treated in Rhode Island. In the Rev. Dr. McSparron's time numbers of wealthy land-holders in Narragansett were slave-holders and slave-dealers. As late as 1804,

[1] Beloved Cuba.

Rhode Island had 59 vessels engaged in the slave trade (fifty-nine). The glebe house occupied by Dr. McSparron for over thirty years, is still standing. For a long time, the slaves were practically barred out of the protestant church. They were not instructed, baptized, or admitted to Communion.

But Dr. McSparron, " the great-hearted Irishman," protested against this unchristian exclusion of slaves, and ultimately prevailed in their behalf.

" Journal of the American Irish Historical Society," Vol. 3, 1900.

Dean Berkley, the famous " Kilkenny Scholar," was a friend of Parson McSparron, and often visited the Episcopal ministers of that place, when he settled near Newport, 1729. Berkley was subsequently recalled to England and made Bishop of Cloyne, an ancient see in Co. Cork.

CHAPTER IX.

Most visitors enter Florida when its glories are somewhat veiled by the gentle frosts that silver its palmetto and pine-barrens. But I had my first glimpse of the Land of flowers through the soft haze of a June sunrise. Thirty years ago, traveling from New Orleans to Florida was mostly by water; June 27, we steamed from New Orleans through an artificial outlet called the New Basin, and through lakes bearing the historic names of Maurepas and Ponchartrain, which give a pleasant water way to Western Florida. Till evening, we were in sight of land. The magnificent oaks and magnolias of Bay St. Louis, the white villas of Pass Christian, Deer Island half concealing Biloxi beach, were faintly visible in the luminous atmosphere.

When opposite the sandy wastes of Pascagoula, we bent over the side of the vessel to catch the tender cadence, of the mermaid's song, and we looked into the waters for the towers and caverns of the gentle Indian whom her seductive music is said to have lured beneath the wave:

> "He sees the round towers of other days
> In the waves beneath him shining."

We thought of the priest who is yet to sail on these mystic waters at twelve of the clock some Christmas night. And well doth the legend say that neither he

nor his frail canoe will ever again be seen by human
eye, for no frail barque could long drift on these
treacherous waves. We were now really at sea, no
land being visible. About daybreak we had our first
glimpse of Florida. The red round sun was coming
slowly out of the water, and a raw breeze attended the
unfolding of the morning. A broad ribbon of silver
sand separated the green woods from the dark sea.
We passed Florida light-house, the finest on the Gulf,
and the ruins of Fort McRae, whose ramparts, battle-
ments, and posterns, are gradually yielding to the destroying element.

Leaving behind the enormous Fort Barrancas, we
were soon opposite Florida Navy Yard. The snow
white sand was blinding in the summer sun, but the
heat, tempered by the brisk sea breezes, was not unpleasant. A granite wall rises from the water along
the front of the yard, and immense magazine and
machine shops are scattered under the trees. Central
Avenue bounded by giant oaks, with pyramids of shot
between, leads to the beautiful home of the Commo-
dore. Here and there are the handsome residences of
the other officers, each with its garden made of rich,
imported soil, laid on the sand. The fine brick and
stone dwellings of the Yard, and the enormous piles
of the U. S. Barracks and Hospital, are in sharp contrast with the shingle-roofed cottages of the outlying
villages of Warrington and Wolsey.

Having heard mass in the neat, pretty church at
Warrington, we were soon underway for Pensacola.
The harbor looked its brightest, as the vessels had
their colors flying, in honor, we were told, of the Feast
of St. Peter and Paul. We stepped ashore to the
music of the noon-day *Angelus*.

During the civil war, Pensacola and its adjacent Navy Yard were almost entirely destroyed, still, many of the original features survived. Previously, the town had been regarded as a mere appanage of " the Yard " and the Gulf Squadron. But it has since been, with no little success, carving out a destiny for itself. Its antiquated look has almost disappeared.

The Pensacola I saw for the first time in 1877, a quaint old town, slumbering beside its beautiful Bay, Santa Maria, will never more be seen by mortal eyes. Two terrible fires have swept away the last vestiges of its early Spanish days. The long flights of steps leading to old houses, the deep sand of the roadways which muffled the sound of every vehicle, the plank walks enlivened by gophers and lizards—nothing of this is now seen. Pensacola has brick stores, and flagged sidewalks, and electric light like its Northern Sisters. One must ascend the Hill to find the broad verandahs, flower-bedecked windows, and embowering shrubbery that gave the old city its festive appearance in its slumbrous days, when its gay, sweet-voiced people enjoyed life as it glided by, before progress had well-nigh swept all poetry from its borders.

On the Hill, a hill by courtesy, are the ruins of the old Spanish Fort, a building of much interest, near which, tradition says, the first mass was celebrated over two hundred years ago. From the Fort is a magnificent view of the Bay. Looking towards Cuba, about five hundred miles off, one sees the broad shining waters studded with vessels near the land, mostly coming for lumber, though trade is done in other commodities, as grain, cotton, fish. The Pensacolians boast that their bay is spacious enough to hold the navies of the world. The largest vessels load and unload alongside her railroad wharves.

Behind you, as you stand by the Fort, San Miguel, is a wilderness of sand and pine, with a knee high growth of heather and several most unpoetic looking groves of scrub oak, varied by clumps of fan-shaped palmetto, and scraggy cypress, some of the poorest specimens Florida counts of her luxuriant sylva. Before you, is the limitless sweep of water beyond the bay, the blue sea, and the blue sky, divided by the sandy slopes of Santa Rosa, the breakwater of the harbor—a sand key of the gulf, about forty miles long, varying in breadth from a quarter of a mile to a mile, seven miles from the city—the whole shimmering in the noonday sun. The town seemed a strange mosaic of Spanish, American and Indian peculiarities, an irregular mass of lights and shadows. But when the moon effaced the stars, it seemed an enchanted city, seated by an ocean of molten silver.

Though many Spanish names still appear in the directory, as Moreno, Castillo, Gonzales, Sierra, Yniestra, Sanchez, the old city has grown cosmopolitan. Few countries in Europe and few States in the Union are now unrepresented in Pensacola. The colored population equals the white in number.

The pretty, antique church of ancient days, dedicated, like the Fort, to St. Michael, was burned during the yellow fever epidemic in October, 1882. Our visit to these regions awakened a laudable curiosity to learn somewhat of the history, particularly, religious, of this pleasant land so redolent of poetry and romance. Our first visit ended on a bright Sunday morning, in July, 1877. The obliging Captain kindly waited until we had heard mass. The bay was clear as crystal, and

6

swarmed with fishes which we could see disporting themselves in its pellucid depths.

Towards the shore, in several places, were acres of the wonderful green waters which looked so picturesque among the aisles of the Carribean Sea. Farther out were sharks, gars, and porpoises, with big dorsal fins, blowing and spouting like whales —gulls and frigate birds enlivened the air, and whenever we neared land we could hear the clear whistling of the cardinal birds, which looked like sparks of fire among the trees, and the melody that pours from the throat of the gray mocking-bird. Now and then the strains of the banjo or guitar, accompanying sweet songs, fell pleasantly on our ears. The moon was rising gently before we lost sight of the silvery coast of Florida with its crown of dark green trees. The natives of Florida cling to the land that bore them. Yea, even the stranger within their gates must come again, for the saying in these parts is: "Those who get Florida sand in their shoes will surely come back to the flowery land." Pensacola may boast, like Ronsard's friend: "When I was young a poet sang of me." We thought of the poet's song:

> "Now Santa Rosa's snow white sands
> Are fading from my sight;
> Farewell, awhile, to thee and thine,
> Sweet Florida, good-night!"

CHAPTER X.

KING PHILIP II. named Pamphilo de Narvaez
Governor or regidor of the first pueblo he should establish in Florida, but the mission of this great man
was a failure. The lands he discovered were not the
" Fortunate Island " to him. From Willard's History
of America (Barnes & Co. New York, 1859,) we
learn that three hundred Spanish families went from
Vera Cruz to Pensacola to found the capital of Western
Florida. Civilizing influences were at work, and the
priests never lessened their labors. One whole tribe,
the Apalachees, became fervent Christians, having long
enjoyed the ministrations of devoted Spanish priests.

They have given their name to a bay, a town, a
river, and the Apalachian range. At Fernandina, a
church was built in honor of Father Michael de
Auñon, a martyr.

Spain claimed in Florida all land north of Mexico.
The Spanish Governor came from Pensacola to Mobile
to protest against the new settlement. Bienville received him, Señor Guzman, courteously. Iberville
wanted to take Pensacola, but the Spanish Junta would
not give it up. Bienville continued on good terms
with his Spanish neighbor. Jan. 7, 1706, Señor Guzman came to spend four days in Mobile. He was God-
father at a Christening ,and gave largesse bountifully
to all.

When Spain declared war against England, Don

Bernardo Galvez, Governor of Louisiana, surprised Fort Manchac, Sept. 7, 1779. He invested Mobile in March, 1780; it surrendered March 12. Baton Rouge surrendered, March 21. After a vigorous siege, he reduced Pensacola, in May, 1780. Through its young hero, Western Florida once more became thoroughly Catholic, and the services of the Church resumed their former pomp and solemnity.

A new Register was begun by the Capuchin, Father de Velez, a beneficed priest of St. Michaels, Pensacola, and chaplain of the garrison. He belonged to the Capuchin Province of Andalusia. His first funeral was that of Anthony Soler, July 4, 1781. His first baptism was that of Diego John Michael, son of Francis Florin and his wife, Catherine Alois. In 1791, Bishop Cyrillo made an official visit, as is entered in the Register of " San Miguel de Panzacola." May 7, 1798, Right Rev. Bishop Peñalvert officially visited the same. All was probably found in good order, as no particulars are noted.

In 1793, ended the administration of Bishop Cyrillo in Louisiana and the Floridas. The King directed him to return to his Province, Catalonia. In Havana, he awaited means of transportation, leading meanwhile a most edifying life. He was still there in 1799. The King expressed surprise and displeasure that his orders had been disregarded by those who should have supplied the funds for the journey to Catalonia.

Bishop Cyrillo, was a man of saintly life, austere and mortified. In a vicious age and amid evil surroundings, he kept himself pure before God, and endeavored by word and example to correct the prevailing laxity of morals and discipline. By some writers of his day he is represented in an odious light, but not a single fact has been adduced to support such allegations. His duties were of a disagreeable nature, and he, possibly, lacked the ability essential in a great reformer, to do unpleasant things in a not unkindly manner. He may even have been embittered by the slanders of his enemies, mostly, those of his own household, and lacked the mildness and benignity St. Paul recommends to Apostolic men. But he led an irreproachable life, and strove, according to his lights, to make the great God known, loved, and served. For his undeniable virtues and his perpetual labors in an unpromising field, he had no reward in this world. Bitter persecution fell to his lot: even the King, in his high office of " Protector of the Council of Trent," had no protection to accord to this faithful laborer in his master's vineyard. But though his virtues are unsung, and his grave unknown, we may well believe that he now rejoices with exceeding joy in the bosom of his Father, and prays for the lands his feet trod in the search for sinners. Blessed is the man to whom the Lord hath not imputed sin and in whose spirit there is no guile.

When the English took possession of Florida, Lord Thurlow declared: " The free exercise of their religion by the laity, and of their functions by the clergy, are also reserved." But after Galvez' victories in West Florida, and in Louisiana up to Natchez, the Church recovered her former splendor. Many of the Natchez people were Protestants. The historian of Mississippi says:

" No attempt was made to proselytize or proscribe them—nor was there ever any official interference, unless parties in their zeal, or indiscreet advisers, became offensively demonstrative. There was, in fact, more

religious freedom and toleration for Protestants in the
Natchez district, than Catholics and dissenters from
the ruling denomination enjoyed, in either Old or New
England." [1]

The English-speaking people whom the Catholic
King was anxious to convert were chiefly those who
had settled, or might settle, in Southern regions.
Little hope was indulged of converting the English in
the North. Some, indeed, returned in 1607, to their
island home, England, giving the land of the Pilgrims
a bad name: "a cold, barren, mountainous desert,
where they found nothing but extreme extremities."

But the inhabitants of the Florida which Juan Ponce
de Leon had seen rising, a faint white streak between
the blue, flashing waters of the Gulf "a sea of glass
mingled with fire," and the tender green of the young
trees—these had made the country their home. English settlers had cast their lot among the sweet-voiced
señoras and Señoritas, and there were marrying and
giving in marriage; and when children came to bless
the homes by the old Fort, or in the forest, the be-
lieving wife saved the child, often with the concurrence
of the unbelieving husband. The King appointed Irish
priests who spoke Spanish and other languages,
for the convenience of the little mixed settlements.
In St. Augustine, some of these zealous Irish priests
had been selected by the Bishop of Salamanaca to
keep religion alive among the Spaniards and attract
strangers to the One Fold. The Register shows many
baptisms of white and colored. Governor Zepedes
urged the King to establish a parish on each river—
St. John's and St. Mary's,—which he did. Much
power was given the King as " Protector of the Council

[1] Quoted by J. G. Shea in the Life of Archbishop Carroll.

of Trent," and history shows that he used it for the
benefit of the true Church. Father Velez was succeeded by Father Valoria, in Pensacola, in 1785. The
Register continues to show the mixed character of the
congregation. Father Troconis became chaplain of the
Hospital, in 1784. From 1794, Pensacola was attended by Rev. James Coleman, who was appointed
Parish Priest, and Chaplain of the garrison. Spanish,
French, Irish and Scotch names continue to appear in
the Register. March 19, 1790, died at St. Augustine
at the age of sixty, Rev. Dr. Peter Camps, so long the
devoted Pastor of the Minorcans, fortified by the
sacraments of the Church. He was buried in the
Campo Santo, (cemetery), his bereaved disciples, weeping over his grave. Father Font came from Catalonia
to succeed Dr. Camps in the care of the Minorcans,
whom he attended faithfully till his pious death, 1793.
He had tenderly loved his lamented predecessor, and
in death they were not divided. In 1800, the bodies
of these holy men were removed to the Parish Church,
by Rev. Michael O'Reilly, who styles himself "the
unworthy successor of Dr. Camps." It is said that,
"to equal a predecessor one must have twice his
worth." But the people of his day found Father
O'Reilly fully equal to any who had preceded him.
The last resting places of these holy men are pointed
out to visitors to St. Augustine, as sacred spots.

In 1785, Dr. Camps was sixteen years in Florida
In 1789, he was nominated to a canonry in Minorca.
In his petition to the King, he asked leave to return
to his native island, Majorca, October 28, 1786. It
is said that St. Ignatius and St. Teresa always expected great success when they met serious obstacles
in the beginning of a good work. But Dr. Camps had

genuine success, in the beginning and the end, for he taught the Faith to his flock and kept it among them. And it is fitting that his remains should repose among them, as they do.

If the ancient Ponce de Leon sought in vain for the fabled fountain of perennial youth; if other navigators sailed into the bright harbors of Florida to slake their thirst for gems and gold which vanished before their gaze, like the *fata morgana* that often appeared to dazzle their vision in the luminous atmosphere, one thing is certain, wherever the Catholic navigators turned the prow of a vessel, on what shores soever they landed, their priests and brothers were always on the alert to carry the glad tidings of salvation to all the tribes of these Southern regions.

But the English Colonies carried war into the peaceful villages of Florida: Ciudad, Puebla, Presidio, and simple settlements were destroyed. The missionaries and their forest children were sometimes slaughtered; many were reduced to servitude, and others were sold in the slave-markets of the West Indies.

When Spain ceded Florida to England, 1763, the poor savages became as sheep without a shepherd. Deprived of their Fathers in the Faith, many fell back into the barbarism from which Christianity has rescued them. Others fled to the pathless Everglades, and, under the name of Seminoles, or wanderers, became the most powerful foes the whites had yet encountered, till they were conquered under General Jackson (1830), and the remnant forced to migrate to the Indian Territory.

What was done when Spanish valor restored the Country to Spain, was done for the white more than the Red men. Or rather, it is the whites, chiefly, who were benefited, because the poor Indians had been, in most cases, massacred, or outlawed, or sold into slavery.

Spanish domination is a thing of the past. French political influences are no longer at work in these regions. But in the story of early days are facts stranger than fiction which, while they give the charm and fascination of romance to the narrative, grieve the Christian soul that reflects on what has been, and what might have been, indeed, had the dreams of the Apostolic men who labored for souls on this fair Continent, and gave their life-blood for the Faith—been realized.

CHAPTER XI.

Le Moyne d' Iberville, the pioneer of French colonization on the Gulf of Mexico, and the founder of the Province of Louisiana, cast anchor at Ship Island, Feb. 10, 1699. He selected a bluff, *petite montagne,* as the early chroniclers say. He had passed through Maurepas and Ponchartrain to Bay St. Louis. On the small Bay of Biloxi he erected a fort, and planted around it forty immigrants.

He had sought a site at Pensacola but found it occupied. He explored Mobile Point, Massacre Island, and the West Shore of Mobile Bay. Experience soon showed him the necessity of a better position than barren Biloxi.[1] Missionaries visited the French settlements, and the first Mass was celebrated at Biloxi; Easter Sunday, April 19, 1700.

In those days the French Government still held with Plutarch that a city could more easily grow without grounds, than without altars. And through its patronage, churches were usually erected in its newly founded colonies. Thus it was neither commercial enterprise nor royal ambition, that carried the power of France into the heart of our Continent.[2] The motive was

[1] The old fort was burned at what is now Ocean Springs, 1717, New Biloxi, was on the point of land west of the bay, fronting Chip island.
[2] *Monette. Hist. Valley Miss.*

religion. The unwearied Jesuits were always in advance of civilization.

The soil of Biloxi was sandy as the deserts of Lybia. Frogs, mosquitoes and alligators abounded as they do to-day, although Biloxi has become a modern city. The settlers cared little for agricultural pursuits, but devoted their time to a fruitless search for mines and pearls. Iberville sent the veteran, Tonti, to summon the Chickasaws to a conference at the picturesque little settlement. Behind the missioners, followed the fur-traders.

The poverty of Biloxi was apparent. The treasure-galleons of Spain came to the Isthmus of Panama for their golden freight of precious bars and ingots, brought by mule-trains overland, to be collected by the fleet from Peru, but no part of such treasures ever found its way to the sandy gulf coast. The roads were mere trails which mostly followed the water-sheds.

Speaking of these Southern regions,[1] Father du Poisson, S. J., wrote: " The greatest torment, in comparison with which all the rest would be but sport, which passes all belief and has never been even imagined in France, still less actually experienced, is that of the mosquitoes. The plagues of Egypt I think were not more cruel. This little insect has caused more swearing since the French have been in Mississippi than had previously taken place in all the rest of the world."

The daring Jesuits were striving to make a new Paraguay among the Iroquois, as they did later among the Californians. And these zealous missioners, ex-

---

[1] The great body of the Jesuits led most pious lives, and suffered the greatest privations to redeem the savages from heathenism.

celling among the excellent, seldom knew failure. The Aborigines were often brutal and indolent, but the priests, by preaching better things and practising what they preached, brought about a wonderful change.

Marquette and Joliet explored the northern rivers far enough to know that the Mississippi emptied into the Gulf of Mexico. They must have noticed the discoloration of the Mississippi by the fierce muddy Missouri, which Charlevoix pronounced the finest confluence in the world. Certainly, as we know from experience, a grand spectacle.

The great navigator, La Salle, determined to reach the mouths of the Mississippi. He was born in Rouen and educated by the Jesuits of that city. Unlike the pupils of that illustrious body, in general, he conceived a foolish, unreasoning dislike for them, which followed him through life, and was a blot on a noble character.

From the Italian wars, Prince Conti had brought to Paris Henri de Tonty, whom he recommended to La Salle. Tonty showed himself the Bayard of navigators, " without fear and without reproach." He is known in history as " the faithful Tonty." His unwavering allegiance and loving friendship were among the few consolations of La Salle's sorrowful life. Indians La Salle could conciliate and manage; but with his own countrymen, owing to his overbearing, exacting temper, he was rarely successful.

La Salle thought he could make a western passage to China by the Missouri. The estate which the Sulpitians gave him near Montreal he called La Chine, China.

Tonty had lost an arm by the explosion of a grenade in Sicily. The deficiency he concealed by a copper or iron hand, which he usually covered with a glove, and which he is said to have used sometimes on refractory Indians.

Another associate of La Salle was the celebrated Recollect Friar, Hennepin, to whom he gave special instructions for the exploration of the Upper Mississippi. This intrepid missioner was the first to discover coal in America; the primitive mine is near Ottawa, Ills. He explored the river with much success; and he named a beautiful waterfall he met, " The Falls of St. Anthony," after the beloved Portuguese Franciscan, St. Anthony of Padua. Strange things have been told of him, about his claiming the honor of discoveries due to others,[1] for it is certain he never navigated the Mississippi below the Ohio. If he ever made such a claim, it was a blunder, and might even be called by a harsher name. For Hennepin's[2] brilliant activity did enough to secure a respectable share of glory for himself. Many a mariner enjoys high honors who did no more. He has been called the picturesque Hennepin, and the Recollect, who never recollects anything correctly. But this is too severe.

Filled with great projects of exploration and colonization, La Salle underwent many hardships and disappointments in carrying out his plans. True, he had one wonderful triumph. But he had endless discouragements, and more than once tasted the bitter-

[1] La Salle placed Chevalier Tonti in command at Crève Coeur—Rock Fort—an issolated cliff, rising 200 feet above the river, which flows near its base, in the centre of a lovely country, of verdant prairies richly tufted with black walnut, etc. This rocky site may still be seen.

Some years ago a few enterprising Yankees chose it as the site of a town they wished to call Gibraltar. But it remains as it was in the days of La Salle, an impregnable site for a fortress.

[2] The whole distance from the mouth of the Arkansas to the Falls of St. Anthony is about 1500 miles. This distance he crossed twice.

ness of treachery. His richly-freighted vessel, the Griffon, with its cargo was lost. Discontent among his men foreboded mutiny, dispelled his hopes and broke his spirits. His crosses and afflictions may be judged from the name he gave, in the bitterness of his spirit, to one of the later forts he built: *Crève Coeur,* the broken heart.

After having navigated three of the great lakes he found himself launched on the Mississippi with several Franciscans, twenty-three Frenchmen, and eighteen Indians. He steered south, the priests visiting the Indian villages on the banks, and evangelizing them. The vessel kept a southerly direction until the great gulf opened on their enraptured vision.

La Salle and his companion now chanted the *Te Deum* and planted a cross. Then in the name of the King of France, amid volleys of musketry, they took possession of the whole country, and in his honor La Salle called it by the sweet-sounding name, Louisiana, a name on which he had fixed before he left Canada.

" We stand," writes McGee, " sword in hand under the banner of the cross, the tutelary genius of those great States which stretch from the Ontario to the Rio Grande, and from the Gulf to the sources of the Missouri. Every league of that region he trod on foot, and every league of its waters he traversed in frail canoes, or crazy schooners."

April 6, they came to the three mouths by which the river discharges into the sea. People afterwards gave one of these a bad name, saying that it was easier to pass an elephant through the eye of a needle, than a ship through it; that other passes should be closed so that the current thus increased would carry off the bar before the Balize. La Salle examined the Western;

Tonty, the middle; and d'Autray, the other. Soon the water under the boats became brackish, and changed to brine; the breeze smelt salt and they saw the waves of the Gulf so long sought, so long dreamed of. Then came more exploration, and lastly La Salle's taking possession, the grandest event since the Landing of Columbus.

On a dry spot above the passes, they landed, and prepared a column and a cross. On the column they painted the arms of France with the King's name. Then they sang the *Te Deum, the Exaudiat,* the *Domine Salvum fac Regem;* then, salvos of artillery and shouts of *Vive le Roi!* At the foot of the column, La Salle declared: "On part of the high powerful, invincible, and victorious Prince, Louis the Great, by the Grace of God, King of France and Navarre, fourteenth of the name, to-day, April 9, 1682, by virtue of the commission of His Majesty which I hold in my hand, open to the inspection of all whom it may concern . . . . . I take possession of this country of Louisiana . . . . . I call to witness those who hear me, and I demand the certificate of the Notary present for confirmation." La Salle placed in the ground at the foot of the tree to which was attached the cross, a leaden plaque. It has on one side the arms of France and on the other Robertus Cavalier cum Domino de Tonty, legato, R. P. Zenobio Membre Recollecto . . . . . To the proces-verbal, made by Jacques de Metairie Notary, were signed twelve names, including La Salle, Father Zenobio, Henri de Tonty, and Nicholas de la Salle.

La Salle was a great explorer, but he was not an expert in dealing withh men. He was at once unamiable and dictatorial, and while he expected all to

obey him, he suffered none to share his counsels. After
disasters of various kinds, he returned to France,
leaving Tonty his deputy, in America. Tonty did
not share the prejudices of his commander against the
Jesuits.

La Salle was the hero of the day in France, and he
secured all he asked for: he and his colonists sailed
for the Gulf, 1685. They missed the mouths of the
Mississippi, and it is said that his Lieutenant Beaujeu
abandoned him, and sailed back to map the Mississippi
passes.

He went ashore with some colonists near Matagorda
Bay, on Texas soil. Terrible were their sufferings, and
the men mutinied against a leader whom they considered the cause of their miseries. March 19, he was
murdered from an ambuscade, near Trinity River.
When the faithful Tonty heard of La Salle's troubles
he went to the Gulf in search of him, 1686. Not
finding him, he left a letter (speaking bark) which an
Indian was to give him. For a hatchet, the Indian
produced the letter Tonty had written to La Salle many
years before. He produced also an Imitation of Christ,
and a gun, which he said the Iron Hand had given
him.

When Tonty descended to the mouths of the
Mississippi, with twenty-five men, to aid his friend, he
found the cross which La Salle had erected eight years
before, lying half buried in the sand, and set it up
again, but found no trace of his beloved friend. All
the Indians he met going and coming were friendly.
On a tree, standing near the cross, he fixed a sign, and
in the hollow of it, he placed a letter addressed: " A
M. De La Salle, Governeur-General de la Louisiana."
This letter was never delivered.

La Salle's is perhaps the saddest history among the great explorers. His murderers perished deservedly. His plans died with him. The great river had proved fatal to many. It seemed as if the legends were true that evil spirits guarded this stream. Let us hope that the assassin's bullet brought rest to the troubled soul of this great explorer.

"His capacity for large designs," says Sparks, "and for procuring the resources to carry them forward, has few parallels amongst the most eminent discoverers."

7

CHAPTER XII.

MANY richly freighted vessels started on their homeward path and never returned. Tradition points to spots in the ocean where millions of doubloons lie, which will probably remain among the " Treasures of the deep " of which Mrs. Hemans sings. Expeditions were frequently organized to search in Barbadoes, and in the isles of the Carribean Sea, for these buried hoards. Men spent time and money hunting for the lost galleons of Spain, undeterred by the fact that many a serious commercial undertaking has proved a mere " will o' the wisp," and of treasure troves, so far, none have proved available, whether in the palm-covered isles of the Gulf of Mexico, or the coral cays of the Carribean. Thirty-seven millions in gold, and silver sank in the harbor of St. Vigo, in Spain. One company after another vainly sought the treasure. A richly-freighted ship sank off San Domingo, but neither wreck nor prize was ever found.

The first commercial highway in America, and for three centuries the most important, was designed by Cortez, chiefly for the transfer of such treasurers—the romantic calzada or shod-mule track, from Vera Cruz to the City of Mexico. This was a paved highway, one hundred leagues long, from the sea-board to the exterior on which, besides the gems and precious metals, were carried indigo, silk, spices, cochineal, cacas, from

one extremity to the other. The military roads of the
incas were used in the same way, and are often compared, but not aptly, to the famous Roman roads of
yore. These, however, were in a different part of the
country. Good roads or even paths through the forest,
were useful not only in carrying wealth and produce
from one point to another, but in affording passage to
apostolic men, going from tribe to tribe, to convert
souls: " How beautiful are the feet of those who
preach the gospel, who bring to souls the glad tidings
of Salvation!

The first teamster who introduced the wheel in
America, and the driving of oxen, was Blessed Sebastian de Aparicio, an early immigrant, who drove ox-
carts from Vera Cruz to Mexico. He became a
Franciscan Lay Brother, and died in Pueblo, in 1600,
in the odor of sanctity, aged ninety-eight years. He
was all but worshiped by the Indians, and in his
humble state must have converted thousands. He
wrought many miracles and was beatified by Pope
Clement XIII. His life was published some years ago
by the late Very Rev. Dr. Faber. He has been selected
chief Patron of Pueblo, where his ashes repose.

Discovery, exploration, and settlement were the
usual titles to ownerships. Florida was the objective
point of many an expedition which sailed by way of
Jamaica. Narvaez left Spain, June 17, 1527, with 600
men in five vessels. All but four were drowned; these
after weary wanderings reached Mexico, and were received as brethren and friends. De Soto's march as we
have related, is almost without a parallel, in song or
story. He died of wasting fever at the early age of
forty-one. He had crossed the country like a meteor,
and he reposes in his oaken coffin beneath the waves

of the awful Mississippi, until, at the voice of the archangel, the earth and the water will give forth their dead.

The whole valley of the Mississippi was the magnificent domain which La Salle added to the kingdom of France, April 9, 1683. Not a fountain babbled west 'of the Alleghany but was described as being in the French empire.

To colonize this immense region came the famous Lemoyne Brothers, Iberville, Bienville, and the rest. To aid them in this came Crozat, the merchant Prince, born a peasant, in whom lived again the spirit of the Medici, and of the powerful Company of the Indies, which had obtained from the French Government large Colonial grants, and was connected with Louisiana from 1713 to 1732. To-day the name is confined to a single State, and not a very large one.

Needless to follow the career of John Law, the Scotch " Magician of Finance," who failed utterly to do what was expected of him, and, having returned to Europe, died in poverty and obscurity at Venice. He had become a Catholic shortly before. Grants of estates along the river attracted many French gentlemen of family. Peasants were induced to try their fortunes in Louisiana, and Germans settled on the estate of John Law, still called " the German Coast." The country seemed for the time unable to take care of all who emigrated, and, in 1721, the troops had to seek support among the Indian villages.

In Florida, Melendez wanted laborers instead of gentlemen. Too many of the colonists were deserters and galley slaves, and it is only by exception that criminals make good colonists. Those who had only aristocratic blood to recommend them were soon at a discount. In 1573, fifty men with their families came from Asturias, one hundred and fifty from the Azores, fifty from Seville, and one hundred Portuguese laborers, brought much prosperity to Florida.

It is an historical fact that "runners" brought fresh fish from the ocean one hundred leagues inland, in something over two days. Muleteers were of wonderful swiftness. At one period a law forbade any one to ride on mules save children and members of religious congregations. But the people "circulated," to use the new English, as fast as they pleased, and, above all, the missioners seem to have found out their flocks with lightning speed. They went knee-deep, or waist deep, in water. They toiled through the morass, and went forward in the desert, where miniature cyclones swirled and gyrated clouds of dust,—they moved on until they found their flocks, as patiently and as successfully as if relays of horses or oxen awaited them at every post.

In the dim aisles of the forest they pressed forward in primeval silence, carrying their God-given message to savage and slave. The Name of Jesus and the love of Jesus allured them. Like Jogues carving the Name of Jesus on the treees, as he passed on, hungry, cold, and weary, seeking the lost sheep of the House of Israel, the light of divine love on his face, his tortured hands, mute witnesses of the sufferings he had undergone for that Sacred Name, which is above all Names, and through which alone we can be saved!

Between 1528 and 1536, Cabeza de Vaca and three comrades walked ten thousand miles. Andrew D'Ocampo and Lucas and Sebastian Donados trudged over twenty thousand miles of the transcontinental wilderness in the nine years following their escape from Kansas, 1542. The Esquimaux with dog-teams, five hundred sometimes in a pack-train; the incas with their lamas; the kyaks of the North Pacific, could hardly do more. Distance seems to have been annihilated for the sainted missioners and the fearless pioneers.

When De Soto and his men were marching in the vicinity of Macon, Georgia, two Indians near the mounds, Mark and Peter, being assailed by the devil, at night, as the story runneth, asked to be baptized. They were guides, and hence the devils punished them. They showed De Soto the marks on their bodies. He asked the priests to baptize them, so that the devil could no longer have power over them.[1]

[1] Herrera. *Expedition of De Soto.*

CHAPTER XIII.

AGAIN as a crux of the missioners we must mention
that terrible atom, the mosquito. A missioner said he
would rather be devoured by lions than by these insects.
" Many things one gets accustomed to," said another
" but not to the irritation of mosquitoes." Bars of
any stuff are of little use. The boils they raise upon
those they prey on must be lanced, and this severe
remedy scarcely relieves them. Madeleine Hachard,
the youngest of the Ursulines who came in 1727, says
she lived in " perpetual fear of being assassinated by
the mosquitoes," blood-thirsty atoms, to this day the
plague of the Passes. As they ascended the river, they
went ashore every night and slept in the forest, though
the air was on fire with mosquitoes " every one," says
she, " provided with a sting like a red hot-nail." The
ugly fashion of wearing patches on the face prevailed
among the colonial ladies, as among their Sisters by the
Thames, the Seine, and the Liffey. They may have
been useful in concealing the bites of the myriads of
mosquitoes, " which hide in the trees till sundown and
then come out to prey on us all night." Matters were
not improved when they landed from their chaloupes
in New Orleans, August 7, 1727. The monastery the
West Indian Company was building them was far
from completion, and they were hospitably received in

Bienville's Country house, the best in the Colony. The surrounding wilderness full of specimens of the *fauna* of Louisiana,[1] was the home of reptiles, vultures, and wild beasts. But it bred especially fire-flies and mosquitoes, which our novice calls *Frappe d'abord* " which sting without mercy." They hovered about the nuns from sunrise to sunset, never failing to leave their traces.

The religious establishments of Louisiana in 1725, consisted of New Orleans with 600 families, Mobile 60, Apalache 30, mostly Indians, Balize 6, Les Allemands 200, Pointe Coupée 100, Natchez[2] 6, Natchitoches 50. The governors were unanimous in complaining of the troops sent hither from France. Bienville inveighs against their small size, some being only four and a half feet tall, and says their vices equalled their cowardice. The French had generally good leaders. Gravier is one of many who praises Bienville's Government (1700) and Kerlerec was styled the " Father of the Choctaws."

Towards the middle of the eighteenth century the Jesuits received a royal warrant from the King of Spain, empowering them to repeat in California the Reductions of Paraguay. Within sixty years sixteen missions were established. Around each mission were clustered villages of converted savages. A royal decree, signed *Yo el Rey,* expelled the originators of this useful work. This King, Charles III., died December 14, 1788. Solemn services were held for the repose

[1] The tropical forest is almost a solid mass of trailing vines and thorny brush, alive with insects; every insect has a mouth of fire.

[2] Villa Gayoso, a Spanish church and village, was near the bluff, about fifteen miles above Natchez. It always had a resident priest in early days. It was also called Cole's Creek.

of his soul, in St. Louis Church, New Orleans, May 7, 1789.

Many Franciscans came with the saintly Junipero Serra. They led the lives of Apostles, and often met the fate of Apostles. They were ready to go anywhere for the succor of the infant Church. Thus Father Margil having heard that the French at Natchitoches had seldom or never been visited by a priest, went thither from Dolores, on foot, said mass for the people and administered to them the sacraments of penance and the Holy Eucharist. The Vicar General of Mobile, probably the Abbé de la Vente, forwarded to the zealous missioner a letter of thanks for this great charity.

Louisiana was divided into nine districts, by the Company of the Indies, (1721),—Mobile, New Orleans, Biloxi, Alibamons, Natchez, Yazoo, Natchitoches, Arkansas, and Illinois. Mobile was the great rendezvous of the savages. The climate was mild and healthy, and the people kind and pleasant. The Colony of Louisiana had increased from 500 whites to 5000, and from 20 negroes, to 250. The Spaniards conceded that Louisiana of which we shall soon speak more immediately, extended beyond Mobile Bay to the east.

Sauvolle, Governor of Fort Maurepas, at Biloxi, examined and sounded the coast; and, from a daring fighter, became a practical colonizer. From time to time Colonists were brought out, and soon the old forts, were enlivened by women and children. The priests came among them to soothe their sorrows, share their trials, baptize their children, anoint them in their last illness, and invoke the blessing of the church over their graves. When, in 1717, at the command of that grand organizer, Bienville, the capital was removed; another of these matchless brethren was on hand to take his place.

Iberville, a youth in Canada and in France, was educated in schools, and ship. He had taken part in four expeditions in Hudson Bay. In 1694, he and four younger brothers, undertook to capture Fort Nelson. Their chaplain was the Jesuit, Gabriel Marest. When the wind became adverse they made a vow to St. Anne that they would give her part of their treasures, and almost all received the sacraments. Thereupon, the wind became favorable. They were brave and gallant men, but, above all, good Christians. In 1693, Iberville married, and his first child was born off the grand bank of Newfoundland. His wife was often the companion of his voyages. But the chief man who knew how to manipulate both whites and Indians, so as to bring about their allegiance and subjugation, was Bienville.

Iberville returned from France, 1702. The climate of the Tropics had begun to tell on the hardy Canadian, and still more his incessant labors and privations. Sauvolle died at Biloxi, July 22, 1701, of bilious or yellow fever. Iberville was attacked by a similar disease. He died at Havana, whither he had gone to recuperate, July 9, 1706, tenderly nursed by his devoted wife. His remains were laid to rest in the Parish Church of St. Christopher, where for a time reposed the bones of Columbus.

Almost all the Spanish clergy and officials visited Mobile, and it can scarcely be doubted that there were more Catholics in the little town, once the capital of half the continent, than history mentions; the death of Iberville was a severe blow to the infant Colonies.

He had only left Rochelle, October, 1698, and, in January, 1699, made land near the Gulf, stopping at night, and in the fogs. It took their squadron two days to arrive opposite the thin strip of land which half encloses Mobile Bay on the South; a low, flat island covered with sand and bones, suggesting some barbarity on part of the Indians and for this named by the brothers, Massacre Island, (now Dauphin Island). They crossed to Biloxi, built a fort of four bastions upon which were mounted twelve guns, over which waved the lilies of France.

Sometimes a good came, so to say, indirectly to the Colonists. The English settlers in Carolina treated the French Huguenots with much severity, though they finally admitted them to citizenship. About 1695, a vessel from Madagascar touched at Carolina. The captain gave Governor Archdales a bag of seed rice and imparted to him the manner of its culture. This was distributed among many planters and to this accident the State owes its staple commodity. We recall the nursery rhyme

> "Tea comes from China
> Rice from Carolina."

Tobacco became early an article of commerce, and was raised as well as rice in many parts of the country. "What a pity," said poor Charles I.[1]," that so much of our prosperity in America should be founded on smoke.

The United States early took hold of the Indian problem. George Washington, as a youth, had been much with Indians, and, when President, often sought

---

[1] "Charles I. our late most excellent and undoubtedly sainted King.'

to protect them in their rights. He advised them to cultivate the soil, as game would necessarily soon be scarce—an advice the Catholic Bishops and clergy had frequently given them. Indians were removed from Alabama in 1836, but many remained and were found in various places years after, always objects of solicitude to the church. The great fires of 1827 and 1839, almost destroyed the old town of Mobile. Historic points are still shown, but French and Spanish buildings are but little known in the Gulf City.

" The Catholic Church in the United States claims all the early struggles of the first Apostles, their weary marches, their untiring toil to instruct the rude people and the savage; the constant offering of the Holy Sacrifice, the imparting of the sacraments; as part of her glorious heritage to men of all races; the heroic days of her history. Her priests were the pioneers to plod over the Indian trail, to study the vegetable and mineral wealth of the land, and perpetuate in scientific form the unwritten languages of our countless Indian tribes, to discharge unflinchingly the ministry of the altar and the word, and to die, as fully a hundred did, by savage hands while heroically discharging their duty."

In the partition of America between Spain and Portugal, May 4, 1493, Pope Alexander VI., may have had in view to preserve the rights of Columbus and his heirs to the vice-royalty and tenths of the riches of the new continent. solemnly guaranteed to them. Humbolt says:

" The state of science and the imperfectness of all the instruments that could serve on sea to measure time and space, did not permit yet, in 1493, the practical solution of so commonplace a problem. In this state

of things, Pope Alexander VI., in arrogating to himself the right of dividing a hemisphere between two
powerful nations, rendered, without knowing it, a
signal service to nautical astronomy, and to the phys-
ical theory of terrestrial magnetism."

CHAPTER XIV.

WE give here the names of the early priests who labored in Louisiana:

Mons. Le Maire, 1723—1734; C. P. Mathias, 1734 —1739; Mgr. de Mornay, Bp. of Quebec, Sep. 12, 1733; Mgr. Dosgnet, Aug. 16, 1739; C. P. Philippe, 1739; Superior and Grand Vicar; Mgr. Lauberive, 1739—1741; Quebec, 1840.

Mgr. De Ponttriand, sacré à Paris, 7 April, 1741.

Le P. Charles de Ramberrillier, named Superior of the Capuchines, in New Orleans, in 1741, died some years later, (was alive in 1746.) Le Père Dagobert, 1753; Le Père George Fanquemont, 1753.

Le Père Vitry, S. J., Grand Vicar of Upper and Lower Louisiana, in 1730. Succeeded by Le Père Baudouin, Jesuit. He continued till the expulsion of the Jesuits, 1765.

Dagobert named Grand Vicar of Louisiana by l'abbé de l'Isle-Dieu (V. G. in France, for Louisiana, May, 1765.)

GRAND VICARS IN LOUISIANA.			SUPERIORS OF THE CAPUCHINS.		
1723,	Raphael,	1734.	1734,		1734.
1734,	Mathias,	1739.	1734,	Mathias,	1739.
1739,	Philippe,	1741.	1739,	Philippe,	1741.
	Vitry, S. J.,	1765.	1741,	Charles de Kamber-villier,	1765.
	Baudouim, S. J., 1765.		1753,	George de Fauquement,	1765.
1765.	Dagobert,	1776.	1765,	Dagobert,	1776.

CHAPTER XV.

BIENVILLE devoted his labors to the territory contiguous to the Gulf Coast, and founded, on its present
site, the city of Mobile.   Several years earlier, Iberville
began a settlement at Twenty-Seven Mile Bluff.   Here
is the site of the "Vieux Fort."   A well under a
hickory-tree still marks the spot.   It was called Fort
Louis, from Louis XIV. and was safe above ordinary
high water.   Here often assembled many of the early
explorers.   Here Iberville and Bienville, Blondel, and
Pennicant, exchanged their great thoughts, and the
faithful Tonty watched out for his beloved La Salle,
who lay dead in a Texan forest.

In 1709, a rise in the river occurred which overflowed the town and fort.   This destroyed the crops
of the Indians, and, as, of course, it might happen
again, it became necessary to move the site of the
Colony.   A new Fort was built, and the old fort abandoned.   A square facing the sea, was selected for the
Church, and the present space occupied by the   city
was laid out for a fort, barracks, and building lots.
In 1710, the movables and merchandise were brought
down in canoes—cannon, amunition, by floats, and the
old fort abandoned entirely.   The people were followed by their Indian neighbors.   This city was
founded in a time of scarcity due to floods.   Bienville
billited his unmarried colonists among the savages.

Blondel and thirty soldiers spent the period of scarcity among the Indians.

The French and Spanish peasants, soldiers, and sailors, were able to join in the hymns, prayers, and psalms, of the church, which they not only knew in correct Latin, but could sing, as the *Stabat Mater,* the *Te Deum.*[1]

The first Curé of Mobile after it was removed to its present site, was Mons. Le Maire, who was very friendly to Bienville. He acted as chaplain to the Fort. Previously he had been several years on the Louisiana mission.

Bienville knew the Indians thoroughly. He was conversant with all their ways, on land and water, whether in the birch canoes of the east or the rafts of other regions; by horse, mule, or burro; or in the God-given locomotion by which " the Creator had given them a pass over the whole system." It was said each could carry 200 pounds of produce to market 20 miles. He was at home with them on river and forest, and found their climate soft and caressing as a dream. The fur-trading days of the *coureurs de bois* were never forgotten, and even of peltries not a little came from Mexico, " the land of the patient back."

The daily life was picturesque as is its history to-day. The wild Indian and his civilized brother, the daring French and Spanish explorers, the adventurous backwoodsmen; the terrible tragedy of war and revolution, the richness of the Southern surroundings, the thrilling incidents as time rolled on—but, above all, the meek disciples of Christ ready to give their blood for

[1] Suppose the *Vexilla Regis* or other hymn, were given out in one of our schools or churches to-day, how many of the pupils or congregation could respond, without words or notes ?

the souls of strangers, even of enemies, formed the
poetry entwined with daily life, in forest and on ocean.

The whole missionary Church of America sustained
a loss by the death at San Carlos, in the odor of
Sanctity, of the Saintly Prefect Apostolic, Junipero
Serra, June 3, 1770.

Catholic missionaries had prosperous settlements
long before Santa Fe, the second permanent city, was
established. As the Israelites with no King but God,
entered the promised land, so, many Indians, and
colored brethren not a few, found their way to the
missioners. The Indians renouncing the Great Spirit
whom they knew, but did not worship, soon received
upon their heads from the genuine ambassadors of
Christ the saving waters of the great sacrament of
regeneration. The colored disciples no doubt followed
their example. The holy Fathers who used every
means save roughness, which never led any one to
God, to attract the poor children of the forest, were
always ready to receive them with open arms. At a
late Catholic Exhibit, some stones, the remains of the
first Church erected in the New World, were reverently shown. And the Bronze "Bell of the Fig Tree,"
the first that sounded on American shores, presented
to Isabella Church by King Ferdinand, gave out its
sweetest notes on the same occasion. (World's Fair,
St. Louis.)

The Colonial Empire of Spain was perhaps the
greatest the world has ever seen. In seeking fresh
lands, the chief ambition of the grand discoverers was
to bring souls to Christ. Writing to Pope Alexander
VI., Columbus says: "I hope it will be given to me,
with the help of God, to propagate afar the Most
Holy Name of Jesus and His Gospel." And he de-

8

clares that " by his energy and efforts he has not sought for anything but the glory and development of the Christian religion." And his royal mistress, Queen Isabella, declares that " he realized for the divine glory a most signal honor."

The name and memory of Columbus are connected with prayer and praise. To this day is revered the Templete, in Havana, across the Plaza de Armas, erected in the shade of a Ceiba tree, beneath which, according to the legend, Columbus was wont to retire to pray.

" When thou art dead " says Thomas a Kempis," thou wilt not despair, for they will pray for thee who have read thy works. He who gives a cup of cold water to a thirsty person shall not lose his reward. Much more he who gives the living water of saving wisdom to his readers, shall receive his reward in heaven.

" The only way to convert the Indians, says Las Casas," is by long, assiduous, and faithful preaching, until the heathens shall gather some ideas of the true nature of the Deity, and of the doctrines they are to embrace. Above all the lives of Christians should be such as to exemplify the truth of these doctrines, that seeing this, the poor Indians may glorify the Father, and acknowledge Him who has such worshipers, for the true and only God.

Prescott sketches a beautiful picture of one of the early Indian missioners, which might justly be applied to many of these glorious men:

" Olmedo was a true disciple of Las Casas. . . . . His heart melted with the warm glow of Christian charity. He had come out to the New World as a missioner among the heathen and he shrank from

no sacrifice for the poor, benighted flock, to whom he
had consecrated his days. If he followed the banners
of the warriors, it was to mitigate the ferocity of war,
and to turn the triumphs of the cross to good account
for the natives themselves, by the spiritual labors of
conversion. He afforded the uncommon example
. . . . . of enthusiasm controlled by reason, a
quickening zeal, tempered by the mild spirit of toleration."[1]

It is said that the Spaniard entered on the conversion of the heathen with all the enthusiasm of a
paladin of romance." " With sword and lance, he
was ever ready to do battle for the Faith, and as he
raised his old war cry of St. Jago, he fancied himself
fighting under the banners of the military Apostle, and
he felt his single arm a match for more than a hundred
infidels. It was the expiring age of chivalry; and
Spain, romantic Spain, was the land where its light
lingered longest above the horizon.

[1] Vol. I. pp. 403-4.

CHAPTER XVI.

BILOXI is the oldest settlement on the Gulf, and the first capital of Louisiana. Mobile the second, has now (1908) a population of over 75,000. We shall now speak of the numbers who were baptized into the Church, with notices of the holy men who, though endowed with abilities that would have enabled them to make grand success in the world, renounced all that is transitory and embraced much that is painful, even to choosing for their daily companions the poorest, dullest, and lowliest, of their kind, and toiling, without comfort or reward, so far as earth can give, to win souls to God.

The names of many of these holy men may be seen in the ancient registers so carefully preserved in our Cathedrals. The Records of St. Augustine are kept in Havana. The Records of Natchitoches are reverently guarded in the Cathedral of that city. The New Orleans Registers have a special building to themselves, and one or more care-takers, enthusiastically devoted to their work. Much of the history of the South may be gathered from these venerable papers.

The first clergy who officiated in Mobile kept full accounts of births, marriages, and funerals from 1704, as may be seen by the records of their careful custodians. It has been noticed that the history of the Church after the Ascension of Our Blessed Lord, begins with two Apostles whose backs were adorned with stripes. In like manner, many of our holy men, of whom the world was not worthy, were sufferers in the sacred cause of religion. In one instance appeared among the laborers in the vineyard, a man who showed himself a wolf in sheep's clothing: Dominque Mary Varlet, who had been six years on the Louisiana mission. He signed himself " Apostolic missionary," and " Vicar General of Bishop St. Valier of Quebec." No details of his labors on the Mississippi are given, but his name appears in a few entries in the Mobile Register.

Returning to Europe, he was appointed, 1718, Bishop of Ascalon and co-adjutor to the Bishop of Babylon. As early as 1713, he was found to be a Jansenist in disguise. The Pope recalled him from the east. He withdrew to Utrecht where he became a prominent schismatic. There is not, so far as we know, any record of his conversion. He died near that city in 1742, at the age of sixty-four. It does not appear that he ever preached in Mobile during his short sojourn there, the gloomy doctrine of Jansenism which wrought such havoc to souls wherever it was introduced.

On July 20, 1703, the Bishop of Quebec formally erected Mobile into a Parish, with Rev. Henry Roulleaux de la Vente, as pastor, and Rev. Alexander Huvé as Curate. The first entry in the ancient register is the Baptism of an Apalache girl by the good Father Davion, September 6. He discharged parochial functions pending the arrival of the appointed priests, who came on the Pelican, July 24, 1704. In the same vessel came two *Soeurs Grises,* escorting a number of marriageable girls to the Colony. After seeing them settled, the Grey Sisters returned to Paris.

Besides assisting in the Parish Church. Father Huvé took charge of a band of fugitive Apalaches who, flying from English persecution, settled ten miles from Mobile, 1705. These faithful Indians erected a chapel and a priest's house. Father Huvé afterwards became chaplain to a large church built on Dauphin Island, 1709, which drew many settlers to this region. But he was nearly killed by the English who made a descent on the Island, November, 1710, and he lost all his effects. He afterwards undertook an Indian mission, but having little facility for acquiring Indian languages, he was unable to instruct his congregation in any Indian dialect. He struggled on for some years, however, doing all the good he could, till, having become almost blind, he returned to France, 1727.

Father Huvé spent much time in Mobile where he was greatly beloved. He endeared himself to his flock, French, Indians, Negroes. He was well acquainted with all, and was often at their poor houses. His last entry in the Mobile Register is the baptism of a Negro child, Jan. 13, 1721. The induction of the Curé de la Vente, in 1704, noted in the Mobile Records, is attested by Bienville, Boisbriant, and Nicholas de la Salle.

The good Davion who often assisted Huvé in Mobile, and is mentioned in 1704, 1712, 1713, and, in 1720, signs himself Vicar of Kebec.

About 1714 Bienville gave shelter and a home on the Mobile River to the Taensas, from one of the exterminating wars on the Mississippi. He punished the Natchez for robbing and murdering traders, passing through their territory. In 1720, the French built Fort Rosalie among them.

From 1684 to 1715, the Great King of France,

Louis XIV., and his wife, the *de facto* Queen, gave an example of purity and piety to the rest of the world, including especially their own subjects. This was owing to the celebrated Françoise de Maintenon whom the great King married, June 12, 1584, in the Royal Chapel, Versailles. Madame de Maintenon has been styled the " most influential woman in French history," and her influence was wholly for good. The King and his wife led useful, exemplary lives, without falling away, for 31 years. Louis XIV. died Sep. 1, 1715, aged 77 years; his widow died April 15, 1719, at the age of 84 years. One of her last words was: " I have a great devotion to Extreme Unction." She received it with the greatest fervor, answering all the prayers most piously to the end. " I have spared others," she said, " but I have never spared myself." Both died fortified by the sacraments of the Church.

The Bishop of St. Valier resigned the care of Louisiana to his Coadjutor, Father Mendon, a Capuchine, who never came to America. From 1721, Regular Orders, mostly Capuchins, worked in Mobile. Bishop St. Valier died, Dec. 26, 1727, aged 64, at the Hospital in Quebec, which he had founded. His charity to the poor was immense and incessant. He expended two hundred thousand crowns on the poor of his diocese.

In 1754, the last priest was sent by the Seminary, Father Duverger.

Rev. Mr. Courrier who labored at his post for several years was justly regarded as a man of extraordinary sanctity. Broken by incessant labors and agonizing disease, he went to New Orleans to obtain medical treatment, and died, tenderly nursed by the capuchins of that city, 1735.

There are several instances of the extreme kindness of the New Orleans Capuchins to sick and destitute priests, throughout its history.

The population of Mobile remained, to a great extent, French, though the ruling class was partly Spanish. There may not have been extraordinary progress in church affairs in Mobile, but there seems to have been much peace. None of the disedifying accusations or unseemly dissensions that disturbed the Church on the river border seem to have troubled the peace of the second capital of Louisiana. An intoxicated sleeping sergeant by letting his lighted pipe fall in his tent, started a fire which consumed Biloxi, and so terminated its history as first capital of Louisiana.

During the incumbency of Rev. Mr. Amand, 1738, 1742, the Mobile Church which had never been dedicated, and was now completely rebuilt, was blessed, September 8, the Feast of the Nativity of the Blessed Virgin, Mons. Amand was especially empowered by the Vicar-General of Quebec, for this function. He ordained that the anniversary should be celebrated every year. The Church was styled " Notre Dame de Mobile." Some time later, Governor Galvez styled it La Purissima, and it has since been known as The Church of the Immaculate Conception.

From the precious and venerable Registers of Mobile, it may be gathered that French, Spanish and English-speaking clergy exercised their sacred ministry in this little far away ciudad and presidio, long before the American Republic was born.

The Registers in the custody of the Church of Mobile are evidently originals. They were not issued annually, for each of the old volumes covers several years. The paper and ink are excellent, quill pens were used. The writing is bold and legible, mostly good, and often excellent. Judge Gayarré told the writer he regarded Antonio de Sedilla, whom he knew well, as a prodigy of ignorance. But this would not be inferred from his writing which is particularly good in the Mobile Register. And we noticed the same, in the larger Registers of New Orleans Cathedral, which we had the privilege of examining.

Jan. 21, 1726, Fleurian, of New Orleans, delivered to Brother Matthias, a Register for marriages, baptisms, and burials, containing ninety pages, numbered and initialed. Prefixed is an extract from an ordinance bearing on the subject. Fleurian signs as a royal councillor and Attorney General to the Superior Council of the Province. (Martin's History of Louisiana, page 293.)

CHAPTER XVII.

Nov. 14, 1722, Brother Matthias received the abjuration of heresy of Madeleine Moyennant, from the vicinity of Geneva. She could not write, but five witnesses attest her mark. Dec. 23, Jean Baptiste de Roy made his abjuration of the same, before seven witnesses who signed the document, among the names were some well known in the Colony, as Carrion, Beauchamp, and Durand.

In February, 1736, Brother Raphael de Luxembourg seems to have made a visitation, as Vicar-General of the Bishop of Quebec. Father Matthias was empowered by the same prelate to receive an abjuration, September 8, 1727. Edward Harksall from England, made a profession of Faith in the Holy, Catholic, Apostolic, Roman Church, and publicily abandoned his former Protestant heresy, with the prescribed ceremonies, in presence of several distinguished personages, among them Rev. Mathurin Le Petit S.J. and Mons. Divon, Commandant of Fort Condé.

In some cases owing to a lack of Holy Oils, children baptized are not christened but are said to be *endoyer,* the ceremony being supplied as soon as possible.

In 1730, the Jesuit Father, Francis de Mornay, performed the functions of Curé at the Fort. He sometimes went on a mission to the Coosa River. But when the English, under Oglethorpe, were pushing into the Alabama basin, this excellent Father was recalled to succeed Father Doutreleau in charge of the hospital and Convent in New Orleans, when he died in 1761. He was born in 1701, and entered the Society 1720.

Father Le Roi, one of the last Jesuits who labored in Mobile, had some trouble because he vigorously opposed the sale of fire-water to the Indians. From 1754 until the expulsion of the Jesuits, by decree of the Superior Council, June 9, 1763, Father Jean Jacques Le Prédour, was on the Mobile mission. In 1726, the Alibamons and Choctaws had been definitely assigned to the Jesuits, who occupied the Mississippi up to Natchez.

Several stations higher up were filled by Seminary Priests. Davion built his chapel on a rock—*Roche-à-Davion*.

March 4, 1763, Father John Francis signed as Parish Priest of Mobile, Capuchine; March 26. Father Ferdinand, of the Same Order, signed in the same capacity, April 18, 1769. His name appears for the last time. In Dec. 1777, Father Paul baptized. many Negroes of the Krebs family. All were admitted to the blessings of the Church. " There were no classes or races, but one universal brotherhood."

The Parish Register of Mobile, hitherto kept in French, begins at this point in Spanish.

March 12, 1780, the Fort of Mobile surrendered to his Catholic Majesty, represented by the General of the Expedition, Don Bernardo de Galvez, Knight pensioner of the Order of King Charles III., and Don Jose Espeleta, Colonel of the Infantry Regiment of Navarre.

Father Salvador was Parish Priest 1780, and the services of the Catholic Church were restored to their former pomp and solemnity, Fathers Velez, Notaria, and Arazena, followed, till 1784.

The large residence built for the clergy in 1707, on the left of the Fort, overlooking all the surrounding country, continued to serve its purpose for many years. The Mobile priests were kind and hospitable to their brethren from all parts of the country. Very Rev. Mr. Bergier came to Mobile with tidings of the death of the Canadian Priest of Natchez. On his return he became very ill, and Father Marest, hearing of his condition, hastened from Kaskaskia, and remained a week till Father Bergier seemed out of danger, when he returned to his own mission. He was soon summoned back to celebrate a *Requiem* for his soul. Father Bergier suddenly relapsed, and expired Nov. 9, 1707.

Of the seven thousand Acadians seized as Popish recusants, many found their way to Louisiana. The last French priest to officiate in Mobile was the Acadian, Father Ferdinand. They settled in many parts of Louisiana where their descendants still flourish. Their precious Registers were placed in the Church of St. Gabriel, Iberville, where they are still reverently preserved.

Some few Creole families date back to Spanish times. They speak not Spanish, but French. In marriages, names, ages, quality, and residence of bridal couple are given. In baptismal entries, the date of birth, the names of the child's parents, of godfathers and godmothers.

We have frequently mentioned the zeal of the clergy for their flocks. And this extended beyond the clergy. A distinguished writer says: " The cavalier felt he had a high mission to accomplish as a soldier of the cross. Not to care for the soul of his enemy was to put his own in jeopardy."

The Quebec Bishops usually selected Jesuits for their Vicars-General. The most celebrated of these officials was Nicholas, Ignatius de Beaubois, founder of the Louisiana missions and the New Orleans Ursuline Convent. Born at Orleans, 1689, he entered the Society of Jesus of the age of 17. His labors in America will be frequently noticed. Some opposition on part of the Capuchins of New Orleans was the occasion of his returning to France, 1737. He labored in various houses in the Province of Paris. In 1762, he was occupied in the city of Vanues, Britany, directing several pious works, among them, retreats and sodalities. He was then seventy-three years old. The Society of Jesus was suppressed in France, 1762. After that year all trace of Father de Beaubois is lost.

From 1739, Father Vitry, S.J. was Vicar-General, and in 1757, Father Baudouin who, had previously labored many years among the Choctaws. After the Suppression, Father Baudoin, then old and infirm, gratefully accepted shelter from the wealthy planter, Etienne de Boré, grandfather of Charles Gayarre, chief historian of Louisiana.

Having mentioned Madame de Maintenon as *de facto,* Queen of France, it may not be uninteresting to add that the wife of Etienne de Boré had been a pupil of Madame de Maintenon's famous Seminary of St. Cyr, near Paris, and propagated among the elite of New Orleans the Christian sentiments and the elegant manners she had then acquired.

After the removal of the capital to New Orleans the Mobile curé had often to undertake charge of a large territory. In 1728, the Apalaches and Dauphine

Island, are mentioned as dependent on Mobile Parish. The Registers show many priests assisting in Mobile, among them the redoubtable Antonio de Sedilla.

The history of this section is connected with the chief nations of the globe. Over Mobile have waved five flags, and it was the centre of an extensive Indian civilization. Many of our names are Indian still. It would be difficult to find a region of greater historic interest. The Chateau Bienville, built on the bay which " the literary Carpenter, Pennicant," says " was surrounded by beautiful gardens, filled with fruit trees," a league from the fort, was a splendid mansion. Bienville's country house in New Orleans would be a handsome home to-day. He knew how to build elegant houses. The Mobile streets are still French to some extent—Royal, Conti, Dauphine, St. Louis. The name of the Fort was changed to Charlotte, for the Queen of George III. The Spaniards called it Carlota.

The chief city grants date from the Spanish period—1781—1813; and several streets go back to Spanish times, as St. Emanuel, St. Francis, St. Michael, Esclava. Fire has been very destructive in Mobile. We can see its former glories only through the haze of romance. The grey walls, the tiled roofs, the quiet courts of old New Orleans have nothing analogous in Mobile.

Among the villages that often fell to the spiritual care of Mobile was Pascagoula. Here, on a still summer night is heard the mysterious music of the Gulf Coast, whose sweet tones resemble the music of an Eolian harp, vibrating softly as if stirred by a gentle breeze. Science has investigated it, but without finding a satisfactory solution. The phenomenon has been ob-served also on the Southern Coast of France. Bienville heard it when he visited Pascagoula in 1699, and made a note of it in his records.

Another feature of the same coast is not so pleasant, the oft-mentioned mosquito.

" Mosquitos," Bienville writes, " are here (Biloxi,) almost the whole year. In sooth they have given us but little truce for seven or eight days; at this moment they sting me in close ranks; and in December when you should not be troubled by them, there was such a furious quantity that I could not write a word without having my hands and face covered, and it was impossible for me to sleep the whole night. They stung me so badly in one eye that I feared I should lose it. The French of this Fort told me, that, from March there is such a prodigious quantity of them, that the air was darkened and they could not distinguished each other ten paces apart.[1]

" As for Fort Biloxi, besides the air being better and the country more open, all kinds of garden vege-tables, can be raised there; deer are near and hunting good; and to temper the heat every day, an hour or two before noon, there comes from the sea a breeze that cools the air. Only the water is not so very good."

It is easy to see that neither Biloxi nor Mobile was to become the site of the vast city Bienville dreamed of—extending from the Mississippi to Lake Pouchar-train, which we nearly have to-day, in the fast-spreading New Orleans.

[1] Munsell, Vol. VIII.

CHAPTER XVIII.

THE prophetic wail of the Indian maiden is not far from its realization. In 1718, she beheld the French clearing out the small Indian village, Tchou—Tchouma, to become the site of New Orleans. " The Spirit tells me," she sang, " that the time will come, when, between the river and the lake, there will be as many dwellings for the white man as there are trees standing now. The haunts of the red man are doomed, and faint recollections and traditions concerning the very existence of his race will float dimly over the memory of his successors as unsubstantial, as vague, and obscure, as the mists which shroud on a winter morning, the surface of the Father of waters."

A noted writer says : " History is a voice forever sounding across the centuries the laws of right and wrong. Opinions alter, manners change, creeds rise and fall, but the moral law is written on the tablets of eternity, that we may observe it."

The Mississippi scheme began in 1716, and closed 1723. Many years before had been " the tulip mania " when all caught the fever for tulips and gold. Later, the South Sea Bubble, a fountain of misery to thousands. These passed away with the bankruptcy and beggary they sometimes entailed, and the mighty river flowed on to the Gulf unheeding. Thriving villages and cities sprang up as it were in a night, like the gourd of the prophet.

In our own day things worked still more rapidly than in the more romantic early days. Guthrie, at noon, was an open prairie; at night, it had ten thousand inhabitants. But there was little or no question of helping the crowd to save their souls, as there would have been in the time of the missioners. Many ways of living were tried in early times. Mulberries were planted in Georgia, but silk culture proved a failure near the Savannah. Among the more useful articles of commerce we find wax myrtle and the candleberry tree. The berry was placed in hot water; the wax came off and was skimmed for use. This furnished the only light used in the Colony in early days.

Immigrants came at various times to Southern points from Normandy, Brittany, and the Canaries. Many were little better than hewers of wood and drawers of water, but they served their purpose, and work was always to be found. The people thought it only right to provide them with work, and " Right wrongs no one." A famous philosopher says, that, " In this theatre of men's life, it is given only to God and his angels to be lookers on." May 31, 1789, King Charles IV. of Spain issued a royal decree requiring that on every plantation there should be a chaplain for the negroes. But the authorities in Louisiana urged the impossibility of this, as there were not priests enough for the Parish Churches. Soon after, Father Joseph Denis, O. S. F., with six of his Order were sent to Louisiana. And the Catholic King applied for help to the Bishop of Salamanca who at his request sent out several Irish priests " of great repute," the King wishing to retain the English settled in several parts of the Colony.[1]

---

[1] Gayarré, History, Spanish Domination.

9

Throughout this history are frequently found instances of kindness to the colored race and interest in procuring their conversion. Very often they were slaves only in name. Governor Unzaga forbade the masters of runaway slaves to punish them. He offered them a free pardon. And, indeed, they usually returned to the plantations which they had left. The most intellectual prelates in the country took a special interest in them, as Bishop England in Charleston, S. C., and Bishop James O'Connor of Omaha. To the latter, as Spiritual director of Miss Katherine Drexel, we may be said to owe the Order founded by that lady for the conversion of the Indian and Colored races. The historian of Pittsburg diocese, Father Lambing, writes: "Bishop M. O'Connor[1] was one of the most brilliant lights that ever shed its lustre in the Church in the United States." Both brothers always took a special interest in the poorer and weaker races; as indeed did all the prelates in America, especially those whose chief work lay in Slave States.

The oldest Irish Missionary College in the world is at Salamanca in Spain. It was founded by Philip II. 1592, and was made a royal College in 1610. It received most of its endowment from the famous Irish Chieftain, O'Sullivan Beare. The present Rector is Very Rev. Father O'Doherty, nominated for that office by the Irish Bishops. He has been decorated by the King of Spain with the highest marks of distinction in the power of the Spanish Sovereign to bestow.

We will close this chapter with some account of another associate of La Salle, the celebrated Recollect,

---

[1] Bishop Michael O'Connor was pastor of a colored church in Baltimore after he resigned his see, Pittsburg.

Father Hennepin, to whom he gave special instructions for the exploring of the Upper Mississippi.

The Belgian Franciscan, Louis Hennepin, (born 1640), preached in many cities, and was for a while in charge of the Maestricht Hospital, Holland. At the Battle of Senef, between Condé and the Prince of Orange, 1694, he was present as regimental chaplain to Condé's men.

In 1675, he went to Canada with Bishops Laval and La Salle. He visited the Five Nations and the Dutch at Albany. With La Salle and Tonty, he went to Niagara 1676, said the first mass there, and published the first description of the Falls. They seemed to him hundreds of feet high. Near them is a rock that still bears his name. He erected near the Falls a bark house and a chapel. La Salle sent Hennepin to explore the Upper Mississppi. The river was called the River of Holy Ghost and the Immaculate Conception. Inured to hardship and to forest life, " he undertook an enterprise," capable he says of terrifying any one but me." On a tree near St. Anthony's Falls he engraved a cross and the arms of France. He was imprisoned by the Sioux for several months, and taken to the head waters of the river, where he saw the Source, Lake Itaska. Du L'Hut who gave his name to the city of Duluth—and a party of *Coureurs de Bois* rescued him.

Parkman says: " Hennepin had seen much and dared much; among his failings fear had no part."

On Hennepin's return to Europe, he wrote a book of travels which gained him much renown. Fourteen years later, when La Salle was dead, he wrote another which is said to be a plagiarism on Father Membré. This he dedicated to Willian III., having renounced his allegiance to France. He was not allowed to return to Canada, and is said to have died in obscurity in Europe.

His earlier books are very valuable.

A gentleman famous for his deep research into Hennepin's character and his epoch, thinks he may yet be cleared, and that works of other authors published with his, were added without his authority, and perhaps without his knowledge.

His name is stamped on many places about Minneapolis. Hennepin Co., Hennepin Mills; Hennepin Avenue;—we are not allowed in these parts to forget the energetic Recollect. In this city is the superb water-power of the Falls of St. Anthony—the great river leaping over the limestone rock in a plunge of twenty-five feet, which, with the descent from the rapids above, makes a fall of eighty-two feet, affording water-power for about thirty-four great flour mills.

CHAPTER XIX.

In 1698, two meek men in a frail birchen canoe were seen smoking the calumet with some red men. Canadian priests from the Quebec Seminary, Father Francis Montigny and Antoine Davion. They received little encouragement and had small hope of converts. They proceeded to Biloxi lately colonized by Iberville. In Membré's " Relations," we read: " On Easter Sunday, March 29, 1682, after having celebrated the divine mysteries for the French, and fulfilled the duties of good Christians, we left the villages of the Natchez." It is doubtful if De Soto ever visited Natchez, though it is certain he had intercourse with the Natchez Indians. They proceeded to Biloxi. Buisson de St. Cosme was sent to the Natchez. Montigny passed over to the Taensas, and Davion tried to spread the Faith among the Tanicas. Thus, two years before the site of Natchez was selected the Church had missions for the neighboring Indians.

The hardness of the hearts of the Tunicas constrained Davion to leave them several times, but by earnest entreaties they as often induced him to return. On one occasion they offered to make him their chief.

Father St. Cosme was a general favorite. The royal heir was named in his honor. For eight years he pleaded, and suffered, and prayed, in vain. No doubt his prayers obtained patience for the laborers and some small measure of grace for their stubborn

disciples. In 1707, this zealous priest was murdered
by the Stimachas. The proto-martyr of Mississippi,
Father Foucault, S.J., was treacherously killed by his
Koroas guides.

Iberville, Bienville, and Tonty visited the site of
Natchez. February 11, 1700, Iberville was charmed
with the place. He marked off the boundaries for a
Fort, and laid plans for a city to be called Rosalie, in
honor of the Countess Ponchartrain.

The Natchez were cruel and despotic. The sun was
their divinity, and they were fire-worshippers. Human
victims were offered to their offended deities, and even
mothers sacrificed their babes. The great Sun attended
by 600 braves, received Iberville with all the pomp of
royalty. A treaty of amity was concluded, the first on
the bluffs of Natchez.

Missionaries and explorers from Canada sought the
villages of the Mississippi by way of the great Lakes
and the Wisconsin River. But intercourse with the
mother-country was carried on by vessels plying between France and Louisiana. Northerners sometimes
came South by Montgomery and Mobile and gained
New Orleans by water. In 1779, the Red Cross of
St. George descended from Fort Paumure, replaced,
amid salvos of artillery by the royal standard of Spain,
by Galvez the young conquering hero. In 1785,
Natchez had one thousand five hundred and fifty inhabitants; in 1788, two thousand six hundred and
seventy-nine. Grand Pré became first Governor, under
the new *regime*. Father Davion attended French and
Indians. He labored many years in Mobile, in poverty
and privation. Father de la Vente denounced the
French liquor dealers who almost ruined the Indians
by selling them rum.

At all times spirituous liquor had a wonderfully evil effect on the Indians. Even to-day, Jan. 27, 1906, the Constitution of Arizona prohibits the sale of liquor to the Indians, forever, and the Constitution of Oklahoma [1] for twenty-one years, as a condition for statehood.

The Sulpitian Seminary of Quebec which entered the field as a great missionary body, sent Montigny, Davion, and St. Cosme. Crosses were planted by them in many places. Under the French there was usually a priest at Natchez. Under the Spanish, there was a priest at Villa Gayoso. There was more or less trouble everywhere with the marguilliers or church wardens. But the better class were mostly willing to stand by the Bishop as the lawful head of the Church of Louisiana. The few immigrants who came in were not usually of the true faith.

The King of Spain ordered the erection of a suitable church, and sent Irish priests of zeal and culture to Natchez, the royal treasury assuming all the expense. Messrs. Savage, Lamport, White, and McKenna, embarked at Cadiz and were in Natchez before 1790. In the same year, Manuel Garcia buried " Miguel Lamport, Clerigo, Presbutero y Cura," a great loss to the Colony. Old Memoirs say that Fathers Malone and Brady exercised the ministry at Natchez. They, no doubt, belonged to the large number who came to the Colonies from " the Peninsula." Catholics once more had the consolations of religion, and were edified and delighted by its grand and imposing ceremonies. But one night, Spain withdrew her garrison, March 29, 1798, and next morning the Stars and Stripes floated to the breeze.

[1] Oklahoma.

It is said that, as in European countries, the Church in Natchez had the privilege of sanctuary. It was no uncommon sight to see a Spaniard at the church door, his fingers on the key-hole, trying to avoid arrest for some midnight misdemeanor.

The people long retained a fond recollection of the Spanish domination. The stately rulers had endeared themselves to all by their lenient and paternal sway. Many followed them on their departure. Simultaneous with the recall of the Spanish officials, was the departure of their beloved clergy, the people being left as sheep without shepherds.

The love and veneration of the diminished congregation clung to the poor old Spanish Chapel of the Holy Family. They were deeply grieved when it was destroyed by fire, Dec. 28, 1832. In this Conflagration perished a splendid organ which was viewed in the light of a relic. It had belonged to Louis XVI., the beheaded King of France. Louis XVIII. presented it to Bishop Dubourg, and the Bishop kindly gave it to the Natchez Catholics.

The Spanish Chapel was replaced by " a nondescrip little chapel perched like an eyrie over the one room of the priest's house, and reached by a flight of rickety stairs." Later, the Mechanics' Hall was hired for divine service.

The lower room of the two-story chapel was used as a grocery store. The leasing of this commercial establishment was one of the most onerous duties of the trustees, at least they record little else. To this two-roomed edifice, a facetious, but irreverent, wag, applied the following distich:

> " The spirit above is the spirit divine,
> The spirit below is the spirit of wine."

A wealthy German priest [1] offered to rebuild the church and give his services gratuitously,—Father Kinderling. He continued his charities in New Orleans, and sometimes visited Natchez for baptisms and marriages.

In 1838, Bishop Blanc of New Orleans sent the Lazarist, Father Timon,[2] later Bishop of Buffalo, to give a mission to the Natchez people. Dr. Vandevelt was instructed to ascertain what arrangements could be made for an Episcopal see, and, by an anomaly, prepared the way for his successor.

In 1840, a dreadful tornado left the city almost in ruins. The saintly Father Odin was aboard a steamship in midstream when the tornado rushed by. Struck by a gale, the vessel nearly turned over. He and his companion giving themselves up for lost, fell on their knees in prayer, when the boat immediately righted herself. The good priests rendered heroic service in rescuing people swept overboard from neighboring boats. The mission preached by Father Timon was most successful. In 1839, Father Bogard became Pastor. Like most clergy of the time, he was hampered by the marguilliers, a self-constituted board, who deposed this excellent priest from the ministry! Later the sentence was expunged and a tardy reparation made. Father Badin, the first priest ordained in the United States, paid several visits to Natchez. We learn, traditionally, that he was a bright, original character. But no particulars are recorded of his visits.

The head of the American Church, Right Rev. John

---

[1] We know not why his offer was declined.

[2] Father Timon, Visitor of the Lazarists, was appointed Coadjutor to the Bishop of St. Louis but refused the mitre. He became Bishop of Buffalo, 1847, and died after a life of incessant activity in the Church, 1867.

Carroll, was created Archbishop, and received the Pallium, Aug. 18, 1812, an auspicious event that gave much impetus to Religion. Bishop Cheverus wrote to him, on that occasion: " That you may for many years wear this vesture of holiness is the wish of all your children in Christ. God will, in His mercy, I hope hear their prayers, and prolong the life of one beloved and venerable Father."

Bishop de Neckere was consecrated Bishop of New Orleans, May 16, 1830 by Bishop Rosati assisted by Bishop England. Bishop de Neckere whose health was very delicate, came from the counrty to the city during an epidemic, and, while laboring among the stricken, caught the yellow fever, and died, Sep. 4, 1833.

Fathers Sibourd and Jean-Jean had governed the diocese for two years before Bishop de Neckere's consecration. Father Jean-Jean was mentioned for Bishop, but fled to parts unknown. He returned to New Orleans, and died there, in 1838. November 22, Father Anthony Blanc was consecrated, at a most imposing ceremony, the splendors of which were never forgotten by those who assisted at it. He was forty-three years old, and had been ordained at Lyons, 1817. During his episcopate, New Orleans was made an Archbishopric, and he obtained the Pallium, as first Archbishop. Dr. Carroll of Baltimore requested the Louisiana Bishop to supply a priest for Natchez. But the population had dwindled. Father Timon, C. M. gave another great mission at Natchez, baptized many and heard numerous confessions; piety was revived and much good effected. He also gathered all the priests within his reach and preached them a spiritual retreat. Father Timon was soon after appointed coadjutor to the Bishop of St. Louis, but declined the promotion.

Point Coupée had been without a priest since the departure of Father Brady, Carmelite, 1812. Bishop Dubourg visited this place, 1818. He gave a course of instructions and administered Confirmation. He appointed Father Blanc Pastor, and dedicated a new church in 1823. In 1717, Natchitoches had been established as a French post. Not far off was the Spanish mission, San Miguel at Adayes, founded in 1715, by the Venerable Father Margil.

At New Orleans, Mobile, and the Florida towns, there were missioners of many Orders, among them was represented the Order of Mercy for the Redemption of Captives. In early days the U. S. Government sent money through this Order to rescue from captivity American citizens seized in the piratical States of Barbary.

Bienville's third term was from 1733 to 1751. Towards the close of this period, sixty women came to New Orleans as wives for the soldiers and planters, which they soon became. The church still occupied the square on which it was put up. To the right and left were the barracks, fronting the square were the government buildings. The Indians at all times loved the French and sided with them.

August 7, 1727, was celebrated the Centennial of the arrival of the Ursulines in New Orleans.

Bishop Blanc called on the Society of Jesus for priests, and obtained eight. He also applied to Rev. John Timon, Visitor of the Priests of the Mission, to assume the direction of the diocesan Seminary of New Orleans, which the Lazarists still retain.

Mrs. Pierce Connelly having, with due sanction,

separated from her husband who became a priest, did much for Catholic education in England and America, and founded the Sisterhood of the Holy Child Jesus, to labor in the cause.

Bishop Dubourg sent to the Ursulines from Lyons Mother Seraphine Ray, so celebrated for her generosity. It was said that no one ever applied to her in vain, nor would she wait for an appeal, if she had means to relieve the distress. When the Charleston Convent, near Boston, was burned by incendiaries, she at once sent the nuns three hundred dollars, and invited to her Convent all who wished to make New Orleans their home. In 1847, she founded an Ursuline Convent in Galveston and she established another in San Antonio in 1857.

From the Records, we learn that there was much intercourse between the missioners of Natchez and the Upper Mississippi and those of Mobile. The last foreigner who disturbed the Natchez Church was a Signor Inglesi, who had imposed on Bishop Dubourg.

The news of one part of the church was readily conveyed to another. The Church of Norfolk, Virginia, received from the King of France a copy of Murillo's Asumption; and, from Dr. Higgins, a large Crucifix of great artistic value.

Father Charlevoix, the historian of new France, came to Natchez in 1721. Finding no priest there he remained for some time preaching, exhorting, entreating, and laying the foundations of a Church.

When Mississippi fell under the jurisdiction of the United States, the church property (300 arpents,) was seized by the Federal Government. As the church was not a corporate body and had no official head in Natchez, no claim was presented in her behalf, and thus passed away the property of which she, in equity, had the right of constructive possession.

March 14, 1841, Dr. John Chanche was consecrated Bishop of Natchez, in Baltimore, by Archbishop Eccleston. He had been a member of the Sulpitian body, and when the episcopal office became vacant the honored President of St. Mary's College. The day of his arrival in Natchez, he officiated at the Mechanics' Hall, Ascension Thursday. In 1842, he laid the corner-stone of St. Mary's Cathedral, a noble Gothic structure. In 1852, he went north in the interest of his diocese. In 1853, he went, north a second time. At Frederick, Md. he was attacked by cholera, and on July 22, 1853, he expired, surrounded by loving friends, and fortified by the sacraments of the church, in the 57th year of his age, and the 12th of his episcopate. "He was buried in the Baltimore Cathedral, where he had been ordained priest, and consecrated Bishop. Mgr. Chanche was a most amiable character. His rich treasures of wisdom and erudition fitted him to shine in the councils of the learned, and charm in the amenities of social life. He was devoted to all classes in his extensive diocese, especially the poor slaves.

Right Rev. James Oliver Vandevelt, of Chicago, was translated to Natchez to succeed Bishop Chanche, 1853, and died two years later.

CHAPTER XX.

NATCHEZ was originally under the Bishop of Havana. In 1793, it became part of the see of New Orleans. Later, it fell to the charge of Venerable Archbishop Carroll. He made efforts to save the property but without avail. Father Lennon and Father Blondin remained till 1803, and zealously toiled to keep alive the fire of Faith. While on a sick call, Father Blondin was drowned in the Bayou Lafourche, to the great regret of his flock.

In 1820, Father Blanc, the future Archbishop of New Orleans, spent four months in Natchez. He installed as pastor, Father Maenhaut, who remained till 1824, when Bishop Dubourg gave a mission, and administered confirmation, probably the first episcopal function performed here. He was aided by Rev. Mr. Vidal, brother to Don Jose Vidal, from whom Vidalia took its name. This holy priest led an eremitical life. Poor for Christ's sake, he gave his patrimony to the needy. The Natchez congregation profited by his ministry on his occasional visits to say mass.

Another priest died here in 1825, Rev. Father Gallagher. His well selected library was sold, with his vestments and altar service.

In 1850, on Trinity Sunday, Bishop Chanche blessed a fine bell presented to him by Prince Alexander Torlonio, of Rome. " It came to me," wrote the

Bishop, " free of all expense; such had been the directions of the Prince, through the different merchants through whose hands it was to pass.   I blessed it according to the ceremonial in the Roman Pontifical, and called it Maria Alexandrina, in compliment to the donor and his lady.   It is beautifully decorated and weighs over three thousand pounds."   About twelve o'clock the night it was cast, the Prince left the company he was entertaining, and with his wife and a few friends went to the foundry; the lady threw a gold ring into the glowing, melting mass, and all knelt down reciting the litany of the Blessed Virgin, and other prayers during the fusion.

Miss Emily Harper, of Baltimore, presented to Bishop Chanche the high altar of the beautiful Cathedral.   Among the sacred vessels are some valuable heir-looms.   Five exquisite chalices; " one in 1845, by Gregory XVI, to Bishop Chanche, of the Cathedral Church of Natchez, by him recently erected; " another by Pius IX.; a third by Henry F.Weld, brother of Cardinal Weld; a fourth to Bishop Vandevelt, by the clergy of the diocese of Chicago, and a fifth to the same, by Archbishop P. R. Kendrick.   In 1867, a magnificent monstrance was presented by Very Rev. A. Boone, of Bruges, Belgium, to the Cathedral of Natchez.

The French in all parts of Louisiana were singularly barren of vocations to the priest-hood.   The only one in the 18th century was Etienne Bernard Alexander Viel, born in New Orleans, 1736, and died in France, in his 86th year.   After the suppression of the Society of Jesus, he lived in the Attakapas many years and was much beloved.   The chief part of his life was spent in teaching.   Wherever he settled, he taught a school. He was considered the greatest living Latinist. Gayarre, who knew him well, said he was a fanatic in his love of Latin. He thought nothing fit to be published unless written in that tongue.

Father Viel translated "Telemachus" into Latin verse, and the book was splendidly brought out by several distinguished men who had been his pupils. Gayarre saw that *Edition de Luxe* and other works from the same elegant pen.

The first Protestant congregation in New Orleans was organized in 1805, by immigrants, mostly from the Northern and Western States. It was long a landmark on Canal St., but, a few years ago, Christ church was demolished and an episcopal Cathedral built on St. Charles' Avenue.

Lafayette visited New Orleans, in 1824, and as guest of the city was lodged in the old Cabildo. The streets were then in a very bad condition, and the coach and four in which the honored guest went to visit his friends, was stalled at the corner of Magazine and Gravier Sts. Among the guests who called on the distinguished Frenchman, was the famous Pere Antoine. The aged men met with mutual regard. The day was April 13, 1825.

The *Courier* of that date gives an account of the interview between these renowned veterans. The General stated that he was proud to be of the same age as Father Antonio, who was as old as three generations. "For there is not much difference between us," said Lafayette, "I am a man of 76."

Rev. Constantine Maenhaut and Rev. Father Ganilh returned to New Orleans from Mobile, 1827. Their diocese was formed out of the old diocese of Louisiana and the Floridas. Right Rev. Joseph

Rosati, Adm. of New Orleans, *sede vacante* and Right Rev. Michael Portier, Bishop of Olena i. p. i. were invited to the Council of Baltimore. Ere the Council met, Bishop Portier, was made a suffragan of Baltimore.

Before leaving Baltimore the Bishops went in a body to pay their respects to the last surviving Signer, of the Declaration of Independence, Charles Carroll, of Carrolton. The aged patriot, though in his 96th year, appeared to enjoy perfect health and to be full of life. The Bishops admired his retentive memory and his perfect mental faculties.

A few still living heard traditionally of the simple delightful ways of the celebrated nonagenarian, and his elegant manners. Not many years since, we heard them described by his accomplished grand-daughter, Miss Emily Harper, of Baltimore. How he came to the head of the stairs with his guests, like a prince, to the last and the grace and friendliness with which he bowed them out.

The aged prelate bore all his trials in perfect submission to the divine will, and humbly besought the good God to guide His Church aright, and save it from the consequences of human passion and human frailty.

He had a great consolation in the restoration of the Society of Jesus, to which he had belonged in his youth, by Pope Pius VII., Aug. 7, 1814.

It was said that the Archbishop and his coadjutor would gladly have laid down their mitres and croziers, to assume once more the habit they had worn in youth, but they were beyond the time of active labor.

Indeed the years of the patriarch were now numbered. All the summer of 1815, he showed signs of

10

increasing weakness. Early in November, he became alarmingly ill. On Wednesday, 24, the whole Seminary attended the solemn administration of the Viaticum, and Extreme Unction. He expressed a wish to be laid on the floor to die, and asked to have the *miserere* read: Fortified by the consolations of the religion to whose service he had devoted his life, he expired almost without agony, about six in the morning, Dec. 3, 1815. His holy remains repose in the grand structure which he founded for the glory of God, one hundred years ago, and of which the hierarchy recently celebrated the First Centeninal.

Archbishop Carroll's relative, often called " the Signer," survived him many years. Not long before his death, the venerable Charles Carroll wrote: " When I signed the Declaration of Independence, I had in view not only our independence of England, but the toleration of all sects professing the Christian religion, and communicating to them all equal rights. Happily, this wise and salutary measure has taken place, for eradicating religious feuds and persecution, and become a useful lesson to all governments. Reflecting, as you must, on the disabilities, I may truly say, on the proscription of the Roman Catholics, in Maryland, you will not be surprised that I had much at heart this grand design founded on mutual charity, the basis of one holy Religion."

CHARLES CARROLL to G. W. P. Custis.

Feb. 20, 1829.

CHAPTER XXI.

THE genial Charlevoix keenly felt the spiritual destitution of the Southern settlers and the Indians whom they were gradually to replace, and on his return to France pleaded the cause of Louisiana so successfully that several Jesuits came to its aid. "The young French girls," says Father Le Petit, "are in danger of being brought up little better than the slaves."

February 22 eight Ursulines embarked on the *Gironde* at L'Orient; they were accompanied by three Jesuits. After five months navigation, the party arrived at the Mississippi, July 23, 1727.

At the Balize, the Commandant, M. Deverges, offered his house to the religious party.

July 31, Father Doutreleau and Brother Crucy, with Mother de Tranchepain and five Sisters, began the difficult ascent of the river in a pirogue, (dug-out), the others following in a chaloupé, (schooner). The first party reached New Orleans Aug. 6, the second, Aug. 7.

Father de Beaubois, owing to illness, was unable to meet the travelers. He came out of his house, leaning on a cane, to greet and welcome them. He led them to the poor church, where they thanked the good God with hearts full of gratitude and love, for bringing them safe, through the awful perils of their tedious voyage.[1]

They next went to his house where about eleven o'clock they sat down to a comfortable breakfast.

The delight of the good Father at the arrival of the nuns whom he had given up for lost, cannot be described. He conducted them to Bienville's country house, which the Governor lent them while their own was in course of erection. Aug. 9, Mass was offered here for the first time, and the Blessed Sacrament was reverently placed in the humble tabernacle they had devoutly prepared.

Some one had the happy inspiration to assemble the Ursuline Sisters as they stepped from their shaky vessels on landing, and sketch the picture:[2] Father de Beaubois points out the Indians and the Negroes, their future charges. The strong features of the novice, Madeleine Hachard, are shaded by the white veil of her Order. A negress with a solemn black baby in her arms, regards the group with awe and wonderment. A beautiful squaw, decked with beads and shells, half reclines with easy grace, on some logs, and a tall Congo Negro has suspended work, and betaken himself to the top of a wood pile, to gaze leisurely on the scene. A young girl, Claude Massy, carries a cat, which she tenderly carresses. Another girl, styled simply, Sister Anne, is searching eagerly for something in a basket over which she stoops. Both are dressed

[1] For fuller particulars of the voyages of the Ursulines and their early labors, in the Colony, see: " The Old Convents of Orleans Island," Irish Monthly, Twelfth Vol., 1884; "Essays Educational and Historic," O'Shea, New York, 1899, both by the writer.

[2] The sketch was probably made August 8, as the party arrived in two installments.

as peasants and wear the peaked Normandy Cap.[1]
Several priests appears in the distance; Jesuits, in the
ample cloak of their Society; Capuchins, heavily
bearded. The group is shaded by immense trees which
have long since disappeared.

Madeleine Hachard, in her graphic letters to her
father, mentions "well built houses, with pillars of
white-washed masonary, wainscotted and latticed,
roofed with shingles, that is, boards cut to resemble
slates and having all the beauty and appearance of
slates." In the muddy streets were sung songs which
compared New Orleans to Paris. "The city," she
writes, "is very beautiful, but it has not all the beauty
the songs ascribe to it; I find a difference between it
and Paris. The songs may persuade those who have
never seen the capital of France; but I have seen it,
and they fail to persuade me."

Though sometimes reduced to live on cracked corn,
great luxury appeared in their dress. The ladies wore
robes of rich brocade and damask, although such goods
were three times as dear as in France. They daubed
their faces with red and white paint, as some of their
descendants still do.

Bienville's house, the best in the colony, was built
in the square bounded by Bienville, Chartres Custom
House, and Decatur Streets. It was two stories high,
and the flat roof could be used as a gallery or belvidere.
Six doors gave air and entrance to the ground floor.
There were many windows, but instead of glass the
sashes were covered with fine thin linen. On all sides
were found forest trees of prodigious size and height.

[1] Claude Massy when embarking at L'Orient, carried her cat aboard,
saying: "Perhaps there may be rats and mice in New Orleans. The
cat will be useful."

From the roof the nuns could look on a scene of weird and solemn splendor. The surrounding wilderness, with its spreading live oaks and gloomy cypress, cut up by glassy meandering bayous, the home of reptiles, wild beasts, vultures, and many wondrous specimens of the *fauna* of Louisiana.

The Religious began at once to teach the children, instruct the Negroes and Indians, and nurse the sick. The Governor wished them to open a Magdalen Asylum. They received the Orphans of the Frenchmen recently massacred by the Natchez, and the *Filles-a-la-Cassette*,[1] whom the King had sent out as wives for his soldiers. Women were few, and the poor *Filles* had hardly tasted the hospitality of the Ursuline ladies when they were claimed by planters and settlers in need of helpmates. These marriages made on so short an acquaintance, almost invariably turned out well.

Later, the Ursulines received large numbers of the exiled women and children of the wandering Acadians whose descendants are numerous to-day by the Tèche and other streams, especially in the Attakapas. The nuns received under their care not only the unfortunate of their own race, but the gentle Choctaw and the fierce Chickasaw, the coal black Congo, and the comely Yoloff, the intelligent Foulah, and the terrible Mandingo. So deeply were their hearts imbued with the spirit of their divine Master that they sought not so much the rich and the lofty, as the poor and the lowly. A happy change was soon wrought in all, and the hearts of the new teachers overflowed with joy. They opened their arms to unprotected innocence and had a warm place in their hearts for abandoned sinners.

[1] Girls with a trunk or casket.

It is one of the marks of a divine vocation that others readily receive its impulses. Many holy and accomplished ladies felt the inspiration to follow Father de Beaubois across the Sea, and not a few of these gentle apostles were soon called home, having in a short time fulfilled a long space.

Bienville's third term lasted eleven years, 1733-1744. His return to Louisiana was welcomed with delight, for he was deservedly a favorite with the Colonists. Had he been governor earlier there would have been no massacre. Of the Natchez Indians, Father Le Petit writing, July 12, 1730, from New Orleans to his Procurator, in France, Father d'Avengour, gives a description of the character and customs of the Natchez tribe, and an appalling account of the horrible massacre. It began about nine, a. m. Nov. 28, 1729.

Among the victims were two Jesuits, Fathers du Poisson and Souel, of whose zeal and labors the most edifying reports had gone forth. He says there is nothing to fear in New Orleans now, yet a panic has seized all there, especially the women.

CHAPTER XXII.

In 1730 was laid the corner-stone of the new Convent:

In the reign of Louis XV.
King of France and of Navarre,
The first stone of this monastery
Was laid by the most high and most illustrious
Lady Catherine Le Chibelier.

Spouse of Sir Stephen de Perier, Knight of the Order of St. Louis, Captain of the Frigates of His most Christian Majesty, Commandant of the Province and Colony of Louisiana.

In the year of Grace, MDCCXXX. The names of the Sisters followed. Three of them, like Moses, were doomed to die before entering the promised land of the new Convent.

May 28, 1730, sixty married ladies and twenty unmarried, were formed into a Sodality, whose director was Father de Beaubois. They met on Sundays and feasts for instruction and devotional exercises, and did much to spread and nourish piety in all classes. Through the influence of Father de Beaubois, a separate building was erected for a Hospital, where the Sisters devoted themselves to the sick, soldiers and civilians.

In the absence of Father de Beaubois, an Ursuline always presided over the Sodality. Fathers Vitry and Le Petit aided Father de Beaubois, in all his functions, and sometimes officiated in Mobile. The Jesuits had little parochial duty in New Orleans, but they had control of the schools, sodalities, Convent, and Hospital, where the Sisters devoted themselves to all who needed their ministrations.

In these ways an immense amount of good was done for the Colony. Father de Beaubois had an invaluable coadjutrix in the holy and accomplished Mother de Tranchepain. The community suffered an almost irreparable loss by her death, Nov. 11, 1733, which was bewailed as a public calamity. "It was through her energy, address, and tact, that the obstacles to the setting out from France of the nuns, and their establishment in New Orleans were finally overcome."

The chief helper of the Religions, Father de Beaubois, was about this time assailed by many persecutions. "If we had the misfortune to lose him, by illness or otherwise," wrote Sister Hachard, "we should be deeply afflicted and greatly to be pitied." The injustice done her able and holy director was not the least cross of the dying mother.

October 21, 1733, the feast of St. Ursula, Mother de Tranchepain was stricken with a grievous illness. After eighteen days, she asked for Extreme Unction, which Father de Beaubois administered, with leave of Father Raphad, to her great consolation. In death as in life "she gave evidence of all the virtues that could be desired in a worthy and perfect Superior."

Mother de Tranchepain had the highest esteem and veneration for Father de Beaubois. In her first Convent home, at Rouen, she was supernaturally enlightened as to his plans for the regeneration of Louisiana through the wives and mothers of the Colony, and the prayers and labors of the nuns. Her management of these great enterprises brought out all her admirable qualities. She was deeply regretted by the colonists. Her own spiritual children could not easily reconcile themselves to her loss. She had made the yoke of the Lord sweet and His burden light to all who called her mother. But they felt " she was not lost, but gone before," and that she would help them from Zion.

All the Jesuits and Franciscans in the city attended her obsequies. When the Sisters removed to their present Convent in 1824, her remains were carried to its cemetery, where her tomb is still regarded as a sacred spot.

The celebrated Norman, Madeleine Hachard, who has left us so many delightful pictures of the early days of New Orleans, and so many touching examples of " the first fruits of the spirit," lived until 1760. She was found dead in her bed, August 9, to the grief of her religious Sisters. During her whole conventual life, 1727-1760, she had been accustomed to make a daily preparation for death. Another of the foundresses, Sister Angelica Boulanger, passed away, June 29, 1765, " and," says the Annalist, " both had the inexpressible grief to learn, with the whole community, of the iniquitous proceedings against the Jesuit Fathers, the best friends of Louisiana and the Ursulines."

Sister Angelica remained till 1765, to tender a cordial welcome to the heart broken exiles of Acadia, and minister lovingly to their wants. " Charity," says the historian, Martin " burst open the door of the cloister, and the nuns ministered with profusion and cheerfulness to the wants of their sex."

Meanwhile, the troubles of the Jesuits were increasing. The nuns prayed for the persecutors of the Society whose glory it is to have for enemies only God's enemies and those of his holy Church.

A few Acadians were enrolled in the Ursuline Sisterhood as Lay Sisters. One of these Sister Mary Joseph (Gertrude Braud), lived till 1818. Another, not having the qualities necessary for the religious life, was allowed to make her home at the Convent, where she died at the age of a hundred. She was portress, use to wear a cap and veil and was regarded as eccentric. If she felt no consolation in her visits to the Blessed Sacrament, she would say: " Good-bye, dear Lord, I see you have company. I will come back another time when you are free." She was called Sister Mary.

The first American-born nun was Mary Turpin, daughter of an Indian mother and a Canadian father. She died 1761, aged 32. Sister Martha Ladras, a native of Mobile, daughter of a surgeon, entered the Convent, 1776 and died ten years later, aged 28.

Father de Beaubois was on the Illinois mission 1720, and returned to France 1725, to seek more laborers for his master's vineyard. He was also commissioned by Bienville to procure Sisters to teach the Louisiana girls. His projects were eminently successful. Many a good work was done for the souls and bodies of the colonists. The Jesuits aided the nuns in every possible way. We may see to-day the traces of the oranges and sugar-cane they planted in the Ursuline ground.

Their own plantation was the model garden of the Colony. It helped to create the love of flowers, plants, and fruit, characteristic of the Southern people, always common in the Southern metropolis, and an example which wealthy Creoles were not slow to follow.

The Ursuline Schools were crowded from the beginning. They have always maintained a high degree of culture and efficiency. The Boston, New York, or Philadelphia, of those days, was not so well provided with educational facilities as New Orleans under French and Spanish sway. The Mother Superior of the Ursulines, and her disciple, Madeleine Hachard, have, in their diaries, and letters, given proof of their fitness to teach, in the ease and elegance with which they wrote their native language, and the genuine eloquence with which they describe the scenes of a day that is done, but which lives again in their graphic pages.

In the Atlantic States persecution for religion, that is, the Catholic, went on with little intermission. In 1683, Governor Thomas Dongan, an Irish Catholic, presided over the first legislative assembly in which religious freedom and trial by jury, were granted to the Colonists, in " a charter of liberties," in New York. Dongan was appointed Governor of New York, by James, Duke of York, Lord of that Colony. These were called the Duke's Laws. Dongan settled the boundary dispute with Connecticut, and made a treaty of peace with the Indians. Freedom of worship was often promised, but in most of the Colonies it was not practised as regards Catholics.

Mother Duchesne, a French Religious, visited the Ursuline Convent and received multiplied attentions from the Ursulines. " Mothers," said she, " could not do more for their children." Great was the delight of this ardent lover of the Sacred Heart on finding the devotion of which she had hoped to be the first

Apostle in the United States, already fervently practised by the Ursulines and their pupils. Not counting
slaves or their children, their pupils then numbered
more than three hundred. Mother Duchesne took a
special interest in the little negresses, hailing them as
the first fruits of the poor whom she wished to
evangelize. In a letter to Madame Barat, she wrote:

"Alas, we shall not have the glory of being the first
to bring to the United States Devotion to the Sacred
Heart. I have found here a beautiful picture of this
divine Heart, painted at Rome, and I have also seen a
book of prayers in honor of the same, which has been
printed in New Orleans."

The painting to which Mother Duchesne alludes is
now hanging over the Archbishop's throne in the
sanctuary of the Convent Chapel of New Orleans, just
beneath a marble slab bearing the inscription that there
repose the hearts of Right Rev. Bishops Dubourg and
De Neckere. It is interesting to know that this picture
commemorates a vision vouchsafed to Mother Gensoul,
who beheld the Sacred Heart of Jesus burning with
love for mankind, adored by angels, the chief figure
being the Eternal Father, under the appearance of a
venerable old man, who seemed to say:

"Behold the Hope of Christians."

"Among other acts of kindness, the Ursulines gave
the Sacred Heart Religions a gift of fifteen hundred
dollars. Mother Duchesne had been a Visitation nun
before the Revolution, and it is well known that since
the days of Blessed Margaret Mary, of Paray, the
Visitation nuns regarded it as their special mission to
propagate devotion to the Sacred Heart of Jesus.

CHAPTER XXIII.

EARLY in the 18th century, a feeling adverse to the Jesuits appeared in many parts of Europe. Several provincial parliaments had condemned them, and measures were taken to Suppress them. Following this evil example, the Superior Council of Louisiana, an insignificant body of officers, issued a decree declaring the Society dangerous to royal authority, to public peace, and safety. The members were forbidden to use its name or its habit. An order was issued to sell its property, save books and clothing, at public auction. Their chapels the only places in many many instances, where Catholics could worship, were leveled to the ground.

The alleged crimes of the Jesuits were: 1. They had neglected their missions: 2. brought their plantation to a high state of culture: and, 3. usurped the office of Vicar General. This last, if done, could be done by only one, but all had to suffer. The Jesuits were arrested; their chapel was demolished, even to exposing the bodies of their dead, and other profanations committed by men assuming to be Catholics.

Of course, the guilt of the accused was a foregone conclusion, but the Jesuits made a spirited defence which bore upon its face the certainty of truth. This was known in France as well as nearer home. " There is hardly any province in France," wrote one, " where

there is not some prominent person who has lived in
Lousiana; there is not one who has not known the
Jesuits there, and most of them have been able to
scrutinize these Jesuits very closely. " And nothing
but edification has resulted from this scrutiny. Several of the Jesuits assembled in New Orleans to await a
vessel to bring them to France. As they had no longer
house or home near New Orelans, they depended on
the charity of strangers. All manner of kindness was
shown them by the natives. The chief people of every
district lavished kind attentions on the pious fugi-
tives. Near New Orleans, they came to the estate
of Monsieur Macarty, former lieutenant of the king
in that city, who by his benevolent efforts recalled to
their remembrance the goodness he had always shown
them in Illinois, when he had been Major Command-
ant-general. When in town he gave them many tokens
of his friendship.
Meanwhile, the Capuchin fathers hearing of the
arrival of the Jesuits, had come at six o'clock in the
evening, (it was December 21.) to the landing place
to show sympathy in their misfortunes, and their in-
tention of rendering them all kinds of good offices. To
the Jesuits, this was an urgent motive to leave the next
morning, to thank these Fathers who received them
with all the demonstrations by which charity can make
itself known. They begged them not to take their
meals anywhere else but with them. The Jesuits accepted, with great joy, the invitation that had been
given them, and during the six weeks which elapsed
before they embarked, there were no marks of friendship which they did not receive from these Reverend
Fathers. Touched by deep gratitude, they wished to
show it in some way. The books that had been spared

to them formed a little library, valuable in a country
newly established, and they prayed the Capuchine
Fathers to accept it.

The retributive justice of God soon overtook the
sacriligious wretches that had profaned the holy places
and the sepulchres of those who died with the sign of
Faith. They were guilty, too, of the odious vice of
ingratitude. The Jesuits had been the best friends of
the Colony. Every special blessing and comfort the
people enjoyed had come through the Jesuits.

One hundred and sixty colored men worked on the
Jesuit plantation. These were instructed and bap-
tised, and required to comply with their duties as
practical Catholics. It is said that fourteen adults is
equal to a family. It is easy to see what a charge the
unbaptised were to the Jesuits.

When the Jesuits were driven out, with every species
of indignity, there were only five Capuchins left in
New Orleans for four thousand people, two hospitals, a
large Convent, a boarding Academy, orphans, free-
schools. Mobile had been ceded to England and
Father Ferdinand, an Acadian, was to leave as soon as
the French flag was lowered. He was still doing duty
in Mobile, in 1773. About that time the old citizens
closed his eyes, and in or near the church he had served
so long, laid to rest with tears the beloved form which
had connected for them this half deserted British out-
post with the Mobile of Bondel and Bienville.[1] The
church has gone, its very site is uncertain; the grave,
its contents unknown. But, somewhere between our
St. Emanuel St. and Theatre St. lies the dust of Father
Ferdinand. (P. J. Hamilton.)

[1] Bienville's "fort belle maison avec un jardin," was on the Mobile
Shell Road. But no trace of it has been seen for generations.

No more spiritual aid was to be expected from the Jesuits. They had left their flocks, praying for their persecutors.

In 1765, some six hundred Acadians who had been wandering about as Helots or paupers, since their dispersion, 1755, made their way to New Orleans, where they were received with open arms. Their sorrowful faces as they drew up on the Levés and in the old *Place d' Armes,* awoke the deepest sympathy in their compatriots in the little city over which the French flag still waved. The Convent on Chartres St. offered its hospitality to the women and children, and every house opened its doors to the rest.

Nothing could well be imagined more different from the smiling meadows and snug farm houses of Acadie, " the home of the happy." But the Acadians deemed themselves fortunate to hear their native tongue once more, and live again under the white flag of the Bourbons. As they had been mostly farmers, a tract of land, on the river, with farming utensils, and a year's rations, all at the king's expense, were allowed to each family. They became once more a happy peaceful people, and their descendants are found by hundreds on the prairies near the Louisiana rivers.

It has often been said that the Ursulines were able, if they so desired, to write a more truthful and pathetic account of the Godfearing Acadians than that left us by Longfellow in his exquisite " Evangeline."

In 1763, France transferred Louisiana to Spain, and in 1764, Louis XV wrote to governor Abbadie, relating the terms of the Cession. But the colonists, deeply attached to France, besought the king to keep them, and sent Jean Milhet, the richest merchant, to Paris, to plead their cause. Bienville, then in his 86th year, backed their petition. But the king would not even see them. Choiseul the minister utterly refused to keep Louisiana. In the eyes of the evil ignorant woman who then presided at court, the American possessions were but " a few acres of snow."

Don Antonio Ulloa, a distinguished scholar, was appointed governor. He arrived in New Orleans, March 5, 1766. Discontent soon culminated in Revolution, although he had done nothing to offend the people. The letter the king wrote to the governor Abbadie is " In consequence of the friendship and affection of his Catholic Majesty, I trust he will order his governor and all other officers employed in his service, in said colony and city of New Orleans, to continue in their functions the ecclesiastics and religious houses, in charge of parishes and missions; as well as in the enjoyment of the rights, and privileges, and exemptions granted them by their original title.

Ulloa was driven from Louisiana by a decree of the Superior Council. He retired on board one of the king's vessels then moored opposite the city where he remained until the night of the following day, when the cables were cut by the populace and the vessel set adrift! A murderous act, and more than king Charles III. would endure. Ulloa and his wife, (Marchioness d' Abrado) and their children, escaped the terror, of the awful river, and rested in Havana, *en route* for Spain. In Havana he met the Spanish Intendant who, hearing of Ulloa's adventures, declined to sail for New Orleans.

The king, determined to reduce the rebellion, sent out an officer of the highest rank, in whom he had implicit confidence, Count Alexandre O'Reilly, with a fleet of twenty-four sail, and two thousand six hundred of his best troops to quell the insurrection.

When the people heard of this armament, they were filled with terror, July 23, 1769. On the following day, Governor Aubrey received by express a dispatch from Don Alexander O'Reilly, commander of the Spanish forces, notifying him that he was authorized to take formal possession of Louisiana for the king of Spain.

The people shut themselves up in their houses with every sign of abject terror. But O'Reilly quieted their fears, declaring that only ring leaders would be arrested, tried, and if found guilty, punished.

The last French Governor, Aubrey, handed the keys of the city to O'Reilly, who received them for the king of Spain on the Place d' Armes. The white banner was lowered, and the colors of Spain ascended. The prolonged shouts of Viva el Rey could be heard distinctly in the Ursuline cloisters. The great man who represented the potent Majesty of Spain was received with royal honors by the French clergy, the head of whom, Father Dagobert, solemnly welcomed him, and promised fidelity for himself, and his brethren and the people at large, with utmost enthusiasm, having previously bestowed the benediction of the church on the Spanish flag. Within the sacred walls, a grand military function was performed, and it was observed that the rather austere countenance of O'Reilly was radiant with devotion during the singing of the *Te Deum,* Laudamus!

Judging from the official reports of the French Governor, complete anarchy had reigned in the colony for several years. Governor Aubrey expresses surprise that "the mere presence of one individual, (O'Reilly) should have restored good order, peace and

tranquillity. When O'Reilly's actions were rigorously
examined by the Council of the Indies these gentlemen unanimously declared that every one of his official
acts deserved their most decided approbation," " and
were striking proofs of his extraordinary genius."

There is no character in American history more
basely calumniated than Alexander O'Reilly. " The
worst kind of lies are those which have a semblance
of truth, and the worst kind of liars are those who
succeed in rendering falsehood more plausible than
truth itself. This the slanderers of this truly great man
have well proved.

O'Reilly was the friend of the Indians. He amel-
iorated the condition of the slaves. He encouraged
immigration. He made regulations that greatly improved Commerce. " In substituting the Cabildo for
the Supreme Council, he not only took away a cause
of disturbance, but replaced it by an effective means
of government." " The Colonization of the South."
p. 431 says: " The severity of O'Reilly, there can be
little doubt saved Louisiana much subsequent trouble."
P. J. Hamilton.

Several of the officers who had made trouble in
New Orleans, among them, Lafrénière, went down
to the mouth of the river to visit O'Reilly on his flag
ship, and learn what could be learned of his intentions.
They knew they had been guilty of many acts of
treason. O'Reilly received them courteously, and invited them to dine with him. Looking back on recent
events, as the expulsion of Ulloa, it must have struck
them that some measure of punishment awaited the
guilty. Yet O'Reilly treated them with the utmost
courtesy, as the law had not yet declared them guilty.
His long stay in the river gave them every opportunity

to escape, had they so wished. It has been told to me
by a descendant of one of these men that he even gave
them warning.[1] As all were recreating on deck, after
dinner, he struck his heart and said: " I have orders
here from the king. Flee, gentlemen, flee!" The authority for this incident is still living, and showed a letter from his ancestor which recorded it, and which the
writer saw.

The prisoners seem according to law to have deserved their fate. None appears to have been above
reproach, according to Gayarre, almost a Contemporary. Their defence was that Spain had not formally
taken possession, that Ulloa had not shown his cre-
dentials; that they had not taken the oath of allegiance
to Spain. But it was proved that the Spanish flag
had for years been floating over every post from the
Balize to Illnois, that several of the accused held their
commissions from Ulloa; and were in office under the
king of Spain, drawing their salaries from him while
exciting revolt against him.

Felix del Rey, the king's lawyer, spoke of Lafrénière with withering contempt, as an unfaithful
officer, and the chief instigator of conspiracy against
the king, whose money he was receiving while driving
his fellow citizens into conspiracy against him.

The behavior of the prisoners in the days of their
power, to the suppressed Jesuits, rather lessens the
sympathy and compassion we should like to feel for the
unhappy culprits. O'Reilly was then only thirty-four
years old,[2] yet he remained inexorable to the most

[1] A Mr. St. Martin who died at a great age.

[2] So Gayarre says, but later information makes him older. O'Reilly
was born in Baltrasna, Meath, 1722. He early entered the service of
Spain, won high distinction as a commander in war and a governor in

earnest entreaties from persons of every rank that he would suspend the sentence of death until the royal clemency could be implored. The only concession he would grant was to commute the sentence of death by hanging to military execution. It is a pity that so humane a ruler should have felt himself unable to spare the traitors to whom the law decreed death. But it is almost certain that he had no choice in the matter. Six were condemned to death, one died in prison, the rest were imprisoned but afterwards released. The poor men were escorted by grenadiers to the place of execution near the Ursuline Convent, where the firing could be distinctly heard. Several of their relatives were in the convent chapel where the nuns kindly did all in their power to console them. As all were Catholics, there is no doubt but their spiritual wants were attended to, and, it is probable, by their friend, Father Dagobert. One of the unfortunate men shot was a relative of one of the nuns whose name or rank is not given; but to the end of her life the poor lady could not hear a shot fired without going over again the horror of that dreadful evening. Yet bitterly as the nuns felt, no one ever said a word of blame to O'Reilly. They felt there was no other course open to him.

O'Reilly was undoubtedly among the ablest of the foreign Governors of Louisiana. He was educated by a wandering school-master of the time; he early made his way to Spain, and having enlisted in the armies of the Catholic king, soon rose to high rank.

peace. In a popular tumult in Madrid, he saved the life of King Charles III. He was created Field-Marshal, sent to Havana to restore the fortifications, 1769. He was in command of the army of the Pyrenees, but died, March 23, 1794, on his way there, aged seventy-two, near the small city of Chinchilla.

Other brothers followed him, and one became a Franciscan Friar in Dublin, where he died in the odor of sanctity.   O'Reilly married a Spanish lady of rank, and their descendants still live in Cuba.   After his sojourn in America, he returned to Spain and was raised from post to post by Carlos III, who could never forget the day of his slaughtered Walloons, when the brave Irishman saved his life.   He served with distinction in Italy where he received a wound which lamed him for life.

He was appointed Governor of Cadiz where he showed the talents of a great administrator. " O'Reilly " says Michand, " had always been an object of malignant envy.   He had many enemies whom the flexibility of his temper and the soft influence of his conciliating manners could not reconcile to his advancement.   He received a last promotion in 1794, and died suddenly en route for his army."

During O'Reilly's government of Louisiana, almost a famine broke out in the State.   Oliver Pollock, an Irish merchant, acted with princely generosity to his countryman.   He offered the whole cargo of flour on his brig, to O'Reilly, on his own terms, at a time when flour was so scarce that the price had arisen to twenty dollars a barrel.   O'Reilly accepted the offer, but paid him fifteen dollars a barrel, and allowed him to trade in Louisiana as long as he wished, without paying duty.

During their negotiations on the price of wheat, these gentlemen discovered that they were countrymen, had been boys together, and even spoke English with the same accent.   It is no wonder that Mr. Pollock had been so liberal: " I cannot refuse quarter," said a brave soldier, " when I hear it asked in my native tongue."

With great liberality and profound policy, O'Reilly

placed Frenchmen in all the chief offices, and in the
Regiment of Louisiana, only Creole troops were enlisted.   In all the circumstances of his office he acted
with a fairness, and even generosity, surprising in a
man so recently come to the country, nor can we find
any trace of cruelty in his administration.   In private
life his manners were perfect.

Like other Governors, O'Reilly is commemorated in
the historic streets of New Orleans.   And in Havana,
one of the principal retail shopping districts of the
city is called to this day, " Calle O'Reilly," O'Reilly
St.   In 1804 the upper portion of Louisiana was the
District of Louisiana with St. Louis for its capital;
the lower only the Territory of Orleans, with New
Orleans for its capital.

Miniatures of this celebrated man, preserved among
his descendants, show him to have strongly resembled
his august contemporary, George Washington, in personal appearance.   A small picture of O'Reilly was
given to the writer by the grandson of his Contador,
Hon. Charles Gayarre.   This the writer transferred to
an evident admirer of Count O'Reilly, John Boyle
O'Reilly.

CHAPTER XXIV.

MUCH has been said of the laxity that prevailed among the French Capuchines about the middle of the 18th century and later. But this is possibly greatly exaggerated. The fact that O'Reilly lived near the monastery and met the inmates every day, would appear to show that, had grave abuses existed, they could scarcely have escaped his eagle eye, and in his case to recognize abuses would be to correct them.

O'Reilly instructed his commandants at St. Louis and St. Genevieve to make it their special care that the Government of the king should be loved and respected, justice administered promptly and impartially, and the Indians well treated. It may be said that this princely ruler was almost the last High Priest of expiring chivalry. In the oath of office delivered to his subordinates, there is a promise to defend the Immaculate Conception of Our Lady,[1] and never to accept of any fee from the poor. Mutual good feeling and amicable intercourse prevailed between the civil and military authorities which was commemorated by the Spanish Commandant opposite Fort Panmure, by designating his post as Fort Concord. The name has since been perpetuated in the rich parish of Concordia.

[1] From the siege of Limerick to the French Revolution it is said that three-quarters of a million Irish served in the armies and navies of Europe.

The suppression of the Jesuits was a severe blow to the Ursulines. It deprived them of their spiritual Fathers and directors, who, having brought them to New Orleans, worked incessantly for their advancement. Towards the close of the Spanish Domination, the community had become Spanish to such an extent that the majority refused, when Spain returned the Colony to France, 1803, to live under the French flag, and besought the Catholic king to give them a home in some other part of his vast dominions.

The Capuchins continued their usual functions awaiting the arrival of a reinforcement of Spanish clergy. O'Reilly's attention was given to everything regarding the divine worship. He even requested the Commandant to keep the church clear of dogs during divine worship, at Natchitoches.

In the first record of baptisms, carefully preserved among the achives of New Orleans, there is an entry in French, a simple concise document in the shape of an affidavit, signed: GUEBO,[1] CANTRELL. These are the only two survivors of the massacre by the Natchez Indians of the white settlers at Natchez, 1729. They saved a tiny babe of four months, of whom a kindly squaw took care. When they reached the city, the ecclesiastical authorities inquired whether the babe had been christened according to the rites of the Holy Roman Catholic Church, which was answered in the affirmative.

Among other good works, Bienville tried earnestly to have a superior school for boys established in New Orleans. But this project was doomed to failure until Colonial times had passed away. In the nineteenth century, Bienville's scheme was realized by the opening

---

[1] *Guebo* does not appear again, *Cantrell* has left descendants.

of the College of the Immaculate Conception in New
Orleans by the Fathers of the Society of Jesus by
which, with Spring Hill College, Mobile, they have
done for the youth of these cities all that the sagacious
Bienville desired to do in darker days.   In the interim,
attempts were made with varying success to open
schools as needed.

The first educational establishment incorporated by
the Louisiana Legislature was the College of Orleans,
Cor, Hospital and Claude Sts.   Early in the 19th century the forest primeval came to its gates.   In spring
the thorny arms of the blackberry bushes, spangled
with white blossoms, made a tangled labyrinth of
undergrowth as the flowers grew into green, red, or
black berries, and the small boys of the ctiy invaded
the edge of the wilderness to seek the luscious fruit.
Among the contributors to the College were the Ursuline nuns.[1]   The pupils were celebrated for their
classical attainments and courteous deportment.   Unfortunately, an apostate priest, Joseph Lakanal, who
had voted in the National Convention for the death of
Louis XVI., was appointed President before 1810, ar
office for which he had no qualification but scholarship.
The people indignantly withdrew their sons, nor could
they be induced to send them back.   The institution
declined, and was, finally, closed.   A Church, St.
Augustine, was erected on its site, perhaps in a spirit
of reparation.   To this is attached a Catholic school.

Lakanal felt that his presence in New Orleans was

---

[1] A paper still exists in which the Ursulines are mentioned as contributing three hundred dollars to the establishment of the College of
Orleans. Of course they withdrew their patronage on the appointment of Lakanal. They are frequently mentioned as contributing in
epidemics and other visitations.

not desired. He withdrew to Mobile, where the people do not seem to have discovered his crime, for he lived quietly in a small cottage, near the Convent grounds, none of its inmates ever heard of him. He planted vegetables which he sold to his wealthier neighbors. He was later among those who would turn Marengo Co. into the land of the Olive and Vine. But the project failed. He returned to France where he lived to a great age, dying 1843. He is among those who entered into contract with the U. S. government to lay out the town of White Bluffs, which they called De-mopolis, the city of the People. But, as has been said, the culture of the Vine and the Olive became a failure. Lakanal had a tract of several thousand acres, granted, March 3, 1817.

A Father Maréchale, "a great scholar," who was adorned with medals and distinctions from many uni-versities, established a school for boys on land below the city, which belonged to the Ursuline ladies. The early Ursulines in the new Convent describe them as well drilled and most devout,—particularly edifying in carrying out processions of the Blessed sacrament from one point on the estate to another. The situation of the ancient church is still remembered and pointed out. All this we learned on the spot.

The poor Acadians suffered the horrors of an exile unexampled in history. But persecution, in the house of bondage, broke their spirits, nor could they with-stand the worse ordeal of intimacy with free-thinking Frenchmen. Archbishop Carroll notices the deteriora-tion of the Acadians in Baltimore. Something similar was observed even in the remote Attakapas. They even became the accomplices and tools of the vile men who arrogated to themselves supreme power in church and state, before the coming of O'Reilly. They were among the armed insurgents who paraded New Orleans, and sustained the Superior Council when that body expelled Governor Ulloa, in 1768. In a report to his government, Ulloa charges the Acadians with ingratitude, " they having received nothing but benefits from the Spaniards." It is probable, however, that among the whole body there were many faithful Acadians. When the Acadians complained to O'Reilly, he listened gently to their grievances and rectified them as far as he could. As to the Indians, he officially declared that " it was contrary to the mild and beneficent laws of Spain to hold them in bondage." On their part, the Indians, assembled in Congress in Pensacola and Mobile, resolved : " We, (the Indians,) renounce forever the custom of raising scalps, and making slaves of our white captives," (May, 1784.) To evade O'Reilly's merciful law which forbade the enslaving of the Indians, these poor people were sometimes classed with mulattoes, as colored. The great distinction always kept up in the South between the colored and people of unmixed European origin, may be seen in the registers of Mobile, New Orleans, St. Martins, Natchitoches. Bishop Penalvert styles the mixed races, *browns, morenos.* There were Mestizos, (children of the white and the Indian,) griffe, (of the African and the Indian,) mulatto, mulatre, mulatresse, of the white and black. Later, cognizance was taken but of two classes, Europeans and their descendants, and the colored. This good Bishop notices the moral superiority of the women of the Colony over the men, and he attributes it to the training and influence of the Ursuline schools.

CHAPTER XXV.

On March 3, 1591, a college was incorporated by charter, as: "The Mother of a University: The College of the Holy and Undivided Trinity, near Dublin, founded by Queen Elizabeth; whereby knowledge and civility might be increased by the instruction of our people there, whereof many have usually heretofore used to travail into France, Italy, and Spain, to get learning in such foreign universities, whereby they have been infected with poperies, and other ill qualities, and so become evil subjects."

These words concerning Trinity College prove that it was founded to be a powerful engine of proselytism for the Catholic youth of Ireland.

To meet the requirements of a region in which the Spanish and English languages are used, the king of Spain continued to send Irish priests to Florida, Louisiana, and other parts of his dominions. The regiment of Hibernia, belonging originally to the Irish Brigade, in the French service, was stationed at St. Augustine, late in the 18th century. Irish names appear through rank and file, as Curtis, Delany, Barrow, O'Reilly, O'Connell.

There are few princes more disliked than Philip II. Many, so called, historians have expatiated on his cruelties, though they have little to say of those of his contemporaries, as the terrible Henry VIII., and his

more terrible daughter, Elizabeth. But King Philip
did much good as king. And the writer cannot forget
that he supported and educated hundreds of bright
Irish youths, who fled like " wild geese " from their
native land, on account of persecution, and became
Apostles[1] and evangelists in many parts of America
and other countries.

This king continued to the end of his days to take
the greatest interest in the young Irish Levites, for
whom " a refuge from famine and danger " was provided in his hospitable dominions. His pious Queen
wrote, herself, to the Pope to beseech His Holiness to
open a college at Rome for young Irish students,
which was done later.

This was his saintly Queen, Isabella of Valois,
whose death, in her 24th year, says Gayarre, caused
" the simultaneous weeping of a whole people ; " " the
sobbing of a universal sorrow, from the Pillars of
Hercules to the Pyrenees ; she was hailed as a rainbow
after the storm, and was passionately beloved by her
husband's subjects throughout his vast dominions."

Philip II. was married four times. He married Isabella of Valois, by proxy, in 1560, when she was only
fourteen. Her sweetness, piety, and charity, made her
universally beloved. Born at the conclusion of a
treaty of peace between France and Spain, the French
styled her " the Olive Branch," " La Branche 'd
'Olivier, and the Spaniards, " La Princessa de la Paz "
" the Princess of Peace." Like his other Queens,
Anna of Austria, mother of Philip III., he was most
generous to the Irish students as was the king, her son.

Far into the nineteenth century, the Spanish-Hiber-

[1] Apostles preaching Christ to men, evangelists bringing men to
Christ.

ian clergy were still found toiling throughout the American States, in the interest of the church to which they had consecrated their lives. In 1841 Bishop England was asked by two Bishops to take charge of East Florida: The Bishop of St. Christopher, Havana, and Bishop Dubourg, of New Orleans.

Louisiana and Florida were part of the diocese of Santiago de Cuba, whose Bishop was Monseñor Echererria. In O'Reilly's time, this Bishop sent Fray Cyrillo, de Barcelona, as his Vicar General with six Capuchines, Spaniards, to New Orleans. Cyrillo was made Bishop of Tricali, and Auxiliar of Santiago, his actual diocese being New Orleans, Mobile, Pensacola and St. Augustine.

In 1785, Bishop Cyrillo appointed Father Antonio de Sedilla parish priest of New Orleans, after six years' residence in the colony. The Bishop issued a pastoral calling for a better observance of Sunday. To his other difficulties, was added race-antagonism, for the French did not soon become reconciled to Spanish Rule.

Father Antonio's appointment was unfortunate. He is known chiefly for his insubordination, and was not so easily managed as his namesake, Father Anthony, the first pastor of New Orleans, 1722. The history of Louisiana about the period of its cession to Spain, presents some painful chapters. The Capuchine Fathers who had hitherto done so well and given much edification in the neighboring town of Mobile, seem to have fallen into laxity. Their Spanish brethren soon thought they had discovered how grievously they had fallen away. The decay of religion was loudly complained of by officials of church and State. The methods or want of method, in the monks was sharply censured. Something, perhaps, may be said on the other side. It is possible that for want of over-seeing, men who had worked so long on one spot, and with careless, easy going people, may have lost some-what of their first fervor, and even become neglect-ful of duty. But the weightier charges against them are not credible. There was, too, the question of national prejudice. Another point was the strictness of Religious Orders in Spain at that epoch; and how easily men could become disedified, if not scandalized, at mere breaches of discipline that could scarcely be classed as sins. In the eyes of the Spanish Friars, their French brethren were assuredly not of the strict observance. Spain was the land of reform. There were reforms of St. Teresa for Carmelite nuns and Carmelite Friars. There were the Alcantarines, whose venerable founder, St. Peter, ate only twice a week, slept but an hour and a half every night, knew his brothers only by the sound of their voices, having never seen their faces. Awful austerity! Even in the royal families and among the highest nobles, many led life of strictness and holiness. Continued carelessness and easy going ways were enough to disedify men ac-customed to a different standard. The forced depart-ure of the Jesuits, at one fell stroke, deprived the people of many excellent clergy. Account, too, must be made of the influx of wild, unstable men, and the lawless of many lands; the *emigrés* who came to seek a home, and transplant to it the blasphemies of the evil days of the French Revolution. The vile books of the so-called philosophers were found in every home.

The Cabildo was made up of *Regidores,* who held honorary offices, Alcaldes, and a syndic, or mayor. The Colony was under the supervision of a Captain

12

General in Cuba. Appeals might be made from him to the Royal Audencia in Santo Domingo, and, ultimately, to the Council of the Indies in Spain. We hear no more of the tyranny of the Superior Council. O'Reilly left the Colony in perfect order and peace.

There had been difficulties between the French and Spanish Capuchins. The people had been prejudiced against their old favorite, Father Dagobert. Gayarre says he had come to the Colony very young. He was a native of Longuy, and a Capuchin of the Province of Champagne.

Very serious is the blame attached to the latest generation of the New Orleans Capuchins. But the charges against them were, at least, grossly exaggerated; especially in case of Père Dagobert. We are credibly informed that "he obtained the esteem of Count O'Reilly and the good will of the Spaniards by the prudence of his deportment." As their homes were contiguous, they must have met almost every day, and, were but a tithe of these accusations true, the Count would have laid them before authority, and insisted on their correction or even the expulsion of the guilty parties. O'Reilly's able successor, Governor Unzaga, expressly exonerates them from the heavier charges. " How comes it ? " he asks, " that the prelate, (Cyrillo,) is acquainted with the existence of crimes . . . which I am unable to detect, though on the spot ? " " Finally the conciliatory action of the Spanish government soon established peace.

CHAPTER XXVI.

As has been already said, priests appointed to administer the affairs of convents, and preside at their ceremonies, are usually men of learning and piety. Père Dagobert was frequently so employed in the celebrated Ursuline Convent.   In a certificate written by the Ursulines, which still exists, he is commended for his zeal and piety.   Previous to the expulsion of the Fathers of the Society of Jesus, it was customary to choose two Jesuits whose names were,—according to the Rules of the Congregation of Paris, to which our Community belonged, until after the retrocession, when sixteen members left for Havana,—sent to the Bishop that he might approve one as Ecclesiastical Superior.   This election was preceded by the Forty Fours' Devotion.   Father Dagobert's earthly pilgrimage was now drawing to a close.

Father Prosper's first signature as chaplain occurs Feb. 24, 1767.   F. Dagobert's first signature occurs in the examination of a novice, April 28, 1768.   "Fr. Dagobert, V. G. Sup. des missions de cette Colonie, Sup. des Dames Ursulines."

The father of the Sister Vezin, the novice examined by F. Dagobert, was well known throughout the Colony, as a model Christian.   He was a member of the Cabildo, and the devotion with which he took the oath of office was often spoken of as a matter of great

edification; it bound him to defend the doctrine of the
Immaculate Conception, and, as a lawyer, never to
take any fee from the poor. My informant says that
O'Reilly who imposed this oath kept it himself most
faithfully; and adds what is important, when we consider how closely the Ursulines were connected with
the city families, and the widows and children of the
members of the defunct Superior Council, who were
tried and found guilty of high treason and suffered the
penalty of the same. " None of these ever complained
of O'Reilly for having, according to the King's order,
suffered the law to take its course on their relatives.
There was then no daughter of Erin or of Spain among
the Religious. The people of the Convent were mostly
French or of French descent, but no word or act of
O'Reilly's was ever found fault with within the Convent walls. The nuns were satisfied to do all in their
power for the suffering.

We may say here that no religious persecution of
any kind was ever practised in Louisiana. All were
free to come and go and worship God according to
the dictates of conscience.

The appointment of O'Reilly was but temporary.
He was sent out to try the accused of the Supreme
Council, acquit them, if innocent, and punish them if
guilty. He fulfilled his commission, and made his
king and his adopted country respected and beloved
through out the Colony. And though he was not
charged with the religious administration, it was well
known that no abuse would be tolerated in O'Reilly's
atmosphere.

Dagobert is described as an easy, ignorant man, and
less complimentary things are said of him. Easy, he
probably was, but he was beloved in the Colony. His

exquisite voice often led the congregation in singing
God's praise. " The Père will always be very glad
to officiate," said one of the governors, " for singing
is with him a passion. " And he sometimes recreated
his friends at the entertainments which celebrated the
marriages and christenings at which he officiated.
Ignorant he was not, and none of his contemporaries
seem to have charged him with ignorance. He wrote
and spoke French and Spanish fluently, and had a
good knowledge of Latin. He was known as a friend
of O'Reilly's and that is surely in his favor.

Count O'Reilly[1] had fine social qualities and was
distinguished as a letter-writer. Jean Bouligny who
wrote a genealogy of the family, referring to their
escutcheon, says : " The principal nobility is to be a
good man, *hombre de bien,* of deeds, without reproach,
to live in the fear of God, in obeying his commandments." By his sons, he sent a letter of introduction
to O'Reilly, and he goes on to say, "to whom I
recommend you, *El conde* offered me to do for you all
that would depend on him." " Apply yourself to do
your duty well, for God is the true patron of honest
people."

Francisco Bouligny to whom the above is addressed,
came to Louisiana as aide-de-camp to O'Reilly, in
1769. A very affectionately-worded letter is extant
from O'Reilly to the wife of Francisco Bouligny.
Many other letters from El Conde O'Reilly to his ancestor are in possession of Mrs. Albert Baldwin, of
New Orleans, née Bouligny, her descendant. Mrs.

[1] The youths of the Bouligny family often spoke of the many advantages they derived from their conversations and correspondence
with Count O'Reilly. There were several letters from the Kings of
Spain, bearing the autograph, *Yo el Rey,* in the Bouligny collection.

Baldwin also possesses autograph certificates signed by Frère Dagobert, and Antonio de Sedilla. The late Charles Gayarre[1] possessed many letters of the first Spanish Governor. They are bright and pleasing, and show a kind and pleasant disposition on part of the writer, who is always ready to oblige, and do favors even for an enemy. No trace whatever, of an unkind, much less cruel, character. They are written chiefly in Spanish or French, and there is great intimacy between the correspondents though seas often divide them. Mrs. Baldwin's collection is quite large. It is most carefully kept and in excellent condition.

The Gayarres, Boulignys Navarros, Loyolas, O'Farrells, were, with the Governors' household, the leading members of Père Dagobert's congregation. There were surely many good practical Catholics among these families. Sebastian O'Farrell, a brilliant youth of eighteen, came to the Colony with O'Reilly, whose heir had married one of the O'Farrells. Sebastian O'Farrell was later well known as the Marquis of Casacalvo whose exquisite politeness embarrassed Claiborne.

The last ceremony presided over by the Jesuits at the Convent was that of Sister Ste Antoine, Lay Sister, Marthe Délâtre, March 25, 1759. She lived till 1820. Father Morand who presided, signs himself " Grand Vicaire en absence du Père Bandouin, Grande Vicaire Général." The act bears the following signatures: " Carette Jesuite missionaire, LeRoy, Jesuite missionaire." It has been said that division of authority was the curse of French America.

---

[1] Mr. Gayarre showed the writer many of these letters. Several of them were from Kings of Spain. Being financially embarrassed, Mr. Gayarre sold some of these letters to wealthy friends.

The Creoles, descendants of French and Spaniards were all Catholics. Under French and Spanish rule, the city officials were appointed by the crown. The original settlers mostly came from Normandy, Brittany, and Canada. In the Spanish *régime* there was some immigration from Spain and some from the Canary Islands. Towards the close of the 18th century, many refugees came from San Domingo. The insurrection of the slaves in the French portion of San Domingo took place on the night of Aug. 23, 1791. Hundreds of families were butchered by the infuriated negroes. Many ultimately came to Louisiana.

The native tribes first known to the early French colonies preserved their friendship in a remarkable manner, excepting only the Natchez and Chickasaw nations. Sad accidents sometimes happened the missioners. The aged René Mesnard was lost in the forest and never seen again. Long after, his cassock and breviary were kept as amulets among the Indians.

The churches were served by Jesuits and Capuchins and occasionally by secular clergy. The state never claimed the churches. They belonged to the parish and to the eccleciastical authorities, though often claimed by the marguilliers or church-wardens. Early in the nineteenth century, there was but one Catholic Archbishop under the American flag, Most Rev. John Carroll, of Baltimore. But long before, Father Dagobert's troubled career had ended in peace. He had sung himself, let us hope, into the heavenly choirs whose music makes the gladness of us poor pilgrims, while we long to sit at the feet of the Queen of Angels, and listen. This we learn from an extract of the Register of deaths, in the Parochial church of New Orleans, in which the holy Bishop, Cyril of Barcelona, says that " he gave ecclesiastic sepulture to the body of Rev. Father Dagobert," missionary Apostolic of Louisiana for sixty-three years and one month. He was eighty-three years old, and it is certain that the holy Bishop who attended him, left nothing undone for the salvation of his immortal soul.

But tradition long affirmed that the people had not heard the last of their favorite. It was rumored that he and his old friends arose every night from their graves, and walked about the ancient cemetery, singing and praying. Many will remember the beautiful description of the music of Tintin Calandro given by that ancient Creole, Charles Gayarre. People listened outside the walls for the wonderful strains of music from the voice of the Père, and the instrument of Tintin:

> " When the weather is warm and sweet,
> And hushed is the sound of passing feet,
> He lingers still in his snug retreat
> By the open wall ! "

On All Saints' Day, all are laden with flowers, wending their way to the city of the dead.

On account of the marshy nature of the soil the dead in New Orleans are usually buried above ground, in receiving vaults. It is said that at midnight the dead arise, and shaking off the cerements of the grave, commune with each other till dawn. Then, in their narrow homes they await their loved ones who will soon come laden with flowers: " Our bed is covered with flowers."

When the shadows of evening fall, the dead will be left covered with beautiful blossoms. In the crowds you will not see one Indian. The dull, swarthy In-

dians of the French market ignore all this, for the
Indians never speak of their dead after burial.

All Saints' Day, the feast of the dead, or its eve,
is one of the curiosities of New Orleans. It reminds
one of the Feast of Our Lady of the Snow,[1] a pretty
way the Romans have of perpetuating the story of the
miraculous snow-fall in August. A shower of blossoms of white Jessamine is made to fall from the roof
of the basilica at mass and vespers! By this means
pious traditions live among the Roman poor. The
graves in the old cemetery of Father Dagobert, Basin
St., used to be strewn with flowers on the Feast of
the dead, so that it was said to appear as if covered
with snow. The flowers used on these occasions were
mostly white. But these weird times may be said to
have passed away, and, though multitudes assemble
in the churches and cemeteries, and flowers are scattered over tombs, the friends of those " who are gone
before us with the sign of Faith," are satisfied to join
in the *Liberas* and *Dies Irae,* and repeat the touching
Requiem, æternum, and, above all to offer mass for
their precious dead. The dead no longer greet the
dead. They rest in the sleep of peace, until the angelic
trumpet will announce: " Arise, ye dead, and come
to judgment.

It will be remembered that a Queen of Philip II
wrote to the Pope to entreat him to open a special
College for the education of Irish youths who had to
fly from Ireland or be forced to accept a Protestant
education. Her request was granted after some delay.
In 1627, Urban VIII. built a College at Rome, to
which students from all quarters of the globe could
come to be trained for a missionary career, and imbued

[1] St. Mary Major.

with the spirit of the church, at the very centre of Catholic Unity.

Even in our own day, in the city of Mexico, in the street of the Sacred Heart, (Calle del Corazon) a great pontifical College, on the site of an old seminary dating from the Spanish Domination, is building. It will cost half a million dollars. French and English are to be taught by native professors. The new building is so conducted as not to interfere with studies still carried on in the ancient edifice.

CHAPTER XXVII.

SPAIN claimed as Florida all land north of Mexico. The Spanish Governor came from Pensacola to Mobile to protest against the new settlement. Bienville received the Governor, Señor Guzman, courteously but declined to acknowledge any right on part of Spain to interfere. Indeed Iberville wanted to take Pensacola, but the Spanish Junta declined to give it up. Bienville remained on good terms with his Spanish neighbor.

When Spain declared war against England, Don Bernardo Galvez, Governor of Louisiana, surprised Fort Manchac, Sep. 7. 1779, and compelled Baton Rouge to surrender, Sep. 21. He invested Mobile early in March, 1780, and it surrendered March 12. After a vigorous siege he reduced Pensacola in May. Through this young hero, Western Florida became once more thoroughly Catholic, and the services of the Church resumed their former pomp and solemnity.

A new Register was begun by the Capuchin Father de Veley, a beneficed priest of St. Michael's, Pensacola, and chaplain of the garrison. He belonged to the Capuchin province of Andalusia. His first funeral was that of Anthony Soler, July 4, 1781. The first baptism was that of Diego John Michael, son of Francis Florin and his wife, Catherine Alois, July 31. Count Arthur O'Neil was the first Spanish Governor of Pensacola. In 1791, Bishop Cyrillo made an official visit to Pensacola, as entered in the Register of " San Miguel de Panzacola." May 7, 1798, Right Rev. Bishop Peñalvert made an official visit to the same. All appears to have been found in good order, though no particulars are noted.

CHAPTER XXVIII.

IN several places remote from the smaller centres
of population, the missionaries almost lived in their
canoes, putting into places where some Red men might
be found, to instruct them and administer the sacraments, as we have seen done in our own day in Central
America. Even in these secluded spots, they sometimes found the unfortunate Indians, with passions
excited and intellects dulled by diabolical fire-water,[1]
and to savages in this condition they mostly preached
in vain. For this deadly fluid was always injurious to
the poor children of the forest, and often maddening.
This is why the men of God who came into their
native wilds so eloquently denounced the sale of fire-
water to the barbarians. Almost from the first the
friends of the Indian had to struggle against this
dangerous abuse.

Ere long the Indian problem was partly solved by
banishing the hereditary owners of the soil to distant
territories where, it was promised them, their wants
would be supplied and their lives unmolested. How
the promises were kept, history records. It is certain
that many Indians remained behind, and some may
be found to this day in their ancient haunts. The
missioners never neglected them even when they had
to perform their sacred ministrations by stealth.

[1] Tafia, a cheap alcoholic drink was a favorite beverage among the
Indians.

CHAPTER XXIX.

In 1840 Bishop Blanc gave a retreat to his clergy
followed by a mission to the faithful. In Jan. 1, 1843,
the Trustees submitted, and received the regularly appointed pastor, an auspicious event which conduced
much to the peace and order of the diocese. No
doubt it pleased the good Bishop, when, about this
time, King Louis Philippe offered eight free places
in the Seminary of Bordeaux for North American
youths, born subjects of the United States.

From the advent of Bishop Portier things went well
in Mobile. Almost all the settlers from early days
seem to have been able to make a living, however
humble, in the little capital. A well-known *Coureur
de bois,*[1] Le Sueur, took his family there, and for a
long time the name was prominent in its simple annals.
The people seem to have been pious. They repaired
regularly to the church, Notre Dame de Mobile, for
the services and ceremonies of their religion. The
climate was mild and healthy.

In the early days of his Episcopate, Bishop Portier
wrote to a friend: "I have a Vicariate as large as
all France, and three churches and two priests." Such

[1] Le Sueur if not a Coureur (wood-ranger) was certainly a remarkable
traveler. Mr. Pierre Le Sueur before his death in 1751, was Major,
and Chevalier of the Order of St. Louis. Several French families
disappeared with the French Flag.

was the condition of the church in this remote corner of the Divine Vineyard when Michael Portier, then a deacon, came to America to devote his life and talents to the struggling Church of the South, 1817.

Teaching, an occupation well adapted to his deep knowledge and energetic zeal, was undertaken soon after his ordination by Father Portier, and, from the Seminary he founded in the old Ursuline Convent, he was taken to become Bishop.

Prior to Bishop Portier, and as far back as 1538, the Holy Sacrifice of the Mass as we have related, had been offered in Alabama. In De Soto's expedition were twelve priests and four Friars. But, carefully organized as this expedition was, it proved a failure, owing to sickness, losses in battle, and other misfortunes. Again, in 1559, Jesuits and Franciscans passed through this place, and finding neither vestments nor altar, they offered the divine sacrifice under the shady magnolias, using the skins of beasts for vestments. For a long time the Indians kept the faith brought them by these devoted men.

Zealous men accompanied Bishop Portier to the new world, to share his labors and suffering. At his first mass in Mobile, in the small dilapidated Cathedral, his followers were seen to shed tears, so striking was the contrast with their own magnificent churches and stately worship.

We have before us a list of the ancient Ursulines among whom the tradition is, that sickness was almost unknown. Most of them died octogenarians, and some older still. The ecclesiastics were also a long-lived generation, and the same may be said even of the servants of this venerable establishment, and also of the neighboring city of Mobile.

Father O'Reilly of St. Augustine willed some land and two small houses to Bishop Portier, to found a monastery of the Visitation. The Bishop earnestly desired to establish a religious house in his diocese, where there were few priests and a dearth of Catholic teachers. He decided to erect the first house for *Religieuses* near his episcopal city. At his request, the Bishop of Georgetown D. C. sent eight fervent nuns to make the foundation. Being the first in his diocese they enjoyed the kindness of the venerated prelate in an eminent degree. Scarcely a day passed that the devoted father and founder did not visit the little colony, founded 1832.

Alabama was not always a land of rest to them, but a battle ground of vigorous conflicts with grinding poverty and stern necessity. Confidence in Providence was strong within them, for difficulties, apparently insurmountable, stared them in the face.

I am with you. In these few words lay the secret of the courage and success of the Founder of the Visitation in Mobile, and the holy souls who seconded his efforts. The Bishop gave the small house and the land on which the Sisters began their work. Five years later, many of their difficulties had passed away, when, in 1840, Alabama was swept by a terrific cyclone. In its course lay the monastery and schools; and in five minutes the work of many years was demolished. No life was lost, but many inmates were severely injured by falling bricks and timber.

At the twilight hour the storm took the roof from over their heads and left them without shelter. The Sisters called this their *noche triste* and sad it was to them. They passed it in the court-yard, exposed to the fury of wind, rain, and lightning.

The tale of woe was conveyed to their faithful Father, and in the early morning he was on the ground. Viewing the havoc made by the angry elements, he said, cheerily: " Well my children, what God sows in sorrow He will not destroy to-morrow," and by words of cheer and encouragement he transfused into his discouraged daughters the faith and courage of his own brave heart. God raised up friends for them in their Southern wilderness, and many came with assistance. The *debris* was removed, order restored, and the nuns resumed their duties. They easily accommodated themselves to inconvenience, for they were little used to comfort.

They desired above all things to procure a small chapel—a dwelling, however humble for Him whose delight is to be with the children of men. Although God consoled them by sending them many fervent aspirants, and their humble possessions increased in value, yet it was many a month before they could make a move towards this cherished project.

The Bishop's watchful eye saw the necessity, and their inability, and made the case a personal one.

In an article written by him and published in the New Orleans papers, he solicited aid to build a chapel for them. A prompt and generous response was the, result, and a substantial chapel was soon erected, large enough to serve as a Parish Church. The good Bishop rejoiced in the realization of his hopes and predicted great things for his cherished community, but, being advanced in years, he did not expect to see the accomplishment of his predictions. He forewarned his daughters that the cross would not be wanting. It would be as a cloud by day, and a pillar of fire by night. But he little dreamed of the great cross to be laid on them: the cross of seeing their labor, sacrifices, and hopes again scattered to the wind.

The morning of May 8, 1854, fourteen years after the cyclone, the monastery and chapel were a heap of smouldering ruins. The evening recreation had been a peculiarly happy one. After night prayers, a novice ascending to her cell, paused to admire the beauty of the scene, and fervent thanksgiving arose in her heart for God's great goodness in bringing her to so holy a home. In a few hours, she was awakened by a fearful glare and the crackling sound of fire. She hastily aroused the Sisters. Already the building was in flames, and but for her prompt action a holocaust of lives would have been the result. Friends and neighbors worked heroically to save the chapel, but in vain. The Bishop was just finishing mass in the Cathedral when the news came. Still fasting he hastened to the scene of the disaster. On gazing on the blackened ruins, all that remained of the monastery, he was unable to check his emotion, and his tears flowed freely. The fire was believed to be the work of the Know-nothings.

Meeting the Sister who had given the alarm, he placed his trembling hand on her bowed head and said:

"Courage, my child, all is not lost. You will live to see a more beautiful chapel than the one we have lost. *I* will not build it. But I shall see it from heaven. More than that, I will help you to build it, for I will ask our Lord to grant me that special favor."

The words were prophetic. The Sister, then in her teens, little dreamed of the great work for which God was fitting her.

The novice was Mary Campbell, daughter of Philip

and Mary Campbell, afterwards so well known and so highly respected as Mother Mary Stanislaus. She was born in Londonderry, Ireland, in 1836. She had come from Boston to Mobile in 1852, in a sailing vessel, the voyage lasting three months.

It is said that the blessing of St. Benedict Joseph Labe, given to Jean Baptiste Vianney, while an infant, in his mother's arms, laid the foundation of the sanctity of the Curé d' Ars. In the years that followed, when God called the young Sister to fill the most responsible offices in the community, she kept the Bishop's words in her heart, and has long since seen the accomplishment of his prophecy. A few years after the fire, the venerable Bishop was called by his master to receive the reward of his life of devotion and self-sacrifice. His name is revered among his daughters as that of a Saint.

He died of dropsy, in the Providence Infirmary, May 14, 1859, R. I. P. His last days were the echo of his holy life. He edified all by the patience and piety with which he bore his long and severe sufferings.

Civil war soon threw its baneful shadow over the southland. The inmates of the quiet cloister had their share in the sufferings by which the South was made desolate. Not a hundred yards from the monastery, entrenchments were thrown up and the stillness broken by signals of war. They expected every day to be driven from their homes to give quarters to the soldiers. Food could scarcely be procured, and they had hardly clothing enough to protect them from the cold. Amid such gloomy surroundings the office was still sung with voices vibrant with love and fervor, and every spiritual exercise faithfully performed.

The first dwelling of the foundresses was a rented house procured by the Bishop. It had only six rooms, with an out-house that served for kitchen and dining-room. Yet parents made application to place their daughters with the Sisters. For these pioneer Religious brought with them a high reputation as teachers. Their first pupil was the daughter of a recently converted Protestant lady. Archbishop Whitfield appointed Mother Madeleine Augustine D'Arréger, a native of Fribourg, superior, 1832 and promised his best aid and support to the enterprise.

CHAPTER XXX.

ARCHBISHOP BLANC of New Orleans called on the Society of Jesus for priests and obtained eight. A Father de la Croix, a Belgian, collected money in Belgium for St. Michael's Church in Louisiana. Like many other zealous priests he was brought out by Bishop Dubourg. He put St. Michael's in excellent order. A flag over the main entrance bears the legend: *Pietas Belgarum erexit.* He returned to Belgium and died there holily in 1869, aged 77.

In Mobile, as in almost everywhere else, the missioners made frequent attempts to teach the children of their flocks. Many families, no doubt, sent their girls to the New Orleans Ursulines. " To my great regret," writes a correspondent, to whom we are much indebted, " the native place of the pupils is not given in the oldest records I have been able to find.

Bishop Portier bought twenty-five acres of land at Spring Hill from Mr. Robinson, Nov. 5, 1828, and later three hundred and eighty adjoining, from the city of Mobile.

The outlook for the monastery and Academy were very gloomy. Bishop Portier's novice was elected Superior. No trial seemed more heart-breaking than this, when *au dedans et au dehors,* nothing seemed probable but ruin and desolation. Yet every effort was made to continue the community exercises as faithfully, as if the hallowed walls of Annecy formed their enclosure. Through all lived the desire to carry out the good Bishop's prophecy, to rear a sanctuary in honor of the Divine Heart, so loving, yet so little loved, an edifice in some manner fit as a thank-offering for the signal favors conferred on the whole Order, and on this little tender plant, the Colony of Mobile, in particular.

During the civil war, Mobile being a sea-port, was blockaded in 1862, and the nuns were forced to keep a continual Lent. Supplies were cut off and they suffered from actual hunger. Besides the inmates of the monastery, there were a number of boarders who had to be provided for without any income from parents who were cut off from all communication with their children. Coffee was made from roasted potato peelings, and for tea they had a drink distilled from the leaves of the Yupon-bush in the forest. Their feet were bare, save when covered with shoes made of scraps of cloth. In August, not knowing when the war would cease, it was decided that two Sisters should go to New Orleans, then in the power of the enemy, to beg provisions and clothing. One of the two selected was the energetic Mother Mary Stanislaus. The grief of the Sisters who witnessed their departure was as great as if they were being borne to the grave.

Great indeed was the necessity which could force cloistered nuns to leave their monastery. It was their comfort to know they were to be accompanied by a Jesuit, Rev. P. Usannez, who was going in the interest of the College, suffering also from the blockade.

After hearing Mass, they set out through a pine forest to a point on the river where was anchored a little vessel having a neutral flag. They hardly dared to hope the Captain would have the hardihood to take them aboard. Constrained by their earnest appeal, he yielded a reluctant consent. Arrived at New Orleans, they sought shelter with friends until they could gain an audience of the officer in command of the city.

Meanwhile, the Captain of their little vessel whose movements were watched by sharp-sighted spies, had been arrested. When the Sisters heard this, they made application to the Federal General for the release of their friend in need. After some annoying preliminaries, Father Usannez and the two Sisters were ushered into the presence of General Banks, who received them courteously and after a few pertinent questions entered into pleasant conversation with them. As soon as they explained the position of the Captain, General Banks sent immediately to have him released. Mother Stanislaus chanced to be from Boston, the General's native city, and he spoke of points and places well known to both. Reassured by his kindness, she stated the deplorable condition of the monastery and asked to be allowed to seek supplies in New Orleans, explaining in her earnest straightforward manner what she needed. "Well, now," said he, with an amused air, "how much money have you to get all these fine things?" "Fifty cents," was the rejoinder. He laughed heartily, and, without more ado, wrote an unlimited order for provisions and supplies of all kinds. Handing her this he accompanied them to the door, and bowed them out with every mark of respect. His order was filled without a murmur wherever presented; and the Rev. Father and the Sisters, returned on a vessel laden with provisions and other necessaries. The name of General Banks is still held in grateful remembrance at the Convent, and every Sister knows this incident by heart.

The end of the war soon came, but not the end of their difficulties. The whole South was left in poverty and disruption, and the outlook for the Convent was gloomy. But everything soon prospered once more.

The Superior and two companions set out for France that they might see the Rules and Customs observed at the fountain head, and obtain the fullest share in the true Visitation spirit. They were received most cordially by their Sisters at Paris, Boulogne, Annecy, Orleans, Amiens, Rouen, Westbury, Versailles, and Paray, also Lyons, Nevers, Dijon. These journeyings to the chief houses of the Visitation were of infinite service to the Sisters of the Mobile Community.

The neighboring city of New Orleans continued to suffer at times from the Church-Wardens. Sister M. Gertrude Young who entered the Ursuline Convent, New Orleans, as a pupil, in January, 1818, told the Sisters there was at that time, besides the Ursuline Convent, only one select school, and that was conducted by an Episcopalian minister. Her uncle, while he was traveling with his son, gave her a choice, and, though a Protestant, she hesitated not to choose the Convent school in preference to the minister's Academy. Previous to that time, she and her cousins had a tutor at home. This was the ordinary practice in Mobile too. The wealthy sent their children away or employed tutors or governesses, who usually came from a distance, to educate them. Miss Young became a fervent Catholic, and was the last nun professed in the old Convent, June 27, 1824.

This lady, Maria Catherine Young, was connected with Mobile, but we have been unable to learn how. In Religion, she was Sister Mary Gertrude. She closed her long and useful life, November 19, 1892,

at the age of ninety years and ten months, seventy-two
years of which she spent in the cloisters of St. Ursula,
having been a pupil in the old Convent before she took
the veil.

An ancient and venerable Ursuline nun of whom
we could say much, did space permit, Sister Mary
Angela Johnson, said that Archbishop Blanc had told
her that, once he believed a man could not suffer all
that *he* was made to suffer, and live.   She also said
that it was after an interview with the marguilliers or
their agents, by whom injurious things were said to
him, and of him, that he entered his room (in the
Convent,) and leaning against his bed, buried his face
in his hands and quivered with emotion.   In this position he was found soon after, almost dead.

Archbishop Blanc, who became Bishop in 1835, and
Archbishop in 1850, died suddenly July 20, 1860,
"after seeing several persons."   His Vicar General,
Father Rousillon, who was hurriedly summoned, had
scarcely time to administer Extreme Unction and the
last absolution.   No words of ours could describe all
that this saintly prelate, who was most sensitive, suffered from the frequent rebellions and litigations of
these unruly, misguided persons.

From the time of Bishop Dubourg the State of
Mississippi had been merged into the diocese of New
Orleans, but in 1837, a see was established at Natchez,
which, with Little Rock, Mobile and Galveston, were
the suffragan sees of New Orleans.   The first Provincial Council of New Orleans was held in 1856.

Religion flourished in Louisiana under Archbishop
Blanc; the sacraments were frequented; and pious
practices became general.   The Redemptorist Fathers
were introduced for the needs of the Germans, espe-

cially in the Fourth District, of New Orleans. The
yellow fever slew its thousands, in the frequent epidemics. In 1858, while hastening to the relief of the
sufferers from this awful disease, the Archbishop
stepped into a hole in the wharf, and broke both bones
of his leg. From this most painful accident he never
fully recovered

CHAPTER XXXI.

"You will succeed," wrote Mother Chappius, of Troyes, to the Mobile Superior, "but by way of the cross." True daughters of Holy Mary, the Sisters *stood* beneath the cross. Bishop Portier's novice, now an ancient professed, was the Mother of this intrepid band. They worked with earnestness and fervor to draw down God's choicest blessings. Trusting in God's goodness, with the kind Bishop's consent, they began to build a monastery such as the exigencies of the Order required.

The school was carried on in a manner to keep up the excellent standard already reached. In thanksgiving for the wonderful mercies which had preserved them amid wars, cyclones, conflagrations, they built to the Sacred Heart a sanctuary as beautiful as generous loving hearts could make it—a monument whose every stone records a sacrifice, whose foundation was laid in humiliation and suffering.

To-day we have before us " the new chapel," grand, beautiful in the dazzling and artistic grace of carven stone. Fifty years ago, almost on the same spot, we see only the blackened ruins of the first Visitation Chapel in Mobile, and, near by, a small group of nuns, with tear-stained, disconsolate faces weeping over the smouldering ashes. The woe this scene depicts can hardly be appreciated by this generation. Only the pen of the Recording Angel can fully tell the tale of courage, heroic devotion, lasting from the foundation. The work is perfect—a marvel of beauty, a picture most fair to look upon. Yet to one who can look through the vista of years, and gaze on the wonderful background of this fair scene, it is plain that to perfect the picture the shadows of the past must be placed upon the canvas, that the beauties of the present may be fully appreciated.

It was fitting to make such an offering in thanksgiving to that divine heart whose tenderest predilection is for the Daughters of the Visitation. This magnificent edifice the crowning of a life of untiring devotion to the fulfillment of good Bishop Portier's prophecy, was begun in 1894.

The flood-gates of Virginia and the Carolinas were now hoisted, and mighty streams of immigration poured through them spreading over the whole territory of Alabama. But the influx was not Catholic.

The Vine and the Olive Company, consisting mostly of friends of Napoleon, settled near Demopolis in 1817, but failed. Some went back to France, others scattered over Marengo County. They did not come in the spirit of religion to teach Christ Crucified. They were rather like the philosophers, so called, than the early settlers. In the towns that sprang up in many quarters education so called was spreading. But it was education without religion which the great O'Connell said, " is worse than ignorance." Fear God and keep his Commandments, for that is the whole man," says the Wise Man, " and if that is the whole man," says Bossuet, " the rest is nothing." The modern education, expressively styled " Godless," is not for the whole man. It does not train the heart with the head, and make an upright Christian as well as a bright

scholar. " The more schools we open in these days,"
says a shrewd observer, " the more jail room we shall
need."

Bishop Portier established schools for boys in
Pensacola and St. Augustine. By 1838, the ecclesiastical troubles of Pensacola, if not quite over, were con-
siderably lessened. The church seemed about to rise,
phœnix-like, from her ashes. For, at the date of the
Revolutionary war, not a mission remained in these
regions of the many founded in the days of old by
Dominican Franciscans, Jesuits, secular clergy, and
others who sowed the good seed throughout the land:
" An enemy hath done this."

The Indians as a rule may be said to have vanished,
but the blacks have long since taken their place, as
special objects of zeal in the Catholic Church here.
The frequent visitations of yellow fever to the Southern cities were a great drawback to the establishment
of schools and churches. The negroes were not or-
dinarily subject to this fever.

This terrible disease retarded the labors of the great
Bishop England in Charleston. He wrote to his
friend, judge Gaston, in the midst of an epidemic in
Charleston: " I have often through weariness fallen
asleep on the ground in the midst of my office. Yet,
thank God, I never enjoyed better health." It was said
in Charleston[1] that in these awful epidemics the Bishop
was scarcely ever absent from the bedside of the
stricken. Yet he never took the yellow fever.

Most of the Jesuits who came to Louisiana were
destined to labor in Mobile, as professors at Spring
Hill College, and in the usual apostolic functions.

[1] One of Bishop England's disciples called South Carolina: " The
land of many horrors and no hopes."

A church and college were begun at Grand Coteau, the foundation stone being laid by Archbishop Blanc, July 31, 1837. The college was opened Jan. 6. It closed the first year with fifty-six pupils. The number of students, and the amount derived from them, depended on the success of the sugar and cotton crops, as in all plantation districts. There was sometimes question of closing the college, and it is said that a holy nun predicted that the Jesuits would never abandon the college. Be that as it may, it still exists, and many pious prayers have ascended to heaven, that it may continue to exist for the welfare of souls.

The Fathers not engaged in teaching did missionary duty in many places under their Rector, Rev. Father Ladaviére. Much good was done that history takes little note of. The Indian Laws—" Las Leyes de Indias—" formulated by the crown of Spain, with the assistance of the Catholic Church—are a glorious monument to Spanish Rule in America. From first to last the Catholic Church was the friend of the Indians, and had these laws been more faithfully observed, history would have a fairer tale to tell of the Aborigines. Yet the Indians were among the whites during the whole Colonial period, always an object of zeal and interest to the Catholic clergy.

Father Constantine Maenhaut was pastor of Mobile from 1823 to 1827. Father Ganilh was there also. One of these holy men said: " As I ponder our exploits I feel that it was not of ourselves we performed them, but that it was the Providence of God guided us." We feared death," said another, " for we were men." But when the honor and glory of God and the salvation of souls were to be promoted, all fears vanished.

Two of the little band who came to America with

Bishop Portier became Bishops, of Dubuque and Vincennes respectively, within a few years. Father Loras was appointed Vicar General, and later, President of Spring Hill College. He worked energetically among the poor, sick, and ignorant and was devoted to the Creoles and half breeds. His bark canoe was well known on the neighboring waters, and he once said: "It seems to me that I am saving a soul by every stroke of the paddle." Being Rector of the Cathedral, he had his share in the crosses of a parish priest, and he cried out in a moment of unusual suffering: "O had I known what is it to be a Curé, I would have buried myself in the shades of La Trappe." He modeled himself on the Curé d' Ars, whom he had known and loved.

At first his lines did not fall in pleasant places, as a Bishop. He was consecrated Bishop of Dubuque, Dec. 10, 1837, by Right Rev. Bishop Portier, assisted by Right Rev. Bishop Blanc, and died, Feb. 19, 1858. In Dubuque he was so persecuted that he seriously thought of asking to have his see transferred to Burlington. Ingratitude cowardice, obstinacy, weakness, insubordination, came into his experience. But he remembered many acts of kindness on part of some good people in Dubuque, and thinking, perhaps, of the few just for whom God would spare the sinful city, he remained to the end, "Angel of the Church" to which he was appointed. And success soon rewarded his devotedness.

Father Bazin, a native of Lyons, came to Mobile as a missionary in 1830, and at the recommendation of the sixth Council of Baltimore, he was made Bishop of Vincennes and consecrated in that city by Bishop Portier, October 24, 1847. In a few months he was attacked by mortal illness, and expired April 23, 1848.

Bishop Loras did much to revive in the North West the missions interrupted since the time of Hennepin in the 17th century. Though the Indians forgot their religion they clamored for the blackrobe. It was easy to almost uproot the religious practices of a people never famous for high sanctity or unusual asceticism.

They do not appear to have found fault with their clergy. Tradition describes their priests as kind and generous, and most charitable to the poor. They were greatly devoted to the celebrated Père Dagobert, who at the period of the arrival of the Spaniards, received, with royal honors at the church portals, at the head of his brethren, the great man Count O'Reilly who represented the potent monarch of Spain. Père Dagobert solemnly welcomed him, and promised fidelity for his clergy and people, with utmost enthusiasm, having previously bestowed the benediction of the Church on the Spanish flag, whose flaming colors had just replaced the lilies of France.

At this time Père Dagobert must have been about seventy-five years of age [1] and had been over fifty years in the Colony. He was, therefore, a venerable figure to welcome the princely Irishman. As they lived contiguous, it is likely that the priest met the Governor almost every day. And O'Reilly would not tolerate anything wrong or even unseemly in the clergy.

The late Judge Gayarre, several of whose relatives were acquainted with Père Dagobert, spoke of him as full of charity, and greatly loved by the people, among

[1] During some little fracas, Dagobert turned toward his assailants and said, says Gayarré, " I have been fifty years among you and have I ever injured any one of you ? "

whom the traditions of him lingered almost into our own day.

For many a year the old Creoles and the Creole darkeys [1] were accustomed to visit, on All Soul's Day, the last resting place of their favorite, Père Dagobert, and beg eternal rest and perpetual light on his immortal soul!

A hurricane destroyed an enormous amount of property in Louisiana, in 1780, and eight years later, New Orleans was nearly consumed by a fire which broke [1] out on Good Friday. It has since been almost drowned by floods, and more than once decimated by Cholera and yellow fever. But, though not seated on a rock, the old city has weathered all storms and is richer and more prosperous to-day than at any period of her past history. The old priests have faithfully chronicled the family events of many generations, and registered with historic accuracy the various transfers of the Colony. Thus does Père Dagobert record the Transfer of Louisiana to Spain, August 10, 1769:

" The Spanish troops entered to take possession of this city and of all the province, the 10th day of August, 1769.

" On Nov. 30, 1803, the Feast of the Apostle, St. Andrew, Father Antonio Sedilla records the transfer by Spain to France:

" And on the 20th of December, same year, the same Father Antonio records the delivery of Louisiana to the United States.

All these transfers are entered in Spanish.

---

[1] Creoles in Louisiana being descendants of French or Spaniards or both, a Creole darkey is one once owned by these families as distinguished from colored servants owned by purely American families.

14

In 1723, the intrepid Bienville established the seat of government in New Orleans, and defined with his good sword a certain plot of ground upon which was to be built a Catholic Church. This site has since been consecrated to the service of God. The little church of wood and adobe was swept away by the hurricane, 1780, and a fierce conflagration consumed its more ambitious successor, in 1788. The third edifice was erected in the last decade of the 18th century, and was the munificent gift of the princely Don Andres Almonaster y Roxas, who is said to have expended four millions on the city of his adoption. Besides St. Louis Cathedral, New Orleans owes him the Charity Hospital, the picturesque buildings flanking the Cathedral, the Chapel of the Ursulines, the large, well proportioned presbytery of the Cathedral and many other gifts of public utility. This distinguished philanthropist, the greatest New Orleans had seen, was born in Andalusia, in 1725, and died in New Orleans, 1798, may he rest in peace. He married, in 1787, Miss Louise de Laronde. Their only child, the richest heiress of the century in Louisiana, Michaela Leonarda Antonia, was born in 1795. In 1811, she was wedded to Monsieur Joseph Xavier de Pontalba, by Father Antonio de Sedilla.[1] The taking possession of Louisiana by Spain under O'Reilly, and the marriage of this lady were the two grandest ceremonies that ever took place in early days. Count Marigny de Mandeville stood sponsor for the bride, and Count Macarthy was among the *élite* who signed the marriage record as witnesses. Although Madame de Pontalba made her home in Europe, she several times

---

[1] In the chapel of the military treasurer, Don Vincente Nunez.

visited the scenes of her early days and was well known in New Orleans as the Baroness de Pontalba.

This lady built, in 1849, on each side of the ancient Place d' Armes, now Jackson Square, on the site of the old Royal store-houses, the picturesque structures known as the Pontalba Buildings. The Cabildo established by O'Reilly, was rebuilt in 1795 and is one of the most imposing edifices left us by the Spaniards. The Civil Courts below the Cathedral were erected in 1810, on the site of the Capuchin Convent, by Baron de Pontalba. The Baroness laid out Jackson Square in the French style of gardening, having first cut down the ancient elms that gave it its peculiar charm.

The stately Cathedral of Almonaster was repaired and enlarged by Archbishop Blanc, in 1850. Its roof was flat, and in the Spanish régime the Seréno or night-watchman, paced to and fro during the night on the look-out for fires. The name Seréno,[1] was extended to all the police. Later they were called gendarmes.

Almonaster was buried in a crypt of his Cathedral. A marble slab of imposing dimensions marks his sepulchre. Upon it is inscribed his coat of arms, and the record of his life, titles, and services, in Spanish. His friends, several of the Counts of Marigny de Mandeville, repose beside him. The marble slab over their remains shows their coat of arms, and gives their epitaphs in French. One of these, Bernard de Marigny, was a princely planter in Louisiana. He received and aided the exiled duke of Orleans, Louis Philippe. After many days De Marigny became poor, but the king of former years, though he knew of his

---

[1] Sereno from calling out the hours of the night and the state of the weather.

benefactor's sore distress, made no effort to assist him. He never retrieved his fallen fortunes. " He died poor, it is said, but without a stain on his proud escutcheon." Many still living in New Orleans knew and revered this illustrious nobleman.[1]

Don Andres Almonaster y Roxas is commemorated every Saturday evening in the Cathedral, which owes him so much, by services offered for the repose of his soul. And, as the sun sets on that day, the sweet but mournful sound of the tolling bell recalls the memory of this great and good man to his fellow-citizens.

The Marignys de Mandeville lived some time in Mobile. Two of them, Antoine and Philippe, were born in Mobile, as is recorded on their respective tombs in the New Orleans Cathedral.[2]

[1] This family was highly considered in New Orleans. Kerlerec, third Governor of Louisiana, arrested Marigny de Mandeville, Bossu, and others as partisans of his intendant,[1] and shipped them to France. His conduct was disapproved at court. For this and other causes, he was imprisoned in the Bastile, and died, it is said, of grief, soon after his release.

[2] Etienne de Boré, another wealthy planter, who placed his home and his purse at the service of the fugitive prince, was rewarded, through his grandson, the late Charles Gayarre, who being in Paris during the reign of Louis Philippe was sought out by that monarch, received into his palace, and treated with every possible kindness and distinction, as Mr. Gayarre often gratefully acknowledged.

[1] The Intendant in those days had really a good deal of power. He was said to be the man in the saddle who managed all.

Governor Kerlerec did so much for the Indians whom he assembled in Congress in Mobile, that they voted him " Father of the Choctaws."

CHAPTER XXXII.

MICHAEL PORTIER, the first Bishop of Mobile, was born at Montbrison, France, in 1795, and even amid the terrors of the French Revolution was trained to piety by his worthy Christian parents. Very soon he entered the theological Seminary at Lyons, a city to which on account of early asociations he was always much attached. Bishop Dubourg of Louisiana coming to France for subjects, young Portier was one of the first to respond to his call. He accompanied that prelate to America, and landed at Annapolis, September 4, 1817, at the age of twenty-two. Having completed his studies under the Sulpitians at Baltimore, he was ordained priest at St. Louis, in 1818. During the next year, his first in New Orleans, he was attacked by yellow fever while attending the sick, and having remained several days at death's door, slowly recovered. Soon after he was made Vicar General. A new Vicariate composed of Alabama and the Floridas was erected, and for its government Very Rev. Michael Portier, V. G., was selected. He was most reluctant to assume this responsibility, but finally yielded, and was consecrated at St. Louis by Bishop Rosati, Nov. 5, 1826, being about thirty-one years old. His jurisdiction included the two old Spanish Catholic cities of St. Augustine founded 1565, and Pensacola, 1696 each with its church and congregation. In Spanish times Florida had been a missionary field, where

Dominican, Jesuit, and Franciscan Fathers had shed their blood in their heroic efforts to convert souls.

The celebrated Bishop England who at this period filled the neighboring see of Charleston, says he does not know a better man than Dr. Portier, and was desirous he might be appointed to the more important see of New Orleans, " where," he says, " he would do well." And he adds that, next to New York, perhaps, New Orleans is the most important diocese on this side of the Atlantic.[1]

The Indian missions had been destroyed by the English and their Indian allies. Catholics of other races were slowly coming in, but the poor young bishop had everything to create or to restore. He was the only priest in his Vicariate. " I need two or three priests," he wrote, " but dare not ask for them, as I am afraid I cannot now support them. I have neither pectoral cross nor chapel, neither crozier, nor mitre," and to add to his difficulties, his little church at Mobile was destroyed by fire, in October, 1827.

Bishop Portier made a visitation of his Vicariate as a missionary, beginning at Mobile, and riding on horseback to Pensacola, Tallahassee, and St. Augustine. His letters show that the fatigues and privations of this journey were such that it seemed little short of a miracle that he survived them. As soon as he could secure one priest to attend to West Florida, he begged Bishop England to lend him another for St. Augustine. He went to Europe in 1829, and God having blessed his labors, he soon returned with two priests and four

[1] The Carolinians, the Georgians, the Virginians, the New Englanders, with much foreign immigration poured into Mississippi and Alabama and laid the foundation of their present population, but this increase was mostly non-Catholic.

ecclesiastics. During his absence the Holy See erected Mobile into an episcopal See, and Bishop Portier was transferred to it. The ancient French city where a parish had been canonically erected, July 20, 1703, thus became the residence of a Bishop.

The Bishop built a modest Church, 20 by 30, in which he was enthroned. A two-roomed frame palace was contiguous. He soon began to erect churches at Montgomery, Tuscaloosa, Huntsville, and other places. He was very successful in collecting congregations and with his small force of priests he met their more immediate wants. He secured some property at Spring Hill, near Mobile, where he opened a College which still exists. Bishop Portier succeeded so well in Mobile that Bishop England seems to continue to regret that he had not been appointed to the more important See of New Orleans, "where," says the Bishop of Charleston, " he was known and loved." He adds that Bishop Portier's College and Convent are supplied with pupils from New Orleans. It was not easy to get Bishops for these southern cities. Although to desire to be a Bishop may be to desire a good thing, still this was a good thing which the southern clergy seldom or never seem to have desired; a command was often necessary to force them to accept the episcopal consecration, and several of the earlier prelates resigned the mitre. Bishop England writes of an excellent priest about this time, " Jean-Jean[1] is away hiding somewhere to escape the mitre."

---

[1] Rev. Aug. Jean-Jean. Bishop England and several other ecclesiastics recommended Père Jean-Jean for the New Orleans mitre, and the bulls came for his appointment, but he returned them and left the city. Bishop Portier, with much difficulty, persuaded the Belgian priest, Leo de Neckers, to accept the bishopric of New Orleans, 1829.

From his arrival in New Orleans, Father Portier was often present at the ceremonies of the Ursulines in their beautiful chapel. April 24, 1823, he preached at the reception of Miss Maria Catherine Young, taking for his text: " He that loveth his life shall lose it; and he that hateth his life in this world, keepeth it to life everlasting." This was the last taking of the white veil that occurred in the old Convent on Chartres St. This lady lived to be almost a centenarian, dying Nov. 19, 1890, retaining to the last the full use of all her mental faculties. She had a vivid recollection of Father Portier's open and benign countenance. Father Portier is mentioned as present at several other ceremonies, the last of which took place in November, 1819, on which occasion were also present Very Rev. Father Sibourg, V. G., Father Louis Moni [1] and others of the early priests. Father Portier was well acquainted with the Ursulines. Mother Seraphina Ray was born in the same year with himself, 1795, and, like him, not far from Lyons. She was baptized in a barn whither she was conveyed in a basket, so as not to excite the suspicions of the vile informers whose business it was to denounce the priests, and the Catholics who dared to give them hospitality. At eighteen, she became a Religieuse of St. Charles. She received the habit, 1813, from Cardinal Fesch, uncle of Napoleon, whose mother, Madame Letitia, stood godmother for the novice, having arrayed her in royal fashion for the occasion. Several personages of the imperial court were present, and the Cardinal's Vicar General, Very Rev. Mr. Aribert, preached an eloquent sermon on the

---

[1] Father Moni was one of the four Italian priests procured for his diocese by Bishop Dubourg in Rome ; the others being Fathers Bigischi, Biglii, and Rossi.

beauty and advantages of the religious state. In 1815, she made her profession, and the following year, Bishop Dubourg invited her to leave Lyons, and join his Ursulines in New Orleans. Mother Seraphina worked incessantly in her holy community till her 85th year. All these excellent women were among the friends of Bishop Portier, and he loved in later years to recall their holy lives. It is hardly necessary to say that good Mother Seraphina had often to rehearse for her bright French pupils her experiences with Madame-Mère, and the court ladies who attended her brilliant reception. Nor did she fail as an antidote to repeat the words: " Vanity of vanities, all is but vanity."

Bishop Portier was of a mild and most amiable character, and would take much pains to serve any person to whom he could be of use. The case of the Frenchman accused of killing young Wyzer, in Eutaw, is not yet forgotten. William M. Murphy, styled " the Curran of the American bar," defended the Frenchman so eloquently that he obtained his acquittal. Bishop Portier sent him a liberal fee, as the Frenchman was unable to pay for his defence, but Murphy returned the money. Bishop Portier laid the facts before the Archbishop of Paris, who acquainted the French government with them. Monsieur Guizot, the premier, wrote to Mr. Murphy a letter conveying the thanks of King Louis Philippe for the humane and disinterested aid he had extended to a French subject in distress. In showing this letter to a friend, Mr. Murphy said: " This is the largest fee I ever received."

Rev. Napoleon Joseph Perché was for twenty-eight years chaplain to the Ursuline Convent. To defend religion with pen as well as voice he founded the journal, *Le Propagateur Catholique,* and was among the ablest adversaries of the trustees.

CHAPTER XXXIII.

It has been said that if the people of these watery regions were wise, they would have an ark or two in readiness for an immediate escape. But the people still go on as they have done for centuries making history. The effects of all this in colonial days had something to do with the progress of religion, in a pre-eminently missionary country.

On Good Friday, March 21, 1788, in the terrible fire which began in the chapel of the military treasurer, Don Vincente Jose Nuñez, on Chartres St., New Orleans was almost wiped out of existence: nine hundred buildings were totally destroyed. The Parish Church, a brick structure dating back to 1725, the adjoining Convent of the Capuchines, the home of Bishop Cyrillo, and the Spanish schools, were among the buildings reduced to ashes. The afflicted people experienced in their measure the truth of the words:

> " A thousand years scarce serve to form a State,
>   An hour may lay it in the dust."

Some time before this conflagration, the Holy See, at the instance of the King of Spain, had erected the Bishopric of Havana, including Louisiana and the Floridas. Right Rev. Joseph James Trespalacio became first Bishop of the new diocese, April 11, 1787.

In the midst of the universal desolation, the greatest benefactor of the Colony appeared, in the person of

a Spaniard who had lived in New Orleans during the
Spanish Régime, and was known as a notary and a
contractor—Don Andres Almonaster y Roxas,—to
whom the spacious Cathedral of New Orleans owes
its existence.

When, in 1779, a terrible hurricane swept away the
humble hospital founded 1737, by a poor sailor, named
Jean Louis, Almonaster had a new one built at a
cost of one hundred and fourteen thousand dollars,
(114,000.)

On March 21, he proposed to the Cabildo to rebuild the Parish Church on a grander scale, the prop-
osition was promptly accepted, and the building began in 1789.

This generous Spaniard became the Saviour of the
burned city. He rebuilt a large portion of it, thus
giving work to thousands of the poorer classes, black
and white. The new church was nearly completed in
1794, and narrowly escaped destruction in a second
conflagration, Dec. 8, 1794. It was to become a Cathedral, with Don Louis Peñalvert y Cardenas for its
first Bishop.

He was born at Havana, April 3, 1749. He received
his early education in the famous College which
the Jesuits maintained for nearly half a century at
Havana. He was studying philosophy there when the
Pragmatic Sanction of Charles III., closed all the Colleges of the Society, in his dominions. The magnificent church of the Jesuits in Havana was built almost
entirely by his parents, who were much revered for
their piety and charity: Don Diego Peñalver, and
Doña Maria Luisa de Cardenas.

The name of this austere and exemplary prelate is
sometimes spelt Peñalver, but probably not correctly.

The historian, Gayarré, spells it Peñalvert, and Gayarré was a contemporary. Peñalvert means green rock. It is customary with Spaniards of rank to add the name of the mother to that of the father: Peñalvert y Cardenas.

Baron de Carondelet, one the ablest of the Spanish Governors, was in office when the first Bishop was expected, and most anxious for his coming. " I regard his coming to these provinces as supremely necessary for the advancement of our holy religion," wrote the Baron. The Bishop reached New Orleans, July 17, 1775. He began at once to study the situation, which was anything but consoling. Some one has said " that a firm seat in the saddle should be acquired before any attempt is made to lead the procession of the Knights-errants of civilization," or, we may add, of religion. The Bishop though a saintly and learned man, seems to have had little of what, a later age called magnetism. He was not liked by all. Though he toiled incessantly for the good of the strange medley of nations, over which he was placed, he had little success as a ruler in Israel. In a letter to His Excellency, the Governor, he gives a heart-rending description of his situation, and the dreadful condition of his flock. The Catholic Church, the oldest organization in America, which had announced Christ to every tribe from ocean to ocean, seemed little more than a failure here. The prelate denounced the sins of his flock in terms, strong and scathing. Much of the evil was due to the circulation of infidel literature of the worst species. Impious works had all but produced that saturnalia of slaughter and licentiousness which had disgraced France and appalled the world. The French had dethroned God and deified

Reason, and, in their ancient Colony, Religion had reached its lowest ebb. But there were many holy souls fired by the burning words of the pious prelate, and sustained by his brilliant example of every virtue; and hopeless as matters now seemed, they felt that virtue would not ultimately be left to be its own reward.

The brightest spot in New Orleans was the Ursuline Convent. The Bishop appreciated the labors of the daughters of St. Angela, and seemed to delight in testifying his esteem and paternal affection for them. He presided over the triennial elections, July 12, 1797, and the Chronicles observe that this was the first time a Bishop was present on similar occasions. The first mention of the saintly Bishop was made in an Act of Profession, February, 1796, but his Lordship was not present, and the act was signed by Antonio de Sedilla, for the Bishop. He was then Pastor of the Cathedral, and he so signs his name.

Bishop Peñalvert traveled much over his vast diocese, preaching, preparing the people for Confirmation, and conferring that great sacrament. We seldom find him baptizing: " God sent me not to baptize but to preach the gospel." The Ursuline Annalist says in a letter: "It may interest you to know "——she speaks of the vicious men, who formed no small part of the Bishop's flock—"that these worthy descendants of the so called Catholics who had banished the Colony's best friends, the Jesuits, rebelled against lawful authority, calumniated and stimatized one of its noblest representatives, O'Reilly, the good and magnanimous while they gave the glorious title of martyr to the arch-traitor, Lafrénière."

Father Sedilla, (Père Antoine) ceased to be in

charge of the Cathedral, when the Bishop, on his with-
drawal from Louisiana, to accept the mitre of Guatemala, left the diocese in charge of Very Rev. Thomas
Canon Hassett, and Very Rev. Patrick Walsh, both
priests of learning and experience, who had long labored in the Colony. This resulted in a schism, excited
to some extent, by the marguilliers. Our Annalist
says: " It is probable that the marguilliers or trustees
of the Cathedral, had more to do with this schism,
than poor, good-natured Père Antoine, whose courage
to resist their unjust pretentions and anti-Catholic
spirit was certainly not equal to that afterwards displayed by Archbishop Blanc, and his faithful champion, Rev. N. J. Perché.

Jan. 25, 1781 Antonia Maria Pesez de Ramos made
her profession in New Orleans Convent, with three
other Spanish ladies. Father Sedilla presided, on part
of Bishop Cyrillo, October 24, 1785. It fell to the lot
of Mother Ramos to lead the Sisters who left New
Orleans for Havana, where the Convent they founded
still flourishes.

The first mention of Père Antoine is his presence
at the profession of Sister Monica de Ramos and Sister
Rita de Castillo, Jan. 25, 1781. He assisted at no
other ceremony from 1785 to 1796, when he was at
the profession of Sister St. Rosalie Bourque. His
signature occurs for the last time at the profession of
two Sisters, Aug. 5, 1802.

Mother Ramos is mentioned as having assembled
the chapter, Aug. 23, 1787, to read to its members a
certificate required by Monseñor Cyrillo, Bishop of
Tricali. It was signed by all the Religious. It was
highly appreciative of the worthy prelate, who, amid
the trials and calumnies which awaited him in the

outer world, was glad to have the testimony of these
guileless souls as to his labors among themselves and
their household, and the exalted sanctity of his life.
May 27th, 1773, occurs the first signature of Fray
Cyrillo of Barcelona, at a reception. He is mentioned
as director and chaplain of the community The above
certificate was given him in gratitude for his services
in every relation in which he had stood towards the
community. He officiated at a profession, May 27,
1775, and signed himself: " Fr Cyrillo de Barcelona
aux. V. G." is on record several times as auxiliary
Bishop of Cuba, under the authority of J. J. Echeverria,
July 19, 1783, and at the profession of two Spanish
ladies, Oct. 16, 1783. Meanwhile the work of the
new Cathedral went on. It was blessed on the day
and in the year appointed, in presence of all the civil
and ecclesiastical authorities, Dec. 24, 1794, all eager
to follow the beautiful ceremonies of the Holy Church.

We here transcribe Rev. Don Joaquin de Portillo's
document concerning the dedication of the New Orleans Cathedral.

" A procession of the chief persons in the city
brought the Blessed Sacrament with all possible ceremony from the Convent to the Cathedral, in presence
of the ecclesiastical and civil authorities. At the opening of the ceremony, the illustrious benefactor presented the keys of the Church to Governor Miro, who
handed them to me, Don Joaquin de Portillo, (the
celebrant). Immediately afterwards, Don Patricio
Walsh, an Irish Priest, chaplain to the royal hospital,
foreign Vicar, ecclesiastical judge of the Province for
the Bishop of Havana—the Bishop elect of Louisiana
not having yet taken possession—blessed the church.
The Holy Sacrifice of the mass was then offered there

for the first time and the magnificent ceremony filled the hearts of the faithful with joy. The Blessed Sacrament was carried with all possible solemnity to the new Church when I had sung the first mass and preached the first sermon. Benediction closed the ceremonies. There were salutes of artillery and the *Te Deum* was chanted by the whole congregation.

The Knight, (Almonaster), so commendable for his piety is almost without an equal. Three churches in this city in which are offered to Our Lord the worship and sacrifice due to Him, are monuments of his piety.

God was praised and our benefactor warmly congratulated for all he had done in the interest of Religion.

It is but just, therefore, that the people, and ministers of the Church, should return perpetual thanks to their illustrious and noble benefactor, Don Andres Almonaster y Roxas. To prevent this work from falling into oblivion, I name him here, for a perpetual remembrance, December 30, 1794."

The glory of Almonaster did not fail to offend some less fortunate, or less generous than he. Some suspected him of ambition, others disputed his right to control the affairs of his Hospital. Governor Miro, his friend, referred the matter to the Spanish King, Carlos IV. who did speedy justice to the princely, benefactor: His majesty writes:

" Having duly considered the above in this, my Council of the Indies, ... the aforesaid Don Andres Almonaster is to be relieved from the obligation of accounting for his administrative acts in said Hospital. . . . . He is authorized to occupy the most prominent place in his church, second only to that of the royal vice-patron, (the Intendant of the Province), and to receive the kiss of peace (La Paz) during the celebration of mass. He is entitled to assistance in case of necessity. And, in order that the faithful fulfillment of the requirements of said ordinances, should meet, with, my royal approbation, it is again ordered that the aforesaid Almonaster, whatever may occur, or he may undertake, is to be treated with distinction, be given support, and aid, and be greeted with solicitous regard, so as in future to preclude all further cause of complaint, as one who has proved grateful to my royal person (grata a me real persona,) by the achievement of great works by drawing so generously upon his own resources for the construction of the parochial church, the nun's Convent, the Charity Hospital, and the government buildings, which had been destroyed by hurricanes and by fire. All of which he has accomplished in honor to Religion and to the State, of his own free will, and for the edification and encouragement of mankind.

"Wherefore, I do hereby order and command the aforesaid Governor of the Province of Louisiana, and also the Intendant of my Royal Exchequer, together with all the judges and justices of the above-mentioned province, to keep, comply with, and execute, this, my Royal Decree, without contravening it, for such is my royal will."

YO EL REY.

Given at San Ildefonso, August 10, 1794.

Nothing is more fleeting than earthly glory. In the same Register in which Don Joaquin de Portillo had written the praises of the founder of the Cathedral,

15

Don Perez recorded the death of Don Almonaster y Roxas. He died suddenly aged seventy-three, without receiving the last Sacraments of the Church. His remains lie under the altar of the Sacred Heart in the Cathedral basement.

CHAPTER XXXIV.

THE Society of Jesus in early days was authorized to found missions in every part of Louisiana and it is not too much to suppose that the Jesuits founded schools with their Churches. But at the Suppression, all were swept away. Bishop Peñalvert bewailed that little or nothing was now done for the Indians. He seems to have forgotten that they were in special charge of the Jesuits, and that the Jesuits had been driven out of the Colony.

By Papal Bull, Sept. 1, 1805, Louisiana fell under the care of Dr. Carroll of Baltimore. But no change was made during the life of Very Rev. Patrick Walsh. Meanwhile the Spanish Governors, Salcedo and Casacalvo, had been replaced by Claiborne, the first American Governor. Writing to him, Father Walsh spoke of Père Antoine as "a refractory monk," "supported in his apostacy by the fanaticism of a misguided populace." The reply of the governor was a sort of lecture, not at all to the point, to the legitimate Pastor though it was certainly plausible:

"If those who profess to be followers of the meek and humble Jesus, instead of preaching brotherly love to men, ... should labor to excite dissention and distrust, there is, indeed, reason to fear that the church itself may cease to be an object of veneration."

Père Antoine and a band of usurpers had already driven out the lawfully appointed Pastors, and done all they could to make the Church itself " cease to be an object of veneration."

A not inconsiderable number of the natives of Louisiana were known from time to time to intrigue for the return of the Spaniards to power. When the loyalty of the unfortunate Spaniard was suspected, while he continued to disturb public tranquillity, Governor Claiborne's eyes were opened: " We have here," he wrote, " a Spanish Priest who is a very dangerous man. He rebelled against the Superiors of his own Church, and would even rebel, I am persuaded, against this government, whenever a fit occasion may serve."

Meekness and humility were not the weapons which the worthy Governor used when he had reason to suspect the incumbent of the Cathedral of being a rebel against the Federal Government. He summoned the Father before him, and compelled him to take a formal oath of allegiance Dec. 29, 1806. Bishop Carroll appointed the aged Father Olivier his Vicar General in Louisiana. The new Vicar General was also resisted in his efforts to remove the recalcitrant Père. He then appealed to the Vicar General in Cuba. His appeal, bristling with charges by no means complimentary to Père Antoine himself, was returned by the Cuban Superior to the accused.

In making arrangements for the diocese he was leaving, Bishop Peñalvert gave no special charge or office to Father Antonio de Sedilla. He was merely one of the four assistants, who usually lived at the Cathedral.

CHAPTER XXXV.

BISHOP PENALVERT Y CARDINAS on leaving for Guatemala established Canon Thomas Hassett and Very Rev. Patricio Walsh, as his Vicars, and Administrators of the Diocese. Father Hassett who had long been delicate and was anxious to leave a climate that had never agreed with him, died rather suddenly, in April, 1804. The administration fell to Father Walsh who had resided twelve years in Louisiana, and whose fine administrative abilities, large experience, and perfect knowledge of French, English, and Spanish, especially fitted him for the important and difficult office. His authority was at once disputed by Father Sedilla, who claimed to be independent of him. Troubles and litigation followed, and he was obliged to withdraw the faculties of Father Sedilla and his pretended Vicars, and to place the Cathedral, of which they had taken forcible possession, under an interdict. He then designated the Ursuline chapel as the only place for the administration of the Sacraments and the celebration of the divine offices. The learned priest then issued a Pastoral of much erudition and eloquence, in which he spoke with no uncertain voice:

PASTORAL LETTER.[1]

MY VERY DEAR BRETHREN:

Patricio Walsh, Vicar-General, Proviseur and spiritual governor of the Diocese of Louisiana: to all

---

[1] This Pastoral Letter is written in French, which we have translated.

the faithful, Catholic, Apostolic, and Roman, of the city of New Orleans.   Salvation in Our Lord Jesus Christ.

In virtue of the powers which have been accorded to us by Monseñor Peñalvert y Cardenas, lately Bishop of this diocese, duly authorized to name one or several grand vicars to replace him until the Sovereign Pontiff would provide in some other manner . . . . . No priest can perform pastoral functions unless he is authorized by ecclesiastical power. . . . . A priest who has been deprived of it, cannot be considered a lawful minister of the Word and of the Sacraments.   This my Dear Brethren, is of Faith and has been decided by the Council of Trent.

" If any one," says the Holy Council, " sustains that ministers who have not received the ecclesiastical and canonical power of the Word and the Sacraments, can administer them, let him be anathema."

The Holy Council decrees that those who, having been called and instituted by the people, or secular power, or the magistrate, have the temerity, to ingratiate themselves into the functions of the ministry, are not ministers of the Church, but robbers, who have not entered by the door of the sheep-fold.

*   *   *   *   *   *

The Fathers of the same Council declare null all marriages made in the presence of any other priest than the true pastor, at least that the priest who blesses them be approved by the true Pastor, or by the Ordinary, that is to say, the Bishop, or his grand Vicar.

Finally the same Council regards as null the absolution given by a priest who has not ordinary jurisdiction or delegated jurisdiction.

"You must not forget, my brethren, that an occumenical Council such as that of Trent, of which you have heard the decrees, is a holy assembly when the Church by the mouth of her chief Pastors forms the decision and purposes to the faithful the infallible rules of devotion, and, for a Catholic not to believe and not to submit to these councils is to renounce the quality of child of the Church, to excommunicate one's-self, to put one's-self in the rank of infidels, as we are warned by Jesus Christ Himself:

"Whoever will not hear the Church, let him be to thee as the heathen and the publican." Matt. XIII. 17.

Whence I conclude, my dear brethren, and if you wish to be Catholics, you must conclude with me, first, that a priest cannot lawfully announce the Word of God, or administer the Sacraments without mission, or ecclesiastical or canonical approbation.

"That acts of authority or jurisdiction which he does, as, to absolve penitents, bless marriages, without mission are null in the eyes of the Church: in fine that all sacraments that he administers are profanation on part of him who administers them and those who receive them.

"I cannot, without rendering myself grievously sinful before God, and before you, leave you in ignorance that a priest interdicted of all ecclesiastical functions, and rash enough to undertake them by his own authority, falls into schism and irregularity. Schism is a culpable and voluntary separation from the Church: irregularity, in this case, an inability to receive any order, any ecclesiastical dignity. It belongs to the Sovereign Pontiff to absolve from schism and dispense from irregularity.

"Such is the invariable doctrine of the Catholic,

Apostolic, and Roman Church of which, without doubt, you do not wish to cease to be children. Nevertheless, my brethren, those who have any difficulty or doubts as to the reality of our powers which, being spiritual cannot depend on change of time or government, let them come to us with confidence. Always ready to answer you and to instruct you, we will destroy your doubts, give reason for our faith, and strive to build up yours. We will instruct and help you, the strong and the weak, the learned and the simple. " Providence has established me your Pastor. Woe to me if I fail to instruct you, but woe to you, if you will not hear my voice. God is my witness that I carry you in my heart.

" Sweetness, persuasion, charity, condescension, but only permissible condescension, will make you the objects of my ministry, and this conduct is not less conformable to my inclination than agreeable to my duty.

" I weep without ceasing till Jesus Christ who is the Way, the Truth, and the Life, be formed in you.

*   *   *   *   *

" Finding ourselves charged with the government of this diocese, under the weight of which we weep before God, we believe it our duty to labor in these evil days to fortify you in the faith. I say, in the joy of my soul, there are among you those who have never belied the promises of baptism, and who rejoice heaven and earth by their fidelity and their attachment to the dogmas of our Holy Faith.[1]

[1] Done at New Orleans, the 27th day of March, the year of grace, 1805, by Mons. the Vicar General, Olivier, Sec. of the Bishopric.

The schism which followed Father Walsh's taking possession, was excited to some extent by the marguillers or Church Wardens. He had been in Louisiana twelve years before the arrival of Bishop Peñalvert, and was appointed co-administrator with Canon Hassett. He took special interest in the Ursuline Convent. When the nuns addressed a memorial to the President of the United States, who sent a most gracious reply, Father Walsh sent copies of these documents to the Editor of the *Moniteur,* asking him to give them space in his paper. His letter is extant in French: We give a translation:

"A l'Editeur du Moniteur: New Orleans, September, 12, 1804:

"A memorial has been addressed by the Ursuline Religious of the city to the President of the United States. As this memorial and the cordial, encouraging reply of the President, would surely give pleasure to the inhabitants of Louisiana, who all, without doubt, take a deep interest in the prosperity of this religious establishment, I beg you to insert them in your next number, in French and also in English.

I remain, Monsieur,

Your humble servant,

Patrick Walsh, Vicar-General.

CHAPTER XXXVI.

THE Vicar-General continued to labor by tongue
and pen for the restoration of peace and charity, but
he labored in vain. He died suddenly after an illness
of five days, August 22, 1806. Posthumous honors
of every description were lavished on a priest who,
during life, had, by his sterling virtue, won the respect
of friend and foe. Father Walsh's official title was:
"Vicar-General and Governor ad interim" of the
diocese. The Cathedral being under an interdict, in
consequence of the usurpation of Father Sedilla, the
Ursuline chapel was the only place in which mass could
be offered, or the sacraments administered. The loss
of this worthy priest to New Orleans was simply indescribable. He was rarely gifted as a linguist and thus
peculiarly fitted to labor in a cosmopolitan city.

By royal çedula, August 1793, was transferred the
right of patronage in the Church of New Orleans to
Don Andres Almonester, by the King of Spain. This
is mentioned in a letter from Baron Carondelet to
the Duke of Alcudia, Jan. 18, 1794.

This Knight so commendable for his charities to the
city of his adoption has not even had consecrated to
his memory the name of a single street. The Church
alone cherishes the memory of this good nobleman,
through the tolling of her bells repeats through history,
his admirable charity, and her eternal gratitude. As

we have mentioned, Don Andres Almonester y Roxas died suddenly in his 74th year, in New Orleans, April 26, 1798. A marble slab over the crypt in which he was buried records his titles and services. But his noblest monument is the Church he raised to the honor of the most High.

The Cathedral has a tenure, to speak in legal phrase, of every Saturday offering services for the soul of its founder, and every Saturday evening as the sun sets, or, after the evening Angelus, the silvery sounds of the tolling bells recalls the memory of the best benefactor of the city he loved so well.

We heard these sweet toned bells on Easter Saturday evening for about half an hour after six, in the ancient Cathedral, and united with the worshipers in prayers for the repose of the soul of the founder. R. I. P. Mar. 30, 1907.

After the lamented death of Father Walsh the Church of New Orleans was without a head. Bishop Carroll wrote, Nov. 17, 1806, to James Madison, Secretary of State: " The only clergyman in Louisiana, in any degree qualified to act with vigor and determination in restoring order in the Catholic Church, is a French emigrant priest, far from any attachment to the present system of his country. This clergyman rejoices sincerely in the cession of that country to the United States."

The war between the usurping parties and legitimate authority was soon at its height.

From another passage in the Bishop's letter we find that a " Mr. Castillon, head of the municipality, employed a certain Castanedo, who was furnished with four thousand dollars, to obtain a recommendation from the Emperor Napoleon for the immediate nomi-

nation of Sedilla to the bishopric of New Orleans! In
his reply, Mr. Madison remarks: " Of the Spanish
Friar, Antonio de Sedilla, the accounts here agree with
the character you have formed of him.   The intrigue
and connections of Antonio Sedilla have drawn on him
the watchful attentions of the government."

About this deplorable schism throughout its whole
history there is much information in contemporary
Catholic literature, as in the United States *Catholic
Magazine,* official organ of the Archbishop of Baltimore—which sincerely deplores the painful events it
recorded.

Above is mentioned a Mr. Castillon who is, probably
the second husband of the young widow of Almonester.
This lady in the early days of her widowhood married
a Creole of that name who may be the person mentioned in the above letter.   The wealth, the beauty, and
the high connection, of the widow, did not save her
from giving offence to her fellow-citizens who could
not forgive the marriage.   They assembled in hundreds about her mansion and treated herself and her
husband to the greatest *Charivari*[1] in history.   It is
said to have lasted four days and four nights, and
nearly killed the young couple who had, by marrying,
provoked their wrath.   We hear little about the connections of Almonester after this.   His daughter, the
Baroness Pontalba, lived chiefly in Paris, where she
purchased the mansion built by Louis XIV, for the
Duc de Maine, and containing 400 rooms.   She died
in 1874, April 20; her three sons inherited the vast
fortune of their mother.

When a priest was named by the ecclesiastical

[1] *Charivari,* a sort of mock serenade at a widow's second marriage,
peculiar to Louisiana.

authorities, pastor of the Cathedral, the marguilliers, as a rule, refused to recognize him. They even claimed the right of patronage formerly enjoyed by the King of Spain. This right had never been transferred to them, nor could they receive it from a federal, or state, government.

In an action which they brought against the Bishop, they were defeated. The Supreme Court, to which they appealed, confirmed the judgment of the lower court. Judge Bullard declared the right to nominate a curate, or the *Juspatronatus* of the Spanish law, is abrogated in this State. The wardens cannot compel the Bishop to institute a Parish Priest of their own appointment, nor is he, in any sense, subordinate to the wardens of any one of the churches within his diocese, in relation to his clerical functions."

The president of the Board of Trustees was also Grand Master of the grand Masonic Lodge, and he and they seemed bent on giving annoyance. They refused to recognize any of the Curates legitimately appointed, and spoke to them in terms of insult. Finally, the clergy were obliged to withdraw from the parochial residence, and the faithful were attended from the Bishop's house and the Convent, and, later, from St. Augustine's Church.

Indeed, it was time to take some such step, for even their personal liberty was interfered with. Once when the venerable Father Perché was about to ascend the pulpit, by order of the Bishop who was present, two young men approached, and forbade him to preach. This put an end to the ceremonies for that occasion.

Outside the Cathedral, services were regularly held in two chapels in New Orleans: the Ursuline and chapel of the Charity Hospital. These were the only places in which mass could be celebrated. The nuns were very uneasy at this state of things.

"I regret," says the Annalist to whom we are so deeply indebted, "not having been more inquisitive during the lifetime of the good mothers and sisters who were the despositaries of the early traditions, having lived several years with some of the pupils and novices of our venerated Foundresses. Some things I heard from them I have kept a note of; but other things have slipped from my memory, or left thereon only a vague idea."

Valuing so highly what we have received, we deeply regret what our scribe could have given under other circumstances. What she has given us, however, we have thankfully received, and transferred as jewels to our own pages.

Abbé Olivier, the successor of Fathers Walsh and Hassett, was past eighty and was scarcely able, from age and infirmity, to control the turbulent elements under his charge; and Rev. Mr. Nerincks absolutely refused to become administrator Apostolic, to which office he was invited. Rev. Mr. Sibourd was sent to New Orleans by Archbishop Carroll. This zealous priest endeavored to collect the English-speaking Catholics at the Ursuline Chapel, but found few to profit by his ministry. His Sunday sermons and his care in preparing candidates for First Communion, produced a good effect. Father Sedilla and his assistants were compelled by his example to preach. Abbé Olivier, had been appointed chaplain to the Ursulines by Very Rev. Patrick Walsh, in which office he succeeded Father Felix Quintana, Capuchin. Father Quintana's signature is found at the reception of a novice, Nov. 21, 1803.

Four novices were received by Abbé Olivier, March
1, 1811.   At Sister St. Angela Johnson's reception,
Oct. 21, 1813, he signed himself chaplain, "aumonier
des Dames Ursulines."   Abbé Olivier was still chaplain to the Ursulines in 1815, when Very Rev. Father
Du Bourg left for Rome.   It is probable that this
saintly priest died soon after, for he was over ninety,
but no details are given, nor is his death even mentioned in the Convent necrology, so far as we can
learn.

The head of the American Church, Right Rev.
John Carroll, was created Archbishop of Baltimore,
and received the pallium, August 18, 1812, an auspicious event that gave much impetus to Religion.
Bishop Chevereux wrote to his grace on that occasion:
"That you may for many years wear this vesture
of holiness is the wish of all your children in Christ.
God will, in His mercy, I hope, hear their prayers and
prolong the life of our beloved and venerable Father."

The Acts of the Provincial Council of Baltimore
(1829) were confirmed by His Holiness, Pope Pius
VIII. September 30, 1830.   The Catholic population
was estimated at half a million in a population of
twelve millions; but it was probably much more.

CHAPTER XXXVII.

THERE were few churches for the thousands of
Catholics and most of them were wretched: "For
precious stones and marbles," wrote one of the early
missioners, "we employed only bark, but the path to
heaven is as open through a roof of bark as through
arched ceilings of silver and gold." They made the
best of their privations and were satisfied till brighter
days dawned. "He who lives content," say an
Italian proverb, "will die singing." They trusted in
the Providence that feeds the little birds of the desert
and clothes the wild flowers of the forest.

The sufferings of the many martyrs of the early
Church in these regions we can understand and ex-
plain. But the sufferings of those who planted the
Faith "once delivered to the Saints," in regions which
our feet tread to-day,—their courage, their tenacity,
their fidelity, even to death, will probably never be
fully known save to Him who was the sole cause and
motive of their agonizing labors: "Jesus, the Author
and finisher of our Faith."

In many parts of the country and at various times
land was purchased by the wealthy or benevolent to be
sold in small parcels, so as to attract industrious
settlers. Captain George Brent purchased of Thomas,
Lord Culpepper, thirty acres of land, and prepared
to bring over a few. They applied to James II. for a

guarantee of religious freedom, and his majesty, by patent, dated Feb. 10, 1687, granted "unto the petitioners and all and every the inhabitants, which are now or shall hereafter be settled in the same town, and tract of land belonging to them, the free exercise of their religion, without being prosecuted or molested upon any penal laws, or other, on account of the same."

The scheme of a grand union of all the American Colonies into one Government, with the broad charter of equal religious rights for all, which emanated from the able mind of James II. was not carried out for a century when the United Colonies shook off the yoke of the Protestant sovereigns of England. So that the liberty of conscience upon which the United States justly prides herself, originated in the liberal policy of poor calumniated James II.

The Code Napoleon was adopted 1808. Louisiana joined the Union 1812.

In encouraging the Marguilliers in early days, Father Sedilla evoked a spirit which he could not quell. It is not to be doubted that he regretted his unfortunate course when too late. Yet blood could scarcely wash out the injury he did to the Church in New Orleans. But "the mercies of God are over all His works" and though he certainly was for a time a schismatic, he never was a heretic.

Monseigneur Anthony Blanc was made Archbishop, July 19, 1850. His trials continued to the end. Archbishop, or, to speak more correctly, Father Perché, by tongue and pen sought to defend the right. But he did not do this with impunity. Every petty annoyance and insult which the enemies of religion could bestow they gave him in public, and even in private.

16

Here is an instance of what one informant calls their spite, as described by an eye-witness, or rather "an ear-witness:"

"We were awakened about midnight by frightful cries, at every moment redoubled. We saw by the light of the moon, a troop of men passing in front of the cloister, and howling like demons. Not knowing what might be the result, we rang the Reveil so that every one might be dressed in case of accident. Several on hearing the bell thought it was the usual hour for rising. Though we were frightened, yet great calm and silence were observed. After having listened and watched from the galleries, some of the Sisters understood it to be a *charivari*. These wretches had no spite against us, but against Father Perché, and, after some hours of tintamarre, the great uproar ceased, to our delight.

On another occasion when Father Perché was writing one of his masterly polemic articles for the *Propagateur Catholique,* the mosquito net surrounding his table and chair took fire. He called aloud to a negro boy who slept in an adjoining room to help him to extinguish the fire. The boy came in such a hurry to the rescue of his master that he did not wait to be quite dressed. He noticed this when the fire was out, and hastened to apologize to his beloved Father. But the kind-hearted priest told him that was of no consequence, and sent him back to bed with many thanks for his prompt and effective action. Some noise and confusion on this occasion made several of the more wakeful occupants, fear it was another *charivari.*

Among other good works, Father Perché was mainly instrumental in winning to the ranks of the priesthood, that true poet, Adrien Rouquette, who, subdued by the fervent zeal of Abbé Perché, renounced the world and its pleasures to become a priest. Bishop Blanc conferred the order of subdeacon on him, Sept. 8, 1843, the first Creole of New Orleans that embraced the ecclesiastical state since the Cession of Louisiana, 1803. On the same day, two hundred and twenty were confirmed at St. Mary's Church.

The periodical to which we have referred writes in 1842 :

" We learn with unfeigned satisfaction that the dissensions in the New Orleans diocese have been brought to a happy termination. The Archbishop of New Orleans has shown throughout these painful transactions such firmness united to condescension and forbearance in the maintenance of his just authority, that the termination is such as to place beyond all doubt the rights that have been assailed."

CHAPTER XXXVIII.

IN 1838, Bishop Blanc of New Orleans sent Father John Timon, later Bishop of Buffalo, N. Y., to give one of his stirring missions to the Natchez people. Dr. Vandevelt was instructed to examine whether arrangements could be made for an episcopal see, and, by an anomaly, prepared the way for his predecessor.

The next anniversary of the victory of New Orleans, 1843, was celebrated with extra solemnity. Bishop Blanc officiated, with the Bishops of Mobile and Natchez. The Mobile Bishop preached in French, and the Bishop of Natchez in English.

Among the good works of Bishop Dubourg is one which has been useful not only to Alabama and the Floridas, but to every diocese in the world in missionary countries—his share in establishing the Association for the Propagation of the Faith. In Lyons, Bishop Dubourg inspired Madame Petit, a pious widow who had once resided in Baltimore, to form a small association in which each would pay a trifling sum weekly to aid his mission. From this, and a little association founded by Mademoiselle Pauline Marie Jaricot, to give aid to the laborers in Asia belonging to the Society of foreign missions in Paris, grew the Association for the Propagation of the Faith, finally organized at Lyons, May 3, 1822, under Very Rev. A. Inglesi, Vicar-General of Monseigneur Dubourg.

The Bishop, who met the cross at all points, had trouble in connection with this official, whom some describe as an unworthy adventurer. " In his strange career," writes Mr. Shea, " his part in establishing this great Association for the aid of the Catholic missions throughout the world, is almost a redeeming trait."

Mademoiselle Jaricot was one of the holiest, most persecuted, most misunderstood, souls of the nineteenth century. To many missioners she furnished means to carry the gospel far and near, and her wealth seemed to increase in proportion as she gave it away.[1]

The Marguilliers or trustees were mostly free-masons. The French free-masons were confessedly atheistic, and, therefore, anti-religious. The English free-masons formally severed all relations with the French free-masons when the French free-masons struck the name of God from their Constitution and their Ritual.

As churches increased the Trustee difficulty diminished. A plain wooden structure consecrated in New Orleans April 23, 1833, for English-speaking Catholics. This was afterwards replaced by the massive imposing St. Patrick's Church, on Camp St., built by Father James Ignatius Mullen, Pastor of that Church for thirty years. His remains lie beneath the floor of the church he loved and served so well. In every way, he had supported the prelates of the city in their just rights, and was their faithful helper in all their good works. During the war he was an ardent champion of the South.

For a short time only postulants of French origin, born in the Colony, were invited to the Ursuline Con-

[1] See *Life* by M. J. Maurin.

vent. But the monastery became, like the city, cosmopolitan, and therefore of more general usefulness than if confined to a single nationality. There were even subjects with Indian blood in their veins. This was the case, too, in the older regions of Canada. Teresa, an Indian maiden, who spent two years with the Ursulines of Quebec, returned to her own people to spread the Faith among them, which she did very successfully.

Coureurs de bois purchased furs and others peltries from the Indians and brought them by canoes to New Orleans, Biloxi, and Mobile. They were said to be a connecting link between the palace of Versailles and the wigwams of America. But the coast bounded by the Mexican Gulf never became famous for mineral wealth.

CHAPTER XXXIX.

IT was during Denis Prieur's administration ('28-'30) that Father Antonio de Sedilla died. His death occurred in a cabin thatched with palmetto leaves, which he had built in the square behind the Cathedral.

The name by which Father Sedilla was known in the world was Antonio Ildefonso Mareno d'Arze. He was born in Sedilla a small town in the province of Granada, Nov. 18, 1748. In early youth he entered the Capuchin Order, where he obtained the title of Lector in *Sacra Theologia*.

In 1779, he was sent, with five of his brethren, to New Orleans, to take the place of the French Monks. Nov. 25, 1785, six years after his arrival in New Orleans, he was appointed Rector of St. Louis Parish. Four years later, 1789, he was sent back to Spain for an alleged attempt to introduce the Inquisition into New Orleans. This so alarmed the fears of the Spanish Governor (Miro) as to induce that functionary to exile the priest. Within twenty-four hours after he heard it, a platoon of soldiers filed into the priest's room, and forcibly carried him to a ship about to sail for Cadiz.

Miro, in a special report to his Government, dated June 3, 1789, gives his account of the affair: " When I read the communication of that Capuchine, I shud-

dered. His Majesty has ordered me to foster the increase of population in this province. . . . .
The mere mention of the Inquisition, uttered in New Orleans, would be sufficient to check immigration which is successfully progressing, but it would also be capable of driving away those who have recently come; and I even fear, in spite of my having sent Father Sedilla out of the country, the most frightful consequences may ensue from the mere suspicion of the cause of his dismissal." In Spain the duties of the Holy Office were sometimes relegated to the Capuchine Monks, of which Order Père Antoine was a member.

Governor Miro has been blamed for his treatment of Père Antoine on this occasion.

" His conduct," says Dr. Castellanos, " in this whole transaction was unjust, arbitrary, and unworthy of the reputation of one of Louisiana's most enlightened governors." Another writer says: " Père Antoine was sent with the title of Commissioner of the Holy Office (Inquisition) in Louisiana. Without the smallest ceremony Miro had him seized, and conveyed on board a vessel which departed with him for Spain that same day.[1] (Andoyo's History, 1785).

Despite the indignation shown in some quarters at the summary action of Governor Miro, it may be that, if the matter were put to the vote of the inhabitants of New Orleans, the Governor would be sustained in his endeavor to keep that, rather political than religious, machine, out of New Orleans

[1] In a recent account of the expulsion of Father Sedilla, we learned, that Governor Miro did not act in this matter on his own responsibility, but consulted the Captain General of Cuba, by whose advice he was guided. This we have from a private source.

at all hazards. Nothing unpleasant happened the Friar. He may even have been pleased to get an unexpected trip to his native land, at no cost to himself or his family. What is certain is that he returned to the watery city in good health and spirits, and probably resumed his former duties.

He was not present in the Ursuline Convent from 1785 to 1796. Part of these years he was absent in Spain, on that fateful journey. He did not, so far as we know, officiate in the Ursuline Chapel after 1802. It was in that year that the disturbances began which culminated in the schism that had such deplorable results, results that did not cease with the life of this remarkable man, though there is reason to hope that he repented of the past.

In 1837, March 11, the Marguilliers obtained from the legislature permission to mortgage the Bishop's Cathedral for their own purposes, for two hundred thousand dollars. They sent delegates to Europe to conclude the business, but they wasted two thousand dollars in the vain effort.

The free-masons desired to erect, in a Catholic cemetery, a masonic monument as a common receptacle, for their deceased members. It is well known that the Catholic clergy do not admit to the sacraments members of secret associations. Those who die without withdrawing from such societies, are not buried with the rites of the Catholic religion, or in consecrated ground.

In a French entry in an ancient manuscript we find: " Mgr. Dubourg, after his consecration 1816, obtained many indulgences for us. Before this epoch, there had been a schism in the Parish, so that all good Catholics came to our Church. This was the origin of our two masses on Sunday. During the schism, our mothers suffered a great deal, so that they were desirous of quitting the country. They wrote to the Holy Father who had the goodness to reply:

" MADAME:[1]

" Your letter of the 2nd of May reached us only towards the end of September. We are very sensible of your good wishes for our preservation and the success of our enterprises, always directed to the glory of God and the advantage of the Church. As to the inquietudes that agitate you, regarding your spiritual direction, they cannot last, for M. Dubourg has received from us Bulls, and has been consecrated at Rome by our order, Bishop of the diocese of New Orleans, to which he will soon return. You may then be tranquil as to your future, and give up the project of going to France; you can do much more for Religion where you are. Therefore, we exhort you to redouble your zeal for young persons of your sex, and for the eternal salvation of your neighbor. We have your Community continually present, especially in our prayers to obtain for you all the graces you need, and we give you, with effusion of heart, our Apostolic Benediction.

Given at Castel Gandolfo, near Rome, the 16th of October, 1815, of our Pontificate, the sixteenth year.
PIUS VII. P.

In 1812, Bishop Carroll sent Rev. William Dubourg to rectify abuses, but he met many obstacles from those who should have aided him, that he was com-

---

[1] To Soeur Thérèse Farjon, Supérieure, and the nuns.

pelled again to close the Cathedral under an interdict. For several years it remained closed, and mass was celebrated in the Ursuline Chapel alone, by the pious octogenarian, Abbé Olivier.

Abbé Dubourg on this visit to Rome represented to the Propaganda the state of Religion in the diocese. He was consecrated Bishop on the Feast of Our Lady of Mercy, Sept. 24, 1815, by Cardinal Doria Pamphili, in the Church of St. Louis of the French. The new Bishop collected in France and Belgium a fresh band of missioners and four excellent priests from Rome.

The French King gave much aid and encouragement, and placed at his disposal the frigate Caravane, to transport himself and his party to America. Bishop Dubourg exerted himself to fill vacancies, and have the gospel preached in the Northern part of his diocese. When traveling in the country parishes,[1] he was nearly drowned while crossing a bayou on a tree.

He reached Natchitoches in time to administer the last Sacraments to Mademoiselle de Mezières, granddaughter of the Duke of Orleans. "We were some time in Natchitoches when a mulatto interrupted our dinner:" "Monseigneur," said he, "Mademoiselle de Mezières is dying, and asks for you." Father Dubourg went to the sick lady. "The good God," said she, "has heard me. For thirty years I have prayed to obtain the grace of not dying without the Sacraments." She made a general confession, received the Sacraments with deep fervor, and died half an hour after.

This lady, Mademoiselle Colette de Mezières, was

---

[1] The mission of Monseigneur Dubourg to Natchitoches was undertaken in 1825. His visits to the country parishes (counties) were always most successful. They took the form of retreats or missions.

cousin-german to Madame de Genlis, and grand-daughter of the Duke of Orleans, father of Egalite.[1]

Near the ancient Ursuline Convent, an edifice of much strength and solidity, is the Ursuline Chapel, so often mentioned in this history. A Spanish inscription, on a marble tablet, in the middle of the façade, says, it was built during the reign of Carlos III., A D. 1787, by Don Andrés Almonaster y Roxas. Don Estevan Miro being Governor of the Province—a plain unpretending, but spacious building. Here the Catholics of New Orleans found a Refuge while the Cathedral was in the hands of the schismatics.

Archbishop Carroll expected Very Rev. Father Dubourg to take possession of the New Orleans Cathedral, and assert his position as head of the church, and Administrator Apostolic. But he did not even attempt to say mass in the Cathedral. When he proceeded to suspend the *soi-disant* vicar, such violence was shown by Father Sedilla's party that the Administrator Apostolic seems to have become alarmed for his personal safety and withdrew from the city.

The time had become worse than usual, and that is saying much during Father Dubourg's connection with Louisiana. Priests had been driven from their

---

[1] The Duke of Orleans having secretly married Madame de Montisson Miss Collette their daughter was married in this country, had five children, three boys and two girls who, not wanting to form a *mésalliance*, were not married. At the time of our arrival at Natchitoches, there were remaining of this family, only M. Ala. de Mezieres, a very aged man, and Mdlle de M., sixty-two years old.

Much good was done for religion at this visit. Sixty were confirmed, who knew the catechism before our arrival, three hundred and fifty children were baptized, several marriages blessed; and arrangements were made for building two or three churches. To this day there is in Nachitoches a " Mézières Street.

parishes. They had been forced into dug-outs and sent adrift on the awful river. His life in Europe was a scene of terror. When little more than a boy he had to flee from Paris, from Bordeaux from Spain. Infidels and rebels had made life a burden to him in America. Some of the worst wretches of the evil days of France lived, moved, and had their being in New Orleans. Lakanal, the regicide, was head of a college, a few streets off.

Father Dubourg seemed always to have feared for his life in New Orleans. He was never popular in America. A famous historian remarks that many persons who are utterly fearless by constitution, are terrified by the thought or fear of assassination.

Yet it was hoped these miserable forms of what, in these days, might, perhaps be described under the generic name of nervousness, would wear away. The climate was mild—in the latitude of Cairo. The weather was seldom extremely sultry or unhealthy. Ice was considered so unwholesome that the mayor ordered the first cargo that arrived to be dumped into the river. Some of the pleasantest people in the world lived in New Orleans as well as many of the most dangerous. The comfort of the city was much increased when its streets were paved with cobble stones, in 1821, and water-works introduced in 1826. To this day drinking water is preserved in immense cisterns, and river water used for cleansing purposes.

At the invasion of New Orleans by the English, Monsignore Dubourg showed courage and determination. He issued a pastoral appointing public prayers in the churches, directing all to implore the protection of heaven, " while our brave warriors, led on by the hero of the Floridas, prepare to defend our altars and our firesides against foreign invasion." (Monsigneur Dubourg to Archbishop Carroll, 1814.)

While the battle raged between untrained American troops, and English soldiers, led by one of Wellington's experienced generals, the ladies of New Orleans gathered in the chapel of the Convent to pray for the success of the American arms.

" The story of the battle is strange. Everything fell out favorably for Jackson, as if by magic. The English lost their way, fired into each other . . . . disobeyed orders, neglected precautions . . . . At night the American works were hardly damaged, while the English works were battered to pieces." [1]

From their galleries and dormer windows the nuns could see the smoke rising from the plains of Chalmette, Jan. 8, and hear the rumbling of cannon and the report of rifles. All night long they watched before the Blessed Sacrament and besought the God of battles to give victory to the American army. Over the front entrance of the monastery was exposed an image of Our Lady of Prompt Succor, brought from France by Mother St. Michael and other holy women, Dec. 31, 1810.

The statue is still religiously preserved in a chapel of its own. Like most miraculous statues, it cannot be called beautiful, if judged by the canons of art. But it is a precious relic, upon which one cannot gaze without emotion. Humanly speaking, there was not a chance of victory for the Americans. Years after, Marshal Soult deemed their victory unaccountable. The Marshal said it was well General Packenham was killed on the field, " otherwise he would have been

[1] Life of A. Jackson, ii, 39.

held accountable for the destruction of that fine army,"
for which he deserved " to be shot as a blunderer."

No wonder then that Jackson, a man of deep religious feeling, attributed the glory of his grand
victory to the God of Armies. By his desire a solemn
thanksgiving service was held, January, 23d. At the
door of the venerable Cathedral, Abbé Dubourg addressed the Conqueror in words that will live forever,
and placed on his head a laurel crown. With a
modesty equal to his bravery, Jackson made a most
felicitous reply, attributing his success to the special
aid of the Most High, and the bravery of his fellow
soldiers. Every year since, on that 8th of January, at
first, in the Cathedral, but, later, in the Ursuline
Chapel, a solemn High mass of thanksgiving is celebrated, and a *Te Deum* sung for the mercy which gave
the American army so grand a victory; and, to this
day, the 8th of January is celebrated as a State Holiday. The Plaza, or Place d' Armes, scene of so many
interesting pageants, has become Jackson Square, and
an equestrian statue of the Victor, commemorates his
fame and the gratitude of Louisiana, in the midst of
that historic ground.

The ovation given the Conquering Hero in the old
Place d' Armes was one of the most exquisite pageants
ever devised. All New Orleans turned out to do honor
to their great deliverer. There were those in the
crowd who remembered when the superb battalions of
another warrior of the same race—a race always
enamored of religious and military glory—paraded the
same square and were received by representatives of
the old Church on the same spot, over forty years
before. But the gallant O'Reilly was compelled to
come as judge and Savior, whereas Jackson came as

Savior alone. There was not, as he poetically expressed it, " a cypress leaf in the wreath presented to
him."

In the midst of the square a triumphal arch was
erected, supported by symbolical figures. Under this,
the General passed to the Church, escorted by the city
authorities, through rows of fair girls, in beautiful
costumes,—eighteen, representing the States of the
Union—their right hands bearing appropriate flags,
stars glittering on their foreheads, baskets of flowers
in their left arms which they emptied at the feet of the
Preserver of New Orleans, as he moved slowly, his
furrowed countenance bearing traces of deep emotion,
through this beautiful avenue.

Four squares off, were many cloistered ladies, whose
hearts were full of gratitude to God, and to the man
of his right Hand, though they were represented in
the parade only by their chaplains, pupils, and servants.
But when all was over the General did not omit to
pay his respects to them, receive their congratulations,
and thank them for their prayers and vows in his behalf. Andrew Jackson was the last great warrior who
passed into the cloisters of the old Convent on Chartres
Street, and the only President of the United States
that ever stood within its precincts. Nor did he fail
to visit the nuns when he returned to New Orleans in
after years.

We will look back for a moment: On Sunday,
Jan. 8, 1815, the early roar of artillery announced
the terrible beginning of the struggle, the faithful
were gathered in St. Mary's Chapel, eagerly praying
for victory. The venerable Statue of Our Lady of
Prompt Succor was placed on the altar, while the Holy

Sacrifice of the mass was offered by Monseigneur Dubourg.

The Feast of Our Lady of Prompt Succor is kept, JANUARY 8. Her chapel is the site of a pilgrimage, the sacred place of assembly for a Confraternity, and even an Archconfraternity. And to many may be again applied the words of inspiration: "Thou art the glory of Jerusalem, thou art the joy of Israel, thou art the honor of our people."

When the Society of Jesus was suppressed in Louisiana, 1763, besides the parish church, there were at either end of the town, the chapel of the Jesuits and the chapel of the Ursulines that, like two rural churches, were frequented by many from the town and vicinity. At the Jesuit oratory, there existed, in 1738, a sodality for men, while at the Convent of St. Mary, a like sodality, bearing the title of Immaculate Conception, was established for women, in 1739, by a Bull of Pope Clement XII.

"To Mary in Heaven," the nuns and their friends, prostrate before the effigy of Our Lady of Prompt Succor, ascribed the power that turned the tide of the battle from their homes. Devotion to her increased so much that her picture was engraved, and indulgences were granted by Abbé Dubourg after his consecration as Bishop, to encourage imitation of her virtues and confidence in her powerful intercession."

General Jackson did his share directly or indirectly, in causing the cessation of the schism. After his glorious victory over Packenham, General Jackson asked Monseigneur Dubourg to have a solemn public service in the Cathedral in thanksgiving to God. It is hardly necessary to say that neither the authors

17

nor the followers of the schism, appeared on this grand occasion. And it was said among the people that Jackson had conquered the Marguilliers and their abettors as well as the British.[1]

[1] Gayarré who was present as a boy of eleven gave the writer some details.

CHAPTER XL.

BISHOP PENALVERT full of zeal for the divine honor and the salvation of souls, after taking possession of his diocese, having visited every part of his episcopal city, and begun a visitation of his diocese; we find is named in the record in several places. He also composed instructions for the parish priests of his diocese pending the opening of a synod, to regulate ecclesiastical matters.

July 20, 1801 this worthy prelate was promoted to the archepiscopal See of Guatemala. Probably some of our readers may be surprised that the first Bishop of New Orleans, who was in every way worthy of his exalted office, and thoroughly equipped for its important functions, should be allowed to retire ere he had completed the reforms he had begun with so much difficulty. During the six years of his episcopacy, he organized a chapter for his diocese, and appointed two canons. He made long and frequent journeys to all parts of his charge, as may be learned from the records of the churches. Owing to his personal holiness and incessant labors, no doubt many of his flock looked for that success which it was hoped would ultimately bless the works of so holy a soul.

But the Bishop was a Spaniard—a born subject of the King of Spain. He had received episcopal consecration as a Spanish Bishop, to labor in the Spanish dominions. And now, it was an open secret, that Louisiana was to be ceded to the French Republic. The treaty of St. Ildefonso, Sept. 15, 1800, was known. French Jacobinism and free-masonry, and the awful horrors of revolutionary times are thought to have so affected the good Bishop, that he could scarcely bring himself to become the subject of such a government. He belonged to a Patrician family of great wealth, and on account of his distinguished ability and unbounded charity, was revered and beloved in his native city. The highest offices were confided to him. And his functions as ecclesiastical judge made him familiar with the diocese to which he was first appointed.

On the voyage to his new See, his vessel was pursued by an English man-of-war, and the Archbishop narrowly escaped being made prisoner. In Guatemala, he founded a Hospital and several schools. But a new affliction overtook him in that beautiful country. He was attacked by what he rather quaintly styles " sight sickness," a malady of the eyes, and, with this affliction, he found the burden of the episcopate too great, and obtained leave to resign, which he did, March 1, 1806.

He returned to his native city, Havana, where he died a holy death, July 17, 1810, having bequeathed what remained of his wealth to pious institutions and the poor.

Besides the Convent and the Spanish schools there were in New Orleans eight private schools for three thousand whites. In 1742, wise Bienville had petitioned the Home Government to establish a College. No doubt he asked for a Christian Seminary and thought of the Jesuits as its founders. But such a request would at that epoch, defeat its purpose. The infidel spirit that ruled France and the evil influences at work in the court, wanted nothing of the sort. And the Colony had no College. Bishop Peñalvert says: " The Ursuline Convent is the nursery of the future matrons who will inculcate on their children what they here imbibe. The education they receive in this institution is the cause of their being less vicious than the other sex." Many of the best citizens were anxious for a Catholic College for their boys. It soon came through Bishop Portier.

The outlook for new priests for the Colony was not so favorable as in earlier days. Many of the continental Colleges were suppressed amid the disturbances of revolutionary times. Maynooth had only begun, and a far greater number had been educated in the foreign colleges than could be received in Maynooth in its earlier days.

Of the Spanish domination the people ever retained a fond remembrance. The stately rulers had endeared themselves to all by their lenient and paternal administration. Many settlers prepared to depart with them, among them several of the clergy. The Catholic Religion was established by law, yet no attempt was ever made to proselytize or proscribe them. April 11, 1804, Very Rev. Canon Hassett gave faculties to Rev. Peter Zamora, who had come to Louisiana with Casaculvo, and had been assigned as chaplain to a Louisiana regiment on its way to Pensacola. It was one of his last acts.

May 1805, Matthew Flannery proposed to publish a city Directory, and this useful work was endorsed by the mayor. In September, 1806, Jean Rénard published a Commercial Gazette.

The bearded monks served the religious purposes of New Orleans for over sixty years, witnessing in turn the successes and the misfortunes of the city, ever growing even amid sorrows, while they gained an extraordinary influence over these people, which more than once counterbalanced the Governor's authority.

CHAPTER XLI.

At New Orleans, Bishop Dubourg at last succeeded in making some progress. General Jackson greatly admired the martial ardor of this valiant ecclesiastic, and his noble bearing during the recent disturbances. The people began to see that, in supinely allowing irreligious men to drive out such a prelate, they had vitally injured their city, as he would naturally cluster around St. Louis whatever institutions he might establish. Even Father Sedilla showed signs of yielding. Some of his worthless associates withdrew; and the congregations trained at the Ursuline chapel soon swelled the petty band that had controlled the Cathedral.

Spain, by treaty, ceded Florida to the United States, 1819, and that ancient province was included within the limits of the Republic. For about fifteen years, it had been governed by the Bishop of Havana. Bishop Dubourg endeavored to make the administration canonical by imparting powers. But the Spanish prelate declined to recognize any acts emanating from Rome, which were not communicated through his own Government, and the Patriarch of the Indies. Even when he recalled his priests and withdrew his jurisdiction, he would not recognize Bishop Dubourg, but wrote to Bishop England of Charleston, S. C., to take charge of the Church of St. Augustine.

Bishop Dubourg was higly esteemed by the Ursuline nuns, to whom he was the kindest of Fathers and friends. About this time there were many old nuns and many young ones, without any of the intermediate link of the middle-aged. He wrote to the Quebec Ursulines for a re-inforcement. "Send us," said he, " three or four nuns of mature age, of good judgment, and formed to the practice of virtue, to fill the interval between the aged and the young."

After much negotiation, three nuns were sent, between the ages of thirty and forty, "a precious acquisition who were received as a boon from heaven." Three of the Ursulines driven from Boston, 1832, took refuge with their New Orleans Sisters, to whom they rendered important services.

Bishop Dubourg presided [1] at the last profession in the old Convent on Chartres St.————Sister M. Gertrude Young, June 27, 1824. On New Year's Day 1821, the nuns had decided, with his approbation, to have a new Convent erected, in one of the healthiest localities in the suburbs, three miles South of the old Convent. The chief cause of this decision was the opening of new streets through the convent enclosure, which it was feared would interfere with the observance of Convent regulations and make the place less suitable for an educational establishment.

The loyal Catholics of New Orleans were deeply pained at the rebellious spirit of the trustees and their abettors. A meeting of the most respectable Catholics was held, and resolutions were passed, deprecating

---

[1] On that occasion the Bishop preached from the text:
"You who have followed me in the regeneration, when the Son of man shall sit on the seat of his majesty, you also shall sit on twelve thrones judging the tribes of Israel.

the outrageous proceedings of these misguided men,
and the insults offered to the venerable Bishop. The
tide of public opinion was setting strongly against men
who defied all authority in the Church, and even con-
tended that the Pastors of the Cathedral should be
chosen by " Call," as is practised in non-Catholic
Churches, instead of being appointed by the Bishop,
who is set over the faithful " to rule the Church of
God."

The Ursulines removed to their new home late in
1824, where they continued to be special objects of
the Bishop's paternal care. Before his departure for
Europe, 1826, he wrote a touching farewell letter to
them, containing a paragraph for each member.
From Rome, he sent them an oil painting of himself
which has since adorned the community room. Several
of his daughters lived to see seven of his equally kind
and venerated successors, whose portraits adorn the
same apartment.

Bishop Dubourg was devoted heart and soul to the
Ursulines and they cordially reciprocated his friendship. They were his chief comfort. The quietest
hours of his life he had passed among them. And
every kindness he could show them was gladly shown.
Their schools, their instruction classes, their buildings
—all interested him, and while with them he felt he
was doing good. And though, as he feared he was in
constant danger of death, he judged life less precious
than the cause for which he toiled.

Still, he felt assured he could do little or nothing for
the city in which he labored so zealously. Things were
changed, but scarcely improved, from the time when
all the Churches from Maine to Louisiana were subject to the Bishop of Quebec. Being thoroughly dis-

couraged, he fancied another could do better than he. He sent his resignation to Rome, urging its acceptance with such earnestness, and apparently good reasons, that the Sovereign Pontiff accepted it. Bishop Rosati was given the Supervision of New Orleans, with his own see, St. Louis.[1] Bishop Dubourg laid down the charge he had held for eleven years. " It is evident," he declared sorrowfully, " that my presence would be more prejudicial than useful. A judicious priest, Rev. Philip Borgna, C. M. wrote:

" We have just received the intelligence of the resignation of Mgr. Dubourg. No one expected this change. Yet all who knew him praise the resolve of that most worthy prelate and rejoice to hear it. It is time to put an end to his sufferings, and just, above all, in the decline of life that he may enjoy a little peace and repose. The prejudice against him in this city is so strong—this sewer of all vices, and refuge of all that is worst on earth—that, in spite of all his sacrifices, and his exalted ability, he could not have effected any good here. The very name, Dubourg, has an irritating sound in the ears of a great portion of this new Babylon. You cannot imagine all the abominations that fill the newspapers of this city."

The news of his resignation, and of his leaving New Orleans forever, was the saddest his spiritual daughters, the Ursuline nuns, could receive. He had spent much of his time in St. Louis, but remained in New

---

[1] A St. Louis cotton merchant, John Mullanphy, a native of Youghal, Cork, may be said to have rivaled Almonester in benevolence. He founded, and endowed many hospitals, orphanages, etc., in St. Louis. It is said that he purchased the bales of cotton used by Jackson in the battle of New Orleans, and sold them for a large sum which he devoted to charitable purposes.

Orleans from 1823 to 1826. He had given many missions in the parishes (counties) and administered confirmation at most of the places where he stopped. His zealous labors along the river-banks revived religion. He was at St. Genevieve the last year of his residence in America, planted a cross, chanted the *Vexilla Regis,* and addressed the people in French and in English. A great concourse came out of New Orleans on his return, and met him six miles above the city. Among them was Father Sibourd and " that calamity of his time," Father Sedilla. Bishop Dubourg showed much charity towards the French refugees from San Domingo. It was he who persuaded Mrs. Seton to form a religious community in this country, rather than go to Europe, and he was appointed by Archbishop Carroll the first ecclesiastical Superior of the Sisters of Charity.

In a house still standing, in Paca St., Baltimore, at the instance of Mgr. Dubourg, Mrs. Seton opened her first institution. Her first scholars were nieces of his, from New Orleans, where some members of his family settled and their descendants still live.

Only last year, I met a venerable lady, a relative of the holy Bishop, who was quite proud that her mother, his niece, had called her Wilheminia Louise, after her holy relative, who died in a foreign land many years before: " Because he had loved justice, and hated iniquity."

Bishop Dubourg was too well known and to highly esteemed to be left long in retirement. He was translated to the See of Montauban in 1826, and, later, promoted to the Archbishopric of Besançon. In both cities he was greatly beloved, and labored much for religion. He died a holy death, Dec. 12, 1833, at the ancient city of Besançon.

There has been no prelate in the country to whom more good works can be traced than Bishop Dubourg. When the Ursulines removed to their new Convent, 1824, the Bishop fitted up a few rooms in the old monastery for the use of himself, his vicars, and other officials. He had schools opened in the larger apartments, which scholars attended in hundreds. This department he placed under Very Rev. Michael Portier, his Vicar-General.

In 1820, the Osage Indians applied to Monseigneur Dubourg to establish a mission in their tribe. After commending the Indian missions to the prayers of the clergy and the faithful, he sent to them Father de la Croix. This zealous priest baptized forty of them, and founded the Catholic band which still exists in the tribe. The Indians scattered along the Mississippi had long been an object of Mgr. Dubourg's missionary zeal.

The last missionary visit which Bishop Dubourg made in the South was to Mobile, in May, 1825. He was soon relieved of this portion of his charge. Pope Leo XII. August 26, 1825, erected the State of Alabama and the Floridas into a Vicariate Apostolic, and assigned it to Rev. Michael Portier, who was consecrated Bishop of Olena, i. p. i.

Bishop Dubourg placed twenty capable priests in the vacant parishes, and there were but two priests in the outlying districts who were not of his appointment. He was aided by several Lazarist priests, among them two were afterwards Bishops, who were instrumental in crushing out the vicious, uncatholic spirit of the Marguilliers.

CHAPTER XLII.

It was, as has been seen, difficult to organize a church in the Gulf States. Bishop Portier at the time of his elevation to the mitre, was head of a College in the roomy old Ursuline Convent. Realizing the difficulties of his position, he at once wrote to Rome to decline the promotion, and returned the bulls. But they were again forwarded.

In his Vicariate, there were only two churches outside Mobile, one at St. Augustine, the other at Pensacola. There were but two priests, one lent from New Orleans the other from Charleston. Mgr. Portier was ordained priest at St. Louis, by Bishop Dubourg, in 1818. Returning, he labored at his usual duties, nearly died of yellow fever, recovered, and rode on horse-back from New Orleans to St. Louis, made a month's retreat at the Seminary, and was consecrated in the Cathedral by Bishop Ròsati, Nov. 5, 1826. He came from St. Louis *via* New Orleans, where he stopped to arrange some business, and reached Mobile, Dec. 20.

His house was not fit to live in, his church was falling for want of repairs. He had everything to create or to restore. Those who have seen any of the wonderful *Trésors* of Europe, say, in the Milan Cathedral, might smile at the Mobile collection: one monstrance, two chalices and patens, a pyx, basin, cruets, bell, holy-water pot, censer, incense-boat, tabernacle, key, oil-stocks, baptismal shell, two vases, two candle-sticks, six sets of vestments, two copes, all in poor condition. Income from pews from one hundred and twenty to one hundred and ninety dollars. He built a modest Cathedral, 20x30, with a two-roomed resi-dence. He went to Europe, in 1829, and returned with two priests and four ecclesiastics. During his absence the Holy See erected Mobile into an episcopal See, in the province of Santiago de Cuba. Mobile had been a parish since 1703. He endeavored to collect Congregations at Montgomery. Tuscaloosa, Hunts-ville, Moulrie and Florence.

Bishop Portier made a visitation of his Vicariate, beginning at Mobile and riding on horse-back to Pensacola, Tallahassee, St. Augustine, till his over-taxed system gave way, as shown in the beautiful letters he published in the Annals of the Propagation of the Faith.

The Bishop was not long at home when the trustees invaded his residence with a modest proposal. They offered to lease him the old graveyard for two hun-dred and thirty dollars a year, for 21 years on condi-tion he should build a church on it, and give bond to transfer it to his successor. At that time the Bishop estimated the Catholics of Mobile at ten thousand.

In early days, Pastors in Mobile usually remained a long time in office. Father Victorin was Parish-Priest from 1728 to 1735, and Father John Francis, "a worker and molder of life" from 1736 to 1755. They journeyed much from post to post, in the exercise of their holy ministry. From the Registers, and other sources, we learn that there was much intercourse be-tween the different missions. The American Revolu-

tion was confined chiefly to the colonies settled, or
occupied by, the English, from Massachusetts to
Georgia.

Among other absurd claims of the Marguilliers was
the right of patronage, which the King of Spain enjoyed in all his American possessions. On the ceding
of Louisiana this ceased. But the Marguilliers had
never enjoyed it. The King of Spain transferred it
in New Orleans to Almonaster, who died soon after,
without having had occasion to use it. Of course the
trustees could not get it.

A writer said of a certain sect: " They do not
chill by early infusion of bigotry the warm feelings of
benevolence." Another, who knew better the spirit
of the church, appealed to the work of those Religious
Orders, by which even Protestant nations profited,
whose chief duty was the Redemption of captives from
the piratical States of Barbary. The United States
Government in early days sent money to the Order
of Mercy, and other Orders, for the Redemption of
Captives, to rescue American Citizens enslaved in the
Barbary States.

The Spaniards have great devotion to Our Blessed
Mother under the title of Our Lady of Mercy. A
bell given by the Spanish King to the Church of St.
Gabriel, Iberville, bears the title: " Santa Maria della
Merced: 1768."

A naval officer quoted by J. G. Shea, writes of the
missionaries of the Mississippi Valley:

" I cannot help doing due justice to the Jesuit
Fathers in regard to their missions. Nothing is more
edifying for Religion than their conduct, and the unwearied zeal with which they labor for the conversion
of these nations. Picture to yourself a Jesuit four

hundred leagues away in the woods with no con-
veniences, no provisions, and frequently with no resources, but the liberality of people who know not
God, compelled to live like them, to pass whole years
without receiving any tidings, with savages who have
only the countenances of human beings, among whom
instead of finding society or relief in sickness, he is
often exposed to perish and be massacred. This is
done daily by these Fathers in Louisiana and in
Canada." (Catholic Church in Colonial days).

The scenic and historic interest of the country
seemed to lessen. The King's Highways—El Camino
Real—were no longer trodden by Padres as when the
land was young. In some places there was even a
scarcity of clergy to solemnize marriage. A strong
feeling against Catholics had crept in, though
Catholics, with scarcely an exception, had rallied to
the cause of freedom. Catholic Indians from Maine
took up the cause of the Colonies. St. Regis Indians
in New York did the same. The French settlers in
the Illinois helped to gain the West for the United
States. Two regiments of Canadian Catholics fought
on the American side during the whole war. But all
seems to have been forgotten.

CHAPTER XLIII.

Bishop Blanc found a most valiant champion in the celebrated Napoleon Joseph, Abbé Perche, who attacked the Bishop's enemies so vigorously and with such cutting logic that they were ultimately compelled to abandon the field. His masterly articles, in the *Propagateur,* are still read with pleasure. He was also celebrated for his charity to the poor and the sick, and the zeal with which he instructed the Indian and the slave. He was worthy to rank with the old Padres, noble pioneers of genuine civilization, when the love of souls gave more than human power to the Apostles of the lowly.

A fine, life-sized oil painting of Père Antoine adorns the New Orleans presbytery. He is garbed as a Capuchine monk. His snowy beard falls to his hempen girdle. His tonsure leaves but a fringe around his bent head. His habit is of the coarsest brown serge, and his bare feet have wooden sandals. Some affirm that, in this splendid painting, he has the holy aspect of a mediæval St. Anthony, while others, we regret to say, could find no trace of sanctity in the lineaments or demeanor of this extraordinary man, as represented on canvas.

In a pamphlet by Messrs Ryan and Augustine, New Orleans (1893), we find the following characteristic anecdote:

18

" The good Father having quarreled with the Vicar-General, the latter suspended him. Père Antoine refused to obey. He appealed to his parishioners, and they stood by him as a unit. He was reinstated. Later on, the irrepressible old priest again gave cause for censure, and was relieved of his pastorate.

" For a few days, he disappeared from the narrow streets of New Orleans, and the children looked in vain for the white beard, the sandalled feet, the brown habit, and the bag of lagniappe.

" Finally, the good folks became uneasy, and resolved to find out what had become of him.

" After hunting for their beloved pastor for several days they found him in a cypress swamp, woeful and miserable. He was kneeling beside a tree-stump, deeply engaged in prayer. The people set up a joyful shout, and carried him to the city in triumph.

" They took him to the church and insisted he should say mass for them, ... but he answered he could do nothing until the Bishop recalled him to duty. Then they rushed out of the church and poured through the streets towards the old Ursuline Convent, where the ancient Bishop dwelt. Father Antonio was promptly restored to duty; and thereafter none ventured to interfere with his spiritual jurisdiction."

Grave are the charges which his Superiors and others made against this Father. But whether they are true, or false, or merely exaggerated, can hardly be ascertained at this distant day. In his later years, he seems to have led a quiet, holy life. And, " if charity covers a multitude of sins," we may surely say of him in the words of the Psalmist: " Blessed is the man whose iniquities are forgiven, and whose sins are covered." One who knew him well in his later years, spoke of him as a man who was forever dispensing alms, whose hand was always stretched out to the needy. He christened, married, and buried, all who had need of these ministrations, and a friend who saw him frequently, told the writer that Père Antoine could hardly have given in alms much less than thirty thousand dollars a year.

His purse was an immense leathern wallet, hanging from his girdle, filled with clinking coins. Into this, people threw money as fast as he gave it away. He was usually followed by crowd of children, who asked for a gift, with his blessing, and he never refused either.

Some time before his death, Père Antoine left the parochial residence, and lived in a hermitage made of planks and boughs, under his direction, in the small garden behind the Cathedral. Its furniture was a bed of boards, a stool, and a holy-water font. Here, he ate, slept and prayed, and here occurred his last sickness and death.[1]

Many aged Creoles to whom the writer spoke, of Père Antoine, mentioned him as being indefatigable in conferring the sacraments, and very good to the poor. " He was a kind, holy old man, was the usual verdict. *Emigrés* from San Domingo said : " He married my parents over again. They could not get a priest in San Domingo." He was well remembered in New Orleans, when the writer first knew it forty years ago. Some said he never acquired any property,

---

[1] The small garden behind the Cathedral, in the midst of which Père Antoine built the hermitage in which he died, still exists. A flagged passage between the little garden and the presbytery is called St. Anthony's Alley.

but others thought the hut in which he died, 1829, was his own.

On the day of his funeral, the whole population turned out to do him honor. The newspapers suspended publication, there were no plays at the theatres, the courts were adjourned, and the warehouses closed. The City Council passed a resolution by which its members pledged themselves to wear crape on the left arm for thirty days in memory of him.

It was, therefore, superfluous that "the masons of all branches," should, in the daily papers, send a public invitation to his funeral. It had often been said that he was a member of this body. But if this were so, he must have withdrawn when preparing for death, else his body would not have received Christian burial. Invitations to the funeral are issued in the papers, by the Church-Wardens, and all Editors are requested to publish them.

A more urgent invitation is issued by "a number of masons," to "masons of all rites and degrees," who are told to remember that "Father Antoine never refused to accompany to their last abode the mortal remains of our Brethren."

In death, Père Antoine might have said: "Save me from my friends." There were several holy ecclesiastics in New Orleans at that date. There was the saintly De Neckere, who was consecrated Bishop that very year, 1829, and Father Blanc, who became first Archbishop of New Orleans. But no one came forward, officially, to send invitations to his funeral but *Marguilliers,* who were in a chronic state of semi-rebellion against their chief pastors, and free-masons, who may be said to have severed themselves from the Church, while bound by the secret oaths of that organization. And his chief eulogist was Edward Livingstone, the free-thinker.

An admirer of the Père, Dr. Castallanas, speaks of "the charges preferred against his ministry as numerous and even now recorded in the archives of the Propaganda at Rome." "Hence the wide divergence of opinion that exists not only among the laity but on part of the clergy at large, as to the verity of the accusations laid to his charge."

The active life of Father Antoine ceased some time before his death, on account of his condition of health. But, in view of all that stands against him, and which was well known in New Orleans, the fulsome eulogies of the papers, of the free-masons, and the free-thinker, Livingstone, were not, to say the least, in the best of taste even if they do not go so far as to remind one of the awful saying of St. Augustine: " Praised where he is not and tormented where he is." Humble fervent prayer for his poor soul would perhaps be more suitable to the wishes of the defunct, could he express them. Well may his real friends be grateful that length of days was given him, in which he could make his peace with God, ere death summoned him before the dread tribunal where flattery avails nothing.

" Behold he cometh, saith the Lord of hosts, and who shall be able to think of the day of his coming, and who shall stand to see him? Matt. iii.

The closing years of his long and stormy life were devoted to the poor. And, " blessed is the man that considereth concerning the poor and the needy." " For alms delivereth from death, and the same is that which cleanseth away sins and maketh to find mercy and life everlasting."

Various are the views taken of this singular man. The best and the worst has been said and written of him. But all who knew him agree as to his generosity to the needy. He surely made " friends to himself of the mammon of iniquity." He was " an eye to the blind, and a foot to the lame, and a tender parent to the poor." And so we may leave him to the tender mercies of Him who has said: " I was hungry and you gave me to eat. Sick, and in prison, and you came to Me. As long as you did it to one of these, my least brethren, you did it unto Me. Come, ye blessed of My Father!"

The funeral services were conducted with unusual pomp and magnificence. Three thousand wax candles[1] illuminated the Cathedral. The whole military service of the city, including the far-famed legion, were arranged in front of the square. When the procession took up its line of march through the streets, every church bell tolled the sad, solemn knells. It is further stated, if we may believe tradition and contemporaneous accounts, that this pageant was the grandest manifestation of a people's grief ever witnessed in New Orleans.

Though his death was not unexpected, it seemed a great blow to many. His corpse was laid out, during three days on a gorgeously decked catafalque, in the centre aisle of the church, attended by a civic and military guard.

Many parishioners in their desire to retain some relic of Father Antoine, had cut into small pieces his humble cassock, and would have proceeded to further extremities but for the exertions of Mayor-Prieur

---

[1] Many of these wax tapers were preserved by Father Sedilla's friends as souvenirs.

who, in person, promptly restored order in the house
of God, and took measures to prevent the recurrence of
further disorder.

The public buildings were draped in mourning, and
the flags of the foreign ships of the various consulates
were hoisted at halfmast.   Crape was hung on the
doors of hundreds of residences.

In the highest story of the City Hall, in New Orleans, are preserved the daily journals that mention the
death and funeral of Père Antoine.   The *Courrier,*
Wednesday, Jan. 21, 1829, says: " In respect to the
memory of Rev. Père Antoine de Sedilla, and in order
to give those in our employ an opportunity of attending the obsequies, the *Courrier* will not appear again
until Friday, Jan. 23."   After more to the same effect, there is a Resolution of the House of Representatives:

" Resolved, that they will attend in a body, the
funeral of the Rev. Father Antoine de Sedilla, whose
death they deem a loss worthy of their sincerest regret . . .   To honor his memory is to honor virtue,
and his remembrance will forever be dear in a country
where he saw three generations succeed one another,
of all of whom he justly enjoyed the love and respect."

The *Courrier* mentions Père Antoine as 81 years
old, but it is probable that he was much older.   No
special disease is mentioned as the cause of his death.
The *Courrier* also says that " though a long sickness
should have prepared all for his death, yet it was very
sensibly felt by all classes of the population."

Early in the morning of the day of the funeral,
Thursday, Jan. 22, the Cathedral and its vicinity were
thronged by an immense assemblage.   At 10 a. m.,
the religious ceremonies began with a solemn high

mass of requiem. Abbe Maenhaut delivered a sermon in which he recalled the virtues of the deceased. After mass, comformably to the arrangements made, all the constituted bodies, and all the individuals invited, formed the procession, and marched through the streets indicated by the programme. They returned to the Church where the coffin was deposited in a vault built for that purpose under the altar of St. Francis. It was resolved to build a special chapel for his remains, but this was never done.

The body of Antoine de Sedilla which was carried with so much pomp and circumstance to the tomb, no longer rests under the altar of St. Francis. In a work of excavation which certain necessary repairs required, the Masons were compelled to disinter the remains of the priests buried near the altar of St. Francis, whence they were carried in wheel-barrows to the cart destined to remove them to the cemetery. Among them are the remains of Père Antoine, which now rest in the Priests' tomb in Basin Street Cemetery. Those who repair to the Cathedral, " and there are thousands," says the Castellanos, " and kneel at his supposed crypt in prayer and repentance, are victims of deceit. The translation has been kept secret and for this there is no excuse."

Among the visitors to New Orleans in the time of Father de Sedilla was the celebrated English geologist, Sir Charles Lyell. He met, and, of course, was interested in the famous Padre Antoine. He asked some of the New Orleans people for an account of him. The answer he received was: " No one could tell you the details of his life." In his account of his second visit to New Orleans, or rather to the United

States, Sir Charles calls attention to a curious memento of the alms-giving priest:

" Walking through one of the streets of New Orleans, near the river, immediately north of the Catholic Cathedral[1], I was surprised to see a fine date-palm, thirty feet high, growing in the open air.

" Mr. Wilde told me the tree is seventy or eighty years old. Père Antoine, a Roman Catholic priest, who died about twenty years ago, told Mr. Bringier[2] that he planted it himself when he was younger. In his will he provided that they who succeeded to this lot of ground should forfeit it if ever they cut down the palm.

Lyell's second visit to the United States, '45-'50., " This beautiful, peaceful memento of Père Antoine has long since disappeared. Pictures of it are common. No doubt it sometimes reminded his friends of the Introit: " Justus ut palma florebit." The just shall flourish like the palm tree: he shall grow up like the cedar of Libanus . . . It is good to give praise to the Lord and to sing to thy Name, O Most High."

---

[1] Sir Charles Lyell says: " Padre Antonio lived to a great age, became quite emaciated, and walked the streets like a mummy. He gradually dried up, ceasing at last to move. I asked a Catholic for the Father's history : He said it could never be ascertained. The city Council, the Legislature, the bench, the learned professions, (even " the masons " whom the Catholic Church excommunicates,) adopted in their several meeting-places eulogistic resolutions, and signified their desire to attend the obsequies of the deceased.

[2] Mr. Bringier was a relative of Bishop Dubourg. The family still live in New Orleans.

CHAPTER XLIV.

WE will conclude our notice of Father Antoine de Sedilla, with the oration of the celebrated Edward Livingstone on the famous Padre:

Jan. 23, 1829. In the court of the first District, yesterday morning, Mr. Livingstone rose and addressed the Court as follows:

" May it please the Court: A Reverend Ecclesiatic has lately departed this life who was endeared to the great mass of the inhabitants of this country by the most interesting recollection of events from the cradle to the grave. He conferred upon them in infancy that title from which they derive their hopes of happiness, hereafter. In this life he united them in the bonds which secured their Conubial felicity, and it was he who performed those solemn rites which connect his memory with the reverence due to that of their ancestors. He was the faithful depositary of their most secret thoughts, their consoler in affliction—their resource in poverty, and their confidential friend in society. His charity and kind feelings were not confined to those of his own Church, and his liberality, both of sentiment and action, were acknowledged by those of a different faith. His holiness and virtues would have entitled him to canonization; and if his title to that distinction were to be tried, as it is said to be in Rome, the advocate of the evil one would burn his brief, and despair of showing even one reason why he should not be received as a Saint in heaven who led the life of one on earth. The death of a man of this character is a public loss, and in order to show the respect entertained for the memory of Rev. Father Antoine de Sedilla, I move that the following resolution be entered on the minutes:

"On the motion of Mr. Livingstone it is ordered that this court will adjourn until Friday morning for the purpose of giving to the Court and the Bar, the opportunity of attending the funeral of the Beloved Father Antoine de Sedilla, a venerable ecclesiastic, whose loss is lamented by the whole community; and that this resolution be communicated to the judges of the Supreme Court and the other Courts in this city, with an invitation to meet in the hall of this Court, for the purpose of attending the funeral, together with the members of the Bar, the officers of the Court at ten o'clock this day.

CHAPTER XLV.

HELP was given to many places in the South by eleven Jesuits who arrived in Mobile in charge of Father Jourdan, S. J. They embarked in the sailing ship, St. Anne, and reached Mobile, Dec. 12, 1847. Among them was the celebrated soldier-priest, Rev. Darius Hubert, S. J., so well known and so deeply revered during the civil war, a chaplain of the Grand Army of Tennessee. The only members of this fervent band now living is the venerable Brother Ignatius, the well-known co-adjutor of the Provincial house of New Orleans. A larger band of Jesuits (22), left Marseilles in October, 1848, and after an uneventful voyage of sixty days reached New Orleans. During the voyage Mass was celebrated daily, the crew joining in the religious exercises, on board the good ship, Tonka. They were escorted by the Superior, Father Cambiaso, to Archbishop Blanc at the Archbishopric, where they were hospitably entertained by his grace for several days. Almost all these priests have been called to their reward. Among the few surviors is the venerable Father de Carrière, in his 89th year, in the novitiate house at Macon, Georgia.

Father Cambiaso, born at Lyons, 1809, was of Italian origin. One of his ancestors had been Doge of Genoa, at an epoch when that free and independent city disputed with Venice the empire of the Mediterranean.

There was now little rapid growth of the Church in Alabama or the Floridas. Catholics sometimes came from distant parts, often from Europe. Occasionally, they remained, often their stay was brief. A brick church was erected in Tuscaloosa, the capital of Alabama, by Rev. Father Hackett, and dedicated by Bishop Portier, 1845. A Gothic Church was erected at Tallahassee, 1846. In 1850, the fine Cathedral of Mobile was completed. It cost over one hundred and eighty thousand dollars. It was dedicated under the title of the Immaculate Conception of the Mother of God, by Bishop Reynolds of Charleston, S. C. Bishop Portier sang the Pontificial high mass, Bishop Spalding of Louisville preached. Archbishops Purcell of Cincinnati and Blanc of New Orleans were present, with Bishop Lamy, Vicar Apostolic of New Mexico

The Apalaches and their country have been frequently mentioned in this work. In May, 1857, the corner-stone of a church in Apalachicola was laid, under the invocation of St. Patrick. A church had been built in Montgomery, in 1834, but it had not always a resident pastor. Apalachicola is built on a sand bed. In 1846, it contained a thousand inhabitants, one hundred of whom were Irish Catholics, who besought Bishop Portier to satisfy their desires for a resident Pastor. Rev. Father Gibbons was sent to them.

It is said that Bishop Juarez and some priests landed on Holy Thursday, 1527, on this coast of Florida, planted the cross according to custom, and said mass, perhaps on the site of St. Patrick's Church. An Indian tradition declares there will be a church built wherever a first mass has been offered.

The chief cities of the territory which formed the

diocese of the zealous Bishop Portier were Mobile and St. Augustine. These with New Orleans are, by excellence, the historic cities of the South. St. Augustine is the oldest city in the country, and in aspect, it may be said to be, despite the modern beauties of the Alcazar and the Ponce de Leon, the most un-American. Its low houses of solid stone, its ancient Convent, its moorish looking church, its romantic fort, over which floated for centuries the gorgeous colors of Spain, its ruins, which eloquently tell its chequered story, transport one to the ancient cities of Europe in its earlier days, the days of its chivalry.

A truly great man, Pedro Melendez, founded St. Augustine. After his death, 1573, its prosperity declined. In 1586, it had made some progress. It had a parish Church and well-cultivated gardens when Francis Drake, in one of his piratical cruises, destroyed it. In 1577, Father Alonzo de Reynoso arrived with a number of missionaries. They worked with such success among the Indians at *Nombre de Dios* and San. Sebastian, that converts were soon regular attendants at the Sunday's mass. Rev. Rodrigo Garcia de Truxillo, parish priest of St. Augustine, who was then old and enfeebled by 28 years of labor in that post, and his previous service as Navy Chaplain.

The Council of the Indies gave free passage to twelve missionaries, with Father de Silvas as Superior, who had already labored faithfully in Mexico. These good priests by their instructions and kindness soon changed the face of the province of Eastern Florida.

The old Franciscan Convent, Santa Elena, was once the cherished home of the missionaries of St. Francis, whence they traveled in all directions to con-

vert the red men, and prayed, studied, and toiled for
the love of Christ and the salvation of souls.

St. Elena was a Mother House for the hard-work-
ing Fathers, and a retreat for the Apostolic men of
the Peninsula.   It was surrounded by broad, airy galleries.   The Spanish colors waved from the tall flagstaff before the large Convent.   Beside this was the
bright Hibernian banner, glittering with the Harp of
Erin, for the Spanish troops were, for a long time,
the Royal Hibernian regiment, with its green standard, and its pastors were long from the land that gave
the American Church some of its greatest names.
For a moment the snowy standard of St. George was
flung to the balmy winds to be lowered when the stars
and stripes rose in triumph from the St. Lawrence to
the St. Mary.

The glorious old Convent became a barracks under
the English, and, later, gave shelter to the United
States troops.   The first colonists came from Spain
more than half a century before the Pilgrims landed at
Plymouth.   The church of St. Augustine was fully organized at that early period, and had full records of
baptisms and marriages from 1594.

The present Spanish inhabitants are chiefly descendants of the emigrants who settled in Florida at
various epochs.   The barracks where a sentinel now
paces up and down, was the centre of the Franciscan
missioners, from which they daily went forth to visit
the Indian villages which then lay on each side of St.
Augustine, both destroyed by the English.

When the English occupied the city, the monks with
most of the citizens passed over to Cuba.   The
invaders seized all their property, and made the ancient
Catholic Church a Protestant Conventicle, which it still
remains.

It would seem that, in this remote region, the emigrants took more example from the Indians than the Indians from them. They were unambitious, as they remain to-day—a little garden and some fishery in the bay, supplies all their wants, as in the time of the stern Melendez. They led the calm, easy lives of the peasantry in other lands, "forgetting the world and by the world forgot," as little concerned in the turmoils of the busy Republic as the Bas Breton is to-day. For a long period Irish priests served the spiritual wants of Florida. Father O'Reilly built the beautiful Church of St. Augustine, and became a founder of the Visitation Convent at Mobile. Father Michael Crosbie who, like the Irish missionary clergy of his day had studied in Spain, succeeded Father O'Reilly in the Pastorate of St. Augustine, and died soon after jackson took possession of Florida.

Father Crosbie's last entry is May 25, 1821. He was assisted by Father Gomez, from 1807. The great Bishop England, always ready to build up the waste places of Zion, came again to the rescue, and sent to the old city by the sea, an excellent priest, Rev. Francis Boland, who remained till 1825. "Who is weak and I am not weak? Who is scandalized and I am not on fire?" are words of inspiration which must often have been on the lips of Bishop England.

Although the English sacked St. Augustine again and again, and preached Reformation doctrines from its most sacred strongholds, it is still, though poor and its spendors vanished forever, a typical Catholic city. Its sacred ruins, its massive garden walls, the sweet tones of its passing bell, "the Agonea," the old fort with its Spanish bastions—the Catalan songs of the light-hearted fishermen, as one watches the dip

of the oar in its shining waters—the oldest conventual building in the territory of the United States,
the balmy climate, the refreshing breezes of the sea—
all this makes the ancient city a Paradise for invalids.
There is, perhaps, no other place on this vast continent
where one feels more consoled by the Communion of
Saints, for there is scarcely a spot on which Saints
have not prayed for sinners, and united their suffrages
to those of Christ, shed their blood for souls in union
with the grand and awful sacrifice of Calvary.

Of the small population about six thousand, perhaps scarcely one third is Protestant. Several non-
Catholics live in St. Augustine for its delightful climate. Some persons said to us when we visited this
dear old city: " I could make more money in other
places, but I could not have good health anywhere
else." Although one no longer sees the brown hab-
ited Franciscans, wending their way from the Convent on errands of mercy, or pious civilians dropping
on their knees on the orange bordered roads, so full
of fragrance, at the music of the *Angelus,* still the
sweet city, with its fading splendors, has a thoroughly
Catholic aspect. It is easy to go back to its early
days, and feel one's self in the ages of faith, and poetry,
and religious enthusiasm.

St. Augustine is flourishing as to religion. The
religious spirit is better than it was twenty years ago.
But, of course, it is not what it was in the old Spanish
times, when only Catholics were here. Those times
we have not seen, but we frequently hear of them.
The ancient cemeteries are as they were long ago, but
are not now used as such.

Some years ago, houses formerly used as residences
for the various Bishops who labored in Florida were

19

still standing on the Church property. These old buildings were torn down, and in their place was erected a large brick block, which is rented out in stores, offices, living rooms. It is said that in time this will bring a large income for religious purposes, but, at present, not any, as the money to build it was borrowed. The church has not yet got the property claimed by the United States. The Franciscan monastery, used as a barracks, is in good condition.

The history of the labors of the Irish clergy in America is, practically unwritten. This is especially true of the clergy who came under the Spanish flag. A grand chapter has yet to be added to the glorious story of the Catholic religion in these ancient colonies, and under the Stars and Stripes.

The good health enjoyed by the Ursuline Community and their household, in colonial times, was most remarkable. There was seldom a case of illness even among their pupils or orphans; the nuns almost invariably lived to a great age. The climate was wholesome, and the laws of health seem to have been well observed. In Mobile and in New Orleans, the most serious disease complained of was " some access of fever," which yielded readily to simple treatment. Every nun had a small flower garden in which she raised a few flowers for the altar, and many medicinal herbs for the sick within the enclosure and outside of it, especially sassafras, which it was thought would cure all diseases.[1]

[1] The medicinal qualities of herbs were well understood by the Ursuline ladies. They knew the plants whose leaves are for " the healing of the nations," and those good for food and pleasant to the eye. And flowers, roots, bark, and fruit, for the care of the various diseases that flesh is heir to, were produced in their well-kept gardens. Their tisanes equalled the " yarrub teas " of New England.

In the first half of the nineteenth century, the Convent was attended by Drs. Carr, Labatut, Stone, Faget, and Rance, physicians who are not yet forgotten by the older Creoles, especially the great surgeon, Dr. Stone. The most distinguished visitor in Bishop Portier's time, was certainly the great Bishop of Charleston, S. C., Right Rev. Dr. England.

CHAPTER XLVI.

By his pen, his preaching, his example, Bishop England did good throughout the whole United States, but especially in the South. He was the most accomplished prelate of his time, and one of the foremost men in the world, the glory of the hierarchy. " If I had Bishop England at my back," said a kindred spirit, O'Connell, " I would not fear the entire world before me." He became Bishop of Charleston, 1820. The three States which formed his diocese were slave states. Most of his children literally sat in darkness and the shadow of death. He spoke of having two millions, but half of them were slaves.

Bishop England's saintly Sister, Mary Augustine, remained in the New Orleans Ursuline Convent for three years during which she was engaged chiefly in the novtiate. Like every member of her gifted family, she was refined and highly educated, and worked incessantly for the glory of God and the welfare of souls.

Before entering the Convent, the young lady, Sister M. Augustine was shown the famous Cathedral, the great monument to the piety of Don Andres Almonaster y Roxas. Her party was received at the main entrance by the Swiss Guard. This official, in bright garb with gold buttons and heavy straps; on his chest is a heavy band in which his sword was firmly fixed.

To no one but Our Good Lord will he take off his cocked hat, in which is a large white feather. He is the terror of noisy children, and the dogs fear him. But address him as " my Captain," and you win his undying friendship.

The besetting sin of the gay Southern Capital was that balls and theatres were so carried on that it was dangerous, if not positively sinful, to attend them. The great orator preached so forcibly on these crying evils that the managers complained of their being deserted by the women. One young lady, whose father had forced her to attend, actually turned her back to the stage during certain plays, and thus relieved herself of the violence done to her principles. For, the father, not wishing to expose himself or his daughter, to public ridicule, ceased to importune her to attend.

The slaves were the Bishop's first care. He said mass for them every Sunday at 7 a. m., and preached for them in the afternoon. He gave them the preference over all others. He tried to have them taught, and to found schools for them. But legislation forbade this, apart from social ostracism, as all dwellers in Slave States know.

Yet Chancellor Kent said: " He restored learning and classical education in the South." " To know him was certainly a liberal education." Bishop England's first effort was to form a domestic priest-hood, animated with his spirit and bound by ties of long-time friendship, and he was eminently successful. It was said of his clergy: " They harbored no thought but religion, no aspiration but missionary toil, no love but God, His holy Mother, His angels and Saints."

The Bishop was a ceaseless, untiring worker. He

trained his disciples by word and example, and with such success that Bishop Persico said that, formed by his training, every one of them was worthy to wear a mitre. His visitation of his diocese was a stupendous labor. Sometimes on foot, occasionally on horseback, no protection from the heat in summer or the frost in winter, often a prey to the blood-thirsty insects of which even the early apostles so eloquently complained. His success was great but dearly bought. He drank the cup of sorrows to the very dregs, and the bitterness of its water was never sweetened save by the wood of the cross.

"Let us kill him and Lazarus also, lest the Romans come and take our country." Mobs bent on rapine and murder, such as had, unhappily, disgraced other cities, were now ready for their evil work in Charleston. But the brave, true men of the city were called out. It became evident that any attempt at mob violence would inaugurate the reign of terror which the persecutors affected to dread. The mayor and city officers without whose connivance matters could not have become so serious, became active peace-agents. Thanks to their great Bishop, the Carolinians were saved from disgracing their city and country by religious riots.

April 11, 1842, this great man, of whom the world was not worthy, passed away, fortified by the rites of the Church he loved so well.

"Consider, O Israel, for them that are dead, wounded in thy high places. The illustrious of Israel are slain upon thy mountains. How are the valiant fallen and the weapons of war perished? There was cast away the shield of the valiant, as though he had not been anointed with oil. I grieve for thee; as the mother loveth her only son, so did I love thee.

All external signs of grief appeared. Thousands visited the sacred remains with every mark of sorrow, as they lay in state in his poor Cathedral. The city was in mourning, the flags on the shipping in the harbor and on public buildings were at half mast. Business was suspended and the bells even in non-Catholic churches tolled mournfully.

The great Bishop Kenrick of Baltimore presided at his obsequies and admonished the people to be mindful of his teachings and example. " He it was," said he, " who had organized the Provincial Councils, framed their decrees, established the discipline of the Catholic Church in America, and was venerated as its Father." Several times Bishop England went as delegate to Hayti, by appointment of the Holy Father, and did much towards creating a revival of Church discipline on that island, where the first bishopric in America had been established.

Bishop Reynolds collected and published the complete works of his great predecessor, in five Octavo volumes, for it was not by preaching alone, but by the pen as well that Bishop England exercised a powerful influence on the whole Church of the United States.

Several years ago, being in Charleston, the writer expressed a desire to see Bishop England's grave. Accustomed from childhood to hear the story of his sublime virtues, from loving lips, we were glad to breathe the atmosphere he once breathed, and gaze on the salient points of " the city by the sea " in which he toiled incessantly for God and for souls. We had heard from his eldest Sister, Mother Catherine England, Superior of the North Presentation Convent, Cork, of his grand intellectual qualities, his love for slaves and free, his superhuman labors among the fever-stricken and the ignorant. Extracts from the beautiful story of his life were printed on white satin, and displayed in the reception-room, where every caller was introduced to the grand prelate. These chaste memorials had been done in his dear city of Charleston, and forwarded to Cork, from which he would have brought his Sister to Charleston to train his beloved children there to the religious life which she so thoroughly understood, and so faithfully practised. But the Bishop of Cork refused to allow her to leave her native soil. And, full of piety, this worthy Sister of a great brother continued to devote her grand intellectual gifts to saving the poor children, who assembled daily in hundreds at the Convent. She died at a great age, in sentiments of tender piety.

Not far from the Convent of Mercy, Queen St., Charleston, was a square of ground in which were three graves, about the same size, covered with ivy. Here, without tomb or cross were the graves of the first three Bishops of Charleston. A Cathedral in course of erection was mentioned as the monument of Bishop England, and the prelates who rested near him. A former Cathedral had been destroyed by fire. The flames shivered into fragments the flags that covered Bishop England's tomb and bared the interior to the light of day. Recently a fine Cathedral has been erected to his memory.

Forty years after the death of the great Bishop, business brought us to several places once under his jurisdiction. We can testify that from the worthy Bishop Becker, who loved and revered his memory, to the lowest of his flock, we found Bishop England spoken of with love and reverence as if he had but recently left them. Every one had some anecdote to relate of his zeal and charity, nor could the people say enough in his praise.

" The souls of the just are in the hands of God, and the torment of death shall not hurt them. In the sight of the unwise they seemed to die . . . but they are in peace."

.   .   .   .   .

" A man is his own star;
Our acts our angels all
For good or—ill."

Bishop Portier was in Charleston in March, 1858, and no doubt prayed fervently by the grave of his revered friend, R. I. P., who had done so much for the Catholic religion throughout the South.

In 1829, Mobile had ten thousands inhabitants. Bishop Portier returned from France, *via* New Orleans with two priests, four subdeacons and two clerics. There was only a rough wooden Cathedral. The people had fallen into lamentable laxity. Father Ponjade, the first priest he ordained, died of yellow fever, 1831.

In 1830, Father Chalon, a relative of Bishop Portier, and Father Loras were commissioned by the Bishop to make a thorough visitation of Alabama. In a seven months' tour they gathered up Catholics wherever they could find them, and enabled them to hear mass and approach the sacraments.

On a beautiful site, near Mobile, Bishop Portier erected Spring Hill College, a brick building 100 x 44. It opened under Fathers, Loras and Bazin, and in its first year had fifty pupils, and later seventy.

During the English domination in Florida, William

Panton, a wealthy merchant, opened branches of his
business at Pensacola, Mobile, and St. Augustine. A
building erected by Panton and Leslie, with a wharf
in front, is still standing. Its solid brick walls are
those of the Hospital of Dr. James Herron, an eminent physican of Pensacola. The handsome dwelling
house of this gentleman stands on the site of the
Council Chambers of Fort St. George, called the old
Fort, or St. Michaels. The business of these merchant princes extended to the Tennessee River, and
even beyond it. Their long lines of pack-horses carried all the supplies the Indians needed, and brought
back all their savage customers provided for barter.
The pony used by these stout traders was a hardy
little animal, which carried one hundred and eighty
pounds and traveled twenty-five miles a day. The
missioners sometimes availed themselves of this mode
of transit.

The entrance to Spring Hill College was from the
South, from the old Pascagoula Road. The central
portion was built of brick. A frame church stood
west of the college. In 1832, there were one hundred
and twenty-five students, and Father Bazin was named
President. Besides the Bishop and Vicar-general
Loras, there was only one priest at that time in
Mobile, Rev. Gabriel Chalon. They not only ministered to the spiritual wants of the faithful, but with
a few laymen, constituted the teaching staff of the
college.

The Bishop was the life of the college. He was
often seen taking part in the games and pastimes of
the boys. The next President, 1835, was Father
Mauvernay, who boasted that he had been a soldier
under Napoleon; he died in 1839. Five Fathers of

Mercy came to the aid of the college. By a decree, Aug. 29, 1840, His Holiness, Pope Gregory XVI, granted the college power to confer degrees in theology and philosophy. In 1841, the Fathers resigned the college, and Bishop Portier again took charge. Despite the efforts of the Bishop and the Eudist Fathers, who came in 1844, the college was closed in 1846.

Bishop Portier finally applied to Very Rev. Father Roothan, general of the Jesuits, who referred him to Father Malliard, provincial of France. Negotiations succeeded, and Father Gautrelet and four other Jesuits arrived in Mobile, January, 1847. Fathers, Yenni and Soller met them from New Orleans.

The college was re-opened under the presidency of Father Gautrelet. Father Bazin was appointed Bishop of Vincennes, Ind. In 1850, Father Matthew, Apostle of Temperance, visited the college, also Father de Smet, the famous Indian missionary. It was visited too by Archbishop Blanc of New Orleans, Bishops, Reynolds of Charleston, Purcell of Cincinnati, Lamy of Santa Fe, and Vandevelde of Natchez. Dr. O. A. Brownson was also among the visitors.

Spring Hill College was incorporated in 1836, by the Legislature of Alabama, with all the rights and priveleges of a University.

While visiting the old Catholic city of Lyons, 1829, Bishop Portier thought of renewing his acquaintance with its Archbishop, Cardinal Fesch, and for this purpose, as well as to receive the Pope's blessing he went to Rome. The Bourbon Government had decreed banishment as the penalty of being the uncle of Bonaparte. The Cardinal was glad to see his friend of former days, now a missionary Bishop, and gave him thirty thousand francs in aid of the college, and, as a mark of personal friendship, presented him with a beautiful painting, now among the treasures of Spring Hill College. In token of gratitude, the college was dedicated to St. Joseph, the patron Saint of the Cardinal.

The Bishop was always the genius of the spot. He might be seen axe in hand, marching into the woods at the head of his young people to fell the forest and prepare the way for future cultivation. " This " he remarked, " may not seem very episcopal, but it is very apostolic, otherwise, St. Paul made a mistake in showing us how to work with our hands." Father Bazin wrote: " Every moment we could spare from our studies and the ministry was devoted to manual labor. Forests had to be felled, gardens and orchards to take their place, grounds had to be fenced, lands cleared, planted, tilled. But always and everywhere, under our eyes, was the stirring example of our Bishop. Not an enterprise in which he, axe in hand, did not lead the way."

Cholera was epidemic in Mobile in 1849 but the college escaped. Several other diseases appeared in the city from time to time, but they touched the inmates of the college lightly, if at all. The old city was not so fortunate. A society was formed in June, 1838, for " the support and education of destitute orphans, and children neglected by their parents, also indigent families or individuals reduced to distress by sickness or other inevitable misfortunes, and though Catholics shall have the first claim, yet others shall not be excluded." To administer these charities, Brothers of the Sacred Heart from France were invited by the Bishop. They had been established in Lyons, 1820, to take charge of schools and Asylums.

Five came in 1847, and began their charitable ministrations among the orphan boys of Mobile, which they
still continue.   The Bishop established a society of
ladies for visiting the sick and poor, so that none
were excluded from his universal benevolence.   Mainly
through the exertions of Very Rev. Father McGarahan, the Providence Infirmary was built, and placed
in charge of the Sisters of Charity.   Three of Mobile's
venerated Bishops breathed their last in this holy Institution: Bishops Portier, Manncy, and O'Sullivan
—R. I. P.

The name of Very Rev. James McGarahan is frequently mentioned in the records of those benevolent works, as aiding them in every possible way, and
his lamented death, in 1865, was bewailed as an irreparable loss.   The orphans for whom he labored for
more than twenty-five years, were deprived of their
greatest benefactor.   Nothing could exceed his kindness to these children.   When they left the Asylum
he continued to watch over them.

We find the following entry in the proceedings of
the Board of Managers, Aug. 6, 1844:

"Resolved by the Board: That the Rev. James
McGarahan be authorized to send to Tuscaloosa for
Mary A. Hines, formerly an orphan in the Asylum.
As the family with whom she was placed have since
left for the North, she is considered by them to be
at present left in a situation, not tending to her good."

The Sisters of Charity came from Emmittsburg to
Mobile, Dec. 16, 1841.

Mar. 3, 1846, the Mother Superior of the Sisters
of Charity notified all concerned, that her Sisters
would be withdrawn from all male Asylums after
April 1, 1846.   At this date there were two hundred

and two children in the Asylums. The Bishop was now obliged to provide for the boys of his flock deprived of their parents.

. . . . .

Alabama has had four capitals: St Stephens on the Tombigbee, Cahaba on the Alabama, Tuscaloosa on the Black Warrior and Montgomery on the Alabama. The Indians were always associated with the missionaries and the fur-traders. The search for some wealthy region was often renewed, caravans moved westward like an army of galleys. But the coast bounded by the Mexican Gulf never was famous for mineral wealth. *Coureurs de bois* brought peltries from the Indians down the rivers to New Orleans, Biloxi, and Mobile. Sometimes they made trouble for the missioners by introducing that most injurious of all imports, fire-water. It was said to be an axiom among some Indians: "Do not strike even with a flower, a woman with a hundred vices." But many a poor industrious squaw felt the weight of her drunken husband's arm. Indian conflicts often meant treachery, assassination, scalping. During the life of the Rouquette brethren, Adrien and Dominique, much impetus was given to labors among the Indians. Adrien was the more intellectual of the pair—*par nobile fratrum,* —Only heaven knows who was the holier. Their labors in the pine regions of Louisiana and Mississippi are famous. Father Adrien was a wonderful singer of nature in all her diversified moods—in sylvan dells, in umbrageous forests, among the moonlit charms of exquisite scenery. Father Rouquette was a friend of every literary character of his day in Louisiana, as Judge Gayarre, Rev. Richard Kane, who admired his genius and revered his virtues. " Some day " says an admirer, " a gifted pen, recalling the legends and traditions of Louisana, will resurrect from the silent tomb the grand poetic leonine face of Father Rouquette and surround it with a halo of sanctified poesy."

CHAPTER XLVII.

MANY Indians sought refuge in Mobile where they were hospitably received.

In the Apalache country thirteen considerable towns were destroyed, each with a good church, and a Convent for the missionaries. They were plundered of plate, vestments, and everything that could tempt cupidity. Fairbank, an historian of Florida, states that "the remains of these mission stations may be traced in several localities" to-day. At Lake City and other places the outlines of the surrounding earthworks can be distinctly traced.

Those who had the interest of religion at heart had long desired the appointment of a Bishop to reside in Florida. Don Dionisio, a native of Havana, was selected for this dangerous dignity and was also made auxiliar to the Bishop of Santiago. He was consecrated at Meriden Yucatan, in 1709, and proceeded at once to Florida. He conferred confirmation, June 26, 1709, in the church of St. Augustine, on a multitude of persons of every rank. July 10th he made a formal visitation of the Church, of which Rev. Lawrence Acevdo, was parish-priest, as shown by the Register. The long pastorship of Father Acevedo ended Aug. 13, 1735.

In the war with Carolina, the Christian Indians were nearly exterminated. Only three hundred survivors were left to represent the numerous towns of native converts.

In 1726, there were three Yemassee missions, each with a Convent and church of palmetto, three of the Ygnasa nation, Guadaloupe, with a church of boards, *Nombre de Dios* had a stone Church, and some others. The heathen Indians, all sided with the English. The occupation of Georgia by Oglethorpe completed the ruin of the Indian missions in this section.

The Governor, Mannel Joseph de Justiz, bears testimony to the zeal and exertions of Bishop Tejada who had aroused piety among the Spanish settlers, having processions of the Rosary on Holidays, reviving the prequentation of the sacraments and omitting no means to draw all to the fear and love of God. His school was the only one in Florida, all the rest having been closed since the terrible English invasion. The chapel was only fifty feet by thirty six. Most of the congregation remained in the street. Though the Catholic King appropriated forty thousand dollars to rebuild the Parish Church, there was nothing to show for this sum but four bare walls. The Bishop and others exerted themselves to have it finished, but it remained unfinished until Florida passed out of the hands of the Catholic King. We were surprised to learn that this poor church had the luxury of a good organ. The King paid the organist two hundred and seventy-five dollars a year, a much larger sum then (1738) than now.

Many fugitive slaves from Georgia and the Carolinas reached Florida, and Bishop Tejada took the greatest care of them. He placed them at Fort Masé and assigned a young priest to instruct them and prepare them for Baptism.

20

It seems that the authorities expected the Bishop to induce these slaves to return. St. Paul so advised a runaway slave. But the circumstances were different. In the Catholic Church, master and slave knelt at the same altar. The Saint taught the slave to serve his master. But he said: " Masters, do to your servants that which is just and equal, knowing that you, also, have a Master in heaven." St. Vincent became a slave, but he escaped at the first opportunity. " In the 13th century," says Lecky " when there were no slaves to be emancipated in France—Christianity had freed the slave—it was usual in many churches, to release caged pigeons on ecclesiastical festivals, in memory of the ancient charity (of freeing slaves), and that some prisoners might still be freed in the Name of Christ."

In 1740, General Oglethorpe, with two thousand regulars, provincials and Indians, and a fleet of five ships and two sloops, laid siege to St. Augustine, but the brave governor refused to surrender. He held out until provisions came for the garrison to save it from starvation, when the founder of Georgia [1] raised the siege. During these days of trial, the Bishop stirred up the faith and piety of the people, and had constant prayers offered for the deliverance of the city.

In 1745, Bishop Tejada who had done so much for religion in Florida was promoted to the See of Meriden, Yucatan, of which he took possession, June 15, 1746. He erected a diocesan Seminary, and rebuilt many churches from his own income. His

[1] Augusta was a general resort for Indian trade. The wealthiest and most conspicuous of Indian traders was George Calphin, a native of Ireland.

charity extended to Spain, where he founded a Refuge for penitent women. In 1752, he was translated to Guadalajara. On taking possession of his Cathedral, he hung his jeweled cross on the statue of the Blessed Virgin, and wore a wooden cross instead. He was one of the holiest Bishops that adorned the Mexican hierarchy.

In 1743, Fathers, Monaca and de Alana, Jesuits, attempted a mission in Southern Florida. With the aid of the sailors they reared a hut for a dwelling and a chapel, and began their labors. The Indians being exceptionally vicious, even to the offering of human sacrifice, showed no inclination to listen to the missioners. Yet the men of God persevered, and a congregation of Catholic Indians was formed. They retained the Faith till the Seminole war, when they were transported to the Indian Territory, although they had taken no part in the hostilities against the whites.

The Indian missions had been again and again decimated till 1753, when there were only four left, all containing but one hundred and thirty-six souls. Reduced as St. Augustine was and almost stripped of the great circle of Indian missions which had been the diadem of the Florida church, it was not left without a Bishop. Bishop Carasce, auxiliar of Cuba, resided in the province from 1751 to 1755. When Havana was captured by the English, Bishop Morell, a learned, zealous prelate, who resided there as Bishop of Santiago, fell into the hands of the enemy. He was treated with great insolence by the Earl of Albemarle, the British Commander. When he refused to force levies from his clergy, he was accused of conspiracy, and summoned to appear before the representative of the British crown.   Declining to acknowledge these arbitrary measures, he was seized by a file of soldiers, Nov. 4, 1762, and carried in his chair to a man of war, which sailed off with him to Charleston, S. C.   After two weeks, he was sent to St. Augustine which was still under the Spanish flag.   He reached it, Dec. 8, 1762. He made his unexpected residence in Florida, a season of revived devotion and discipline.   He began a formal visitation, Jan. 30, 1763, and recorded his approval of the regularity of the parochial services and chronicles.   Between 1762 and 1763, he confirmed six hundred and thirty-nine persons.   His sojourn was a perpetual mission for the faithful.   After Spain had ceded Florida to England, Feb. 10, 1763, the clergy of Cuba sent a special vessel to convey the Bishop back to his See.

After the cession, the Catholics remained, but the tyranny of the English Commanders led to a general emigration.

The first mass said in Charleston, (1786) was said by an Italian priest, chaplain of a ship bound for South America, which put into port, at the solicitation of a few Irishmen.   It is scarcely credible, however, that the above named Bishop remained in that city for two weeks without finding means to celebrate mass (1762), though a close watch was kept on all strangers.   In 1775, two Catholic Irishmen, accused of tampering with the negroes, were tarred and feathered in Charleston.

The arrest of Bishop Morell was the subject of an oil-painting in the Havana Cathedral.   He is represented seated in his chair, in his episcopal robes, and carried by four British soldiers.   This iniquitous arrest is also the subject of a curious poem printed in Havana.

Bishop Morell was born in Santiago de los Caballeros, in Santo Domingo, of which his ancestors were early colonists. He was consecrated Bishop of Santiago de Cuba, Sept. 8, 1755. He founded charitable institutions, distributed eight hundred dollars a month to the poor, and sixty dollars every Saturday. For the negroes he showed special charity and took measures to secure their religious instruction. He died at Havana, Dec. 30, 1768.

CHAPTER XLVIII.

THE Spaniards recovered Pensacola only to lose it a second time, Sept. 18, 1719, when it was taken by Count de Champmeslin, with a powerful squadron. Finding he could not hold the place, he set fire to the Fort and town, not even sparing the church, and carrying off the Sacred vestments and plate. The earlier churches of Pensacola were dedicated to St. Michael. An elegant silver crucifix of ancient workmanship, the gift of some early benefactor, was preserved to our own time in the Pensacola Church.

Spain, by treaty, ceded Florida to the United States, 1819, and it was included in the limits of the Republic. When restored by England to Spain, St. Augustine was in a deplorable condition. The Catholics were mainly Minorcans, from New Smyrna, with some Indians, remnants of the once prosperous native missions, with a few among the English-speaking settlers. The monastery of Santa Elena from which went out the glad tidings of salvation to all the tribes of the South, Creeks of Alabama, Cherokees of Georgia, had become a barracks.

The Franciscans of Santa Elena, through their Custos and delegate, Father Capote, petitioned the King that they should be put in possession of the Convent and missions which had belonged to them when Florida was ceded to England. He set forth that their convent was still standing and they were anxious to resume their labors for the conversion of the Indians.

Governor Zepedes deemed it unadvisable to introduce the Franciscans again, until the country was settled by Spaniards and a larger population there. He averred that " the edifice which formerly served as a Convent, was completely transformed, and had lost all appearance of such a habitation for Religious: that it was too far from the city to allow the Religious to furnish promptly to the faithful any consolation; and that in the event of their return, it would be necessary to rebuild the Convent and Church, and set aside a fund to support the friars, till there were people enough to contribute the necessary alms; and that the four priests already there sufficed for the wants of the people." This reasoning prevailed, and the Franciscans could not revive their work in St. Augustine, or occupy the Convent, which all documents in this affair recognized as belonging to them.

Bishop Calderon had formerly promulgated at High mass an edict requiring Franciscan Fathers versed in various Indian languages to hold a catechism class every Sunday and holiday, to which all masters under penalty of excommunication and a fine of twenty ducats, were to send their Indian servants. Masters were forbidden to force their Indian servants to work on these days. This good Bishop founded many Churches, and supplied them with plate and vestments. He gave alms to Indian chiefs for their poor, and expended eleven thousand dollars among the faithful in this part of his diocese. In a short time, he confirmed thirteen thousand one hundred and fifty-two whites and Indians, including many adults. He declared that the Indians must be paid for all work done by them for the whites.

The history of these times is full of instances of the extreme kindness of the clergy to the Indians. It was no wonder that the chiefs should write to the King of Spain to express their satisfaction with the missionaries and the Governor, for this merciful legislation. It may be remarked that the chiefs were able to sign their own names. There were many schools among the Indians from early days.

And, "looking back," we find it said of an Indian of superior abilities: " The Spaniards who knew Muscozo said of him: ' For grace and discretion, polish of manner and high flown language, this savage chief had nothing to learn from the courts of Kings and emperors.' "

In the history of these people there are many instances of the improvement of the Indians,

CHAPTER XLIX.

ABOUT 1795, perhaps earlier, there was at St. Augustine a Royal Hospital, with its auxiliary Church of Our Lady of Guadaloupe " extra muros," the attending physicians being successively, Dr. Fitzpatrick and Dr. Travers. The chaplain was Rev. Francisco Traconis, of the strict observance, who had arrived in 1785, to teach the school. Hospitals were a very old institution in the Church. The Council of Nice, in the 4th century, ordered the building of a Hospital in every city.

When the King of Spain directed that the income of the property in Havana belonging to the Church of St. Augustine should be paid to it, Rev. Michael O'Reilly, who had become assistant to Rev. Thomas Hassett, resolved to erect a Church worthy of the ancient city. He was a saintly priest, full of zeal, energy, and devotion, and anxious to make sacrifices for God. He obtained a fine site, on the northerly side of the Plaza de Armas, and, in April, 1792, he blessed the corner-stone of a large Church. Material from the ruined shrines of Tolomata and Nuestra Señora de la Leche was employed in its construction. It was a massive, solid structure, of the Spanish type, with a moorish aspect, and was finished in August, 1797. The solemn dedication was celebrated on the Feast of the Immaculate Conception, Dec. 8, 1797. A church was built worthy of the glorious traditions of the place; but it was destroyed by fire, about a century later.

Fathers, Augustus McCaffrey, Michael Wallis, and Michael Crosby, 1791, erected and maintained chapels on St. John's and St. Mary's Rivers, all sent out by the King of Spain. Rev. Michael O'Reilly was born in Longford, 1762. He labored for his flock alone till 1802, when he was joined by another Irish priest, Rev. Michael Crosby. The Regiment of Hibernia which belonged orginally to the Irish Brigade in the French service, was stationed at St. Augustine at this period, and the names of the Irish soldiers, O'Donovan, Curtis, Delany, Barron, O'Reilly, appear through rank and file, besides many from other countries. The States on the Coast, from Connecticut to Georgia, sent Catholics by birth, or converts. Nor were Indians wanting.

After a holy, zealous life, Rev. Michael O'Reilly died at St. Augustine, in September, 1812. He left by will, a house to the Parish Church, and two houses to be used to establish a Convent of Sisters of the Visitation Order, Bishop Portier used this property to establish a Visitation Convent in Mobile, 1833.

Father O'Reilly was buried in the cemetery at Tolomato, where his box-shaped tomb may still be seen, under a moss-draped tree, the root of which seems to be embedded in the grave. Father Crosby who succeeded him in 1812, was aided by Father Gomez from 1807.

In 1791, the observatines were recalled from Florida. Fathers, Mark Barry, Michael Crosby, and the Carmelite, Michael Walles, were to reside at St. Johns and St. Mary's, (Register de San Miguel de

Panzacola) at chapels to be erected. Spanish settlers came gradually, forming a congregation for the official parish priest and his assistant. Father O'Reilly was chaplain to the troops forming the garrison of the fort.

Bishop Verot who was the first of what may be called the modern dynasty of Bishops in these regions, did much to revive the memory of the early martyrs. " Time is the only thing of which it is a virtue to be covetous," and Bishop Verot was avaricious of his time, almost to his last moment, for he died suddenly. But hard as he worked, he never got what was justly his. He put others on the track, however, though little good resulted. Ponce de Leon, after a vain search for the fountain of youth, led the way from Cuba to Florida, and Cortez, from Cuba, conquered the Atzec Kingdom of Mexico or New Spain. The old Catholic history, the names of missionaries, and martyrs, and the sites of ancient shrines were investigated and revived by Bishop Verot.

CHAPTER L.

THE present picturesque Cathedral of St. Augustine is almost a fac-simile of that built of Father O'Reilly. Two wings were erected for the colored Catholics of St. Augustine in Bishop Verot's time, and dedicated to St. Monica and St. Benedict, the Moor. These were pointed out, with some apparent pride, by the chief colored persons of the place, to the writer.

Pensacola had no resident priest when the zealous Bishop Portier accepted the mitre. But it was occasionally visited by the Bishop and priests from Mobile. The congregation soon completed a neat frame chapel. But just as the carpenters had finished it, and were putting the last touches to the roof, a hurricane entirely demolished it.

The Catholics increased rapidly after the cession. Baptisms rose from one hundred and forty-eight in 1818, to three hundred and forty-eight in 1822. Pensacola was attended from 1804 by Rev. James Coleman, Parish Priest, and chaplain of the garrison, with occasional aid from army or hospital chaplains, till Feb. 1822, when he retired with the Spanish officials.

Pensacola was once built on Santa Rosa, near the site of the present Fort Pickens, but floods and storms drove the settlement back to the Continent, 1754, and a town was begun on the unrivaled site now occupied

by Pensacola. Narvaez who discovered the bay, over
three centuries ago, called it St. Mary's Bay, but it
has long since resumed the name by which it was
known to the Indians. It is said that the name Pensacola, was that of an Indian tribe living around the
Bay which was afterwards destroyed. Mr. Fairbanks
says " it was the name of a town of Indians who had
been entirely exterminated in conflicts with neighboring tribes." A third authority derives it from a small
fortified Spanish seaport, in Aragon, on the shores of
the Mediterranean, (Campbell). On a rock, several
hundred feet high, is the fortified little seaport of
Peniscola, which looks out from its eyrie on the
Mediterranean, and its vine-clad cottages. By a
singular accident, De Luna's namesake, Peter de
Luna, of Aragon, an anti-pope, called Benedict XIII.,
reigned at Avignon in the 15th century. It is said
that he would not make the least concession for sake
of peace. This anti-Pope was deposed by the Council
of Constance, 1414, and withdrew to his humble home
in Peniscola, where he lived in retirement several
years, dying in 1424.

It cannot be doubted that the sea-ports of Spain
furnished most of the Spanish sailors to American
enterprise, in the 16th and 17th centuries. And we
can easily believe that some native of the litle town
impressed its name on the beautiful bay in fond remembrance of " Home Sweet Home."

De Luna called the Bay Santa Maria. Another
navigator, Don Andres de Pez, would add in honor
of the Mexican Viceroy, De Galva, Santa Maria de
Galva.

Don Andres took possession of the harbor, 1693.

In 1696, Don Andres d' Arriola, with three hundred

soldiers and settlers, took formal possession of the
harbor, and the surrounding country. He built "a
square fort with bastions," at Tartar point, now
Barrancas, which he named San Carlos. According
to Spanish custom, a church was built called also San
Carlos. It is said, therefore, that the first notes of a
church bell heard within the limits of the United
States, rolled over Pensacola Bay and the white hills
of Santa Rosa, 1559-1562. (Colonial Florida, R.
Campbell.)

Santa Rosa Island a narrow strip of land separated
from the mainland by three miles of water, was com-
paratively free from danger of surprise by Indians.
Fresh water was attainable, by digging wells. Wells
and water pools remain on the Orient unchanged for
generations. But in the western world we cannot expect to find a pool (Indian) as it existed three hundred
years ago. There is no trace of the wells at which the
early Pensacolians quenched their thirst. The artist,
Don Serres, was a resident of Pensacola, in 1743. The
town consisted of forty huts, thatched with palmetto
leaves, barracks for a small garrison, a stockade of
pine-posts. The sketch shows the Fort, the Church,
the Governor's house, the Commandant's house. The
church is octagon in shape. The whole sketch is a
most interesting relic. "The church" says Campbell, "which is so hallowing a feature of the Island
Town, is suggestive of the persevering devotion of
the Catholic Faith to the Spiritual welfare of her
children. In 1559, when De Luna raised his national
flag upon the shores of Santa Maria, his spiritual
Mother raised her cross beside it. With that sacred
symbol, she followed him in his explorations, through
the limitless wilderness, beginning and ending each

day with her holy rites. She returned with Arrivola, and, as he built his fort, her children, under her pious promptings, built her church. As the drum beat the *reveil* to call the soldier to the activities of life, the notes of the bell reminded him of her presence to admonish and console him. The engraving presents the next effort of her zeal. Afterwards, when the wing of the hurricane, and the wild fury of the waves, had swept away her island sanctuary, and left her children houseless on a desolate shore, she followed them to that hamlet just described, where, around a rude altar, sheltered by the frail thatch of the palmetto, they enjoyed her consoling offices. When, in 1763, their national flag fell from the staff, and her people went into voluntary exile, her cross went with them as their guide and solace. She returned with Galvez, and never for a day since, has she been without her altar and her priest on these shores to perform her rites for the living and the dead. For many years after the establishment of American rule, that altar and that priest were the only means by which the Protestant Mother, more obedient to the divine word than to sectarian prejudice, could obey the sacred mandate, " Suffer the little children to come to Me, and forbid them not!"

RICHARD L. CAMPBELL.

We knew traditionally that the old colored nurses of Pensacola were accustomed, into our own day, to bring their little ones to see the priests and get their blessing.

The hostility of the trustees to the discipline of the Church was maintained for years. The rebellion of these troublesome officials was no unusual occurrence.

It was, in Scriptural language " like a tale that is told."
Ps. 90, 9.   An act incorporating the Church at St.
Augustine was obtained from the Legislature, 1823,
and a more mischievous one in 1824. The house once
belonging to the Saintly Bishops auxiliar was given
for Protestant services, with the venerable pilgrimages
of Our Lady. The local authorities declared that all
the powers of the Spanish Kings, under the Bull of
Julius II., had passed to the United States and were
conveyed to the magnates of a single Church!

At last the priests of mercy took charge of St.
Augustine and the missions. In 1847. Rev. Benedict
Madeore obtained documents on which he applied to
Congress for a restoration, and compensation for the
Church property illegally seized and sold. Mr.
Madeore, " a venerable and truthful man," said, " that
the arbitrator asked him what the Catholics were will-
ing to pay for a favorable report, and when he de-
clared they were not able to pay anything the decision
was made against their claim."

The cavaliers in the West helped the monks, since
the main object of both was the saving of souls.
Thousands of Indians were Christianized and civilized
in these wonderful missions. A full history of Spanish
exploration, a most pious and romantic Odessy, has
yet to be written. The caravel of the Genoese Sailor,
who felt himself the agent of the merciful designs of
God to draw new nations to Christ, through His
Spouse the Church, had other caravels to follows in
its wake, with missioners and cavaliers, not unworthy
of Las Casas and the great Admiral.

Missionaries were constantly crossing the seas, not
in search of pearls or gold but to teach the peoples of
new lands the Sacred Name of Jesus, by which alone

we can be saved. They builded better than they knew, and their works remain to praise them in the gate.

Moreover, the Friars were everywhere. When persecuted in one city they fled to another. A Franciscan in brown serge and with sandalled feet, preached the Gospel to the Indians of Western New York.

A most important work, and one which made conversion more easy for the priests, was the building of high-ways, still known as "the King's roads," one was constructed in 1762, from St. Mary's River to St. Augustine, by subscription, and some names indicate that South Carolina families resided on parts of this route. East Florida was called the Tory's Paradise. To this day may be seen about St. Augustine that much use has been made of a clean bright fossil of great strength in walls and paving—coquina, of which Anastasia Island has immense quarries.

How, it may be asked, were the colonists educated? Well, in Cuba and New France, they had as good schools as existed in Europe for the people at the same period. We have seen that clergy of Colonial birth, many of whom never went to European Colleges, as Peñalvert, and some of the Bishops of St. Augustine, were as highly educated as any ecclesiastics who came hither from the universities of Europe. The priests were always ready to undertake the education of the young, when no other provision was made for them. New Orleans had as many schools of superior grade in colonial times as now. Mobile had tutors and governesses, and, a most intellectual lady, Madame Green, taught a fashionable boarding school almost to the date of the coming of the Visitation.

There were many Irish boys at Alcala de Henares who had fled to Catholic realms from persecution at home. These children were sometimes found tired and hungry on the quays of Lisbon and other ports. They were placed in Colleges and educated for the missions in Ireland, and in the world-wide Spanish dominions.

Irish priests educated in Spain for the purpose, by its Kings, from King Philip II. did much to preach and preserve the faith in the Florida peninsula, and Irish names are still plentifully scattered over the directory of the Church in the same region.

The classical school which Bishop Texado opened soon after his arrival in St. Augustine, in 1735, was a great success and a real help to the zealous Bishop. It gave him young clerics whom he trained to assist in the sanctuary, and to whom he gave the habit, probably of an acolyte.

Father Francis Texado was a native of Seville, and a member of the Recollect Reform of the Franciscan Order. He had been professor of philosophy and theology, and guardian of the Seville Convent. Religion flourished in the old city of Melendez during the ten years' incumbency of this holy man, 1735-1745. He gave confirmation to six hundred and thirty Spaniards and one hundred and thirty slaves and free negroes. Thus there were at all times, holy and zealous ecclesiastics in these beautiful regions, even when the spoiler " came and saw " but did not always " conquer." True, dreadful expedients were said to be proposed for the extermination of the Indians. The British Commander-in-Chief, it was alleged, advocated the spreading of the small-pox virus among the savages. Another, Gladwin, suggested killing them off by rum. There was, too, the *divide et impera* policy, partly done at St. Marks, Apalachicola,

When Bishop Rosati received the Bulls of Pope Leo XII. November 4, 1825, appointing him Bishop of New Orleans, he besought His Holiness to allow him to decline that dignity, but without avail. No priest in these regions willingly accepted the mitre. It had proved a crown of thorns to most of its wearers.

General Wilkinson captured Mobile with U. S. Regulars, April 15, 1813, raised the Stars and Stripes over the Fort, and transferred the district to the American Republic. In 1819, Alabama was a State.

In 1857, Bishop Verot became Vicar Apostolic of Florida, Father Aubril and Sheridan, of the Mercy Order, were then at St. Augustine. Looking back, we find a famous native of Florida, Father Francis de Florencia, born 1620, who took the habit of the Society of Jesus at the age of twenty-three, and was sent to Madrid, and then to Rome. He was afterwards appointed procurator at Seville of all the provinces of his Order in the Indies. He returned to Mexico, where he died at the age of seventy-five.

In autumn, 1858, Bishop Verot announced the jubilee and promised to use every exertion to obtain priests to visit all the stations regularly. He next visited Europe and returned towards the close of 1859, with six priests and four Christian Brothers. Meanwhile Bishop Lavialle declined the See of Savannah, and His Holiness transferred Bishop Verot to that city leaving him still Vicar Apostolic of Florida. One of his first acts was the dedication of St. Patrick's Church in Augusta, erected to a great extent by the means of Rev. Gregory Duggan, a native of Wexferd, a most zealous, laborious priest. Pastor of Augusta for seventeen years, his whole life was devoted to works of piety and charity, especially to the Orphans domesticated in his own house. So great was his activity as a missioner that his people described him by the familiar Georgia term, the wheel *horse*. After fifty years of priesthood he died the death of a Saint, Dec. 5, 1870.

CHAPTER LI.

Some tribes retained much of the Christianity preached to their ancestors; they were still clamoring for the black-robes. The Indians were said to be implacable in war. The only man in these regions who ever manipulated them so as to secure their allegiance and subjugation was Bienville. The hostile Creeks were often called Red Sticks, because their war clubs were painted red. Waldo calls the Creeks the most warlike tribe of Barbarians in the universe. The red feather was also a war emblem.

At Spring Hill College Two Military Companies were formed under the command of Major Sands and Mr. Parker, as if the students were preparing for military duty. Jan. 9, 1861, Alabama seceded from the Union. The Confederate Government was organized, and Jefferson Davis elected President. Feb. 8, April 18, great excitement was created by the news of the secession of Virginian. Many of the Jesuits accompanied the troops to various quarters, as chaplains. The Louisiana boys had to return home by Jackson, Miss. and Baton Rouge, La., as the entrance to Mobile Bay was blockaded by the Federals. This cut off all communication between the College, New Orleans and Europe. Mass wine was pressed from the scuppernong grape, and some Brothers went to Mon Louis Island, to evaporate salt from sea-water.

All the members of the College were enlisted in the 89th Regiment of Alabama, but furloughed on plea of teaching. Several boys were withdrawn lest Mobile might be attacked. Great excitement prevailed among the rest. The fortifications of Mobile were begun in May, 1862. Two thousand refugees came from New Orleans to Mobile. Over thirty asked hospitality at the College and were most kindly received. Many youths were sent by their parents to the college to prevent their being drafted into the army. Four men of war were stationed in the Bay. In September, Father Usannez started for Anderson, Georgia, where thirty thousand Federals were kept prisoners. He suffered many hardships and privations.

The Federals took posession of Mobile, April 12. A thousand soldiers occupied the Hill to protect the college. April 9, 1865, General Lee surrendered, and the war was over. In 1867, there was a terrible epidemic of yellow fever in New Orleans and Mobile.

In 1869, a fire broke out in the College, and in a few hours College and Church were a heap of ruins. The students, about ninety, were received at the College of Grand Coteau, where studies were resumed. On the Feast of the Patronage of St. Joseph, April 25, the corner-stone of a new College was blessed by Right Rev. John Quinlan, second Bishop of Mobile, assisted by Rev. C. T. O'Callaghan and many of the clergy. On the Feast of the Immaculate Conception, 1869, the new college opened with fifty-three students. In 1883, Bishop Quinlan died at New Orleans. He may be considered the second founder of the college. It was owing in great part to his kind encouragement and substantial aid, that the college was rebuilt after the disastrous fire.

CHAPTER LII.

BISHOP ENGLAND estimated Catholics in West Florida at two thousand souls. In St. Augustine, where Catholics had once numbered tens of thousands, the vampire policy, of England decimated them again and again until they were little over four hundred. There were one hundred at St. John's River, and about two hundred, mostly fishermen and Minorcans, on Amelia Island. On the death of Rev. Michael Crosbie, Bishop England sent Rev. Francis Boland, another excellent priest, to St. Augustine where he remained till 1825. Bishop Dubourg and the Bishop of Santiago de Cuba had asked Bishop England to take charge of St. Augustine.

Bishop Portier's holy ambition was gratified long before his lamented death. Mobile had a Superior College for boys and a Superior Seminary for girls. The city was within easy reach of many populous centres within his diocese and outside it. The communication between New Orleans and Mobile, two cities of Bienville, was by stage coach between Mobile and Pascagoula, and thence by the Pouchartrain Railroad to New Orleans, the home of many of the pupils of the College and the Convent.

The Perdido River was the dividing line between Florida and Alabama. St. Augustine, the county seat of St. John's Co., and the first capital of Florida, has preserved many of its ancient landmarks, and is one of the few cities in America visited for its history and antiquities rather than business or commerce. It extends nearly a mile from the Franciscan barracks, Santa Elena, to the Castle of San Marco. Fort Marion,[1] the oldest Fort in the United States. A most picturesque ruin is the ancient city gateway, which has thirty feet of the original city wall on each side. Along Orange Street is an ancient moat.

The chief Street, St. George's, is crossed by Treasury Street, which in crossing it narrows to only seven feet. Under Spanish rule it had a population of over three thousand with a garrison of two thousand five hundred. The chief industries are the manufacture of cigars with some curing of fish for the northern markets, and the raising of early fruits and vegetables. Anastasia Island lies across the Matanzas River. Fort Marion is on the River; the Sea may be seen in the distance. There are many cottages on the Island, all rented. St. Augustine is a summer, as well as a winter resort. The transient population is often quite large, many coming from the West Indies, called in early days " the American Isles."

The old Spanish Gate which used to be an illustration in every early history is still an object of interest. Most of the modern houses lie outside the gate, where the streets are much broader. The Plaza de Armas is in the business district. Opposite is the Post Office, built on the site of the Governor's palace, of ancient

[1] Fort Marion, El Castillo de San Marco, the oldest fort in the United States. A tablet over the entrance gives the years of its completion as 1756. It has the Spanish coat of arms and a Spanish inscription. The sea-wall of coquina with granite top, is a splendid promenade extending from the fort to the convent.

days. The famous Fort Marion and the Sea wall, now a graceful promenade, were one hundred years in building. Coquina, a natural concrete of shell and lime, found in large quantities on Anastasia Island, is much used in building and paving.

Among other curiosities at St. Augustine is a coarse, unlovely shed called " The Old Slave Market," a blot on a beautiful scene. A native told the writer it had never been used as such. But it seems one of the permanent monuments of the history and development of this region.

The immense hostelry, Ponce de Leon, is perhaps the largest in America. It is said to have cost over 2,000,000 dollars and is exceedingly beautiful, outside and within.

When the British came in, there were over nine thousand houses in St. Augustine. The old bell dated 1682, still rings out the morning, noon, and night *Angelus*. The gold for which the nations were always searching has been found in our day, in the fertility of the soil and the salubrity of the climate. Fruits and vegetables of all kinds abound. Sugar-cane and pine-apples begin near St. Augustine and continue to where the land stretches into the warm waters that lave Cape Sable.

Vast regions continued to open up to the zeal of the Church, and the church was mostly in advance of the civil explorers. But though the missioners struggled on, under appalling difficulties there was sometimes little return for the arduous labors of the past, and present conditions were not always flourishing or promising.

Self sacrificing priests of different orders never wholly ceased their labors on the Gulf Coast. In the long winter evenings they would talk over with their simple hosts the legends of the history of their orders, embroidered with silken threads of loving memories— memories sometimes mistaken for hopes.

The Catholic missioners were men of unblemished lives, imbued with the learning of the cloisters whence they came. With sandalled feet, and tattered garments, renouncing pomp and splendor, they moved among the aborigines as Fathers and friends, who desired only to draw them to God. And be their faults what they may, every cavalier felt himself a soldier of the cross. Treaties were held and boundaries settled. Creeks and Cherokees warred and made peace. But the holy men who came among them at the risk of their lives thought nothing was done until the children of the forest were gathered into the One Fold, of which Christ is the Shepherd, and confessed One Lord, one Faith, one Baptism, one God and Father of all." Losses in the Old World were repaired by conquests in the New.

The English Colony of North Carolina was a deadly foe at the very gates of Florida. St. Augustine was menaced by the sea which threatened to wash away its fortifications, and by Spain, which proposed to abandon it, and transfer its inhabitants to Pensacola.

A site was selected for a settlement at Pensacola, and a frame church was immediately erected. On St. Mark's day, April 25, 1693, the first mass was said, the Spaniard marching in procession, chanting the Litany of Loretto, to the spot selected, where a cross was set up. This was the beginning of Pensacola. A band of twenty Franciscan Missionaries under Father Lopez was sent to found new Christian Communities in tribes which showed a desire to embrace the Catholic Faith. Success encouraged them at first, but in October, 1696, the heathen Indians of Taroro and other towns rose up against the Spaniards, killed one of the priests, a soldier, and five Indian Converts, burned the church, and fled to the woods. The survivors being left without shelter or flock, withdrew to St. Augustine. Five Religious, however, with an experienced Superior versed in the language, were sent to reclaim the Indians, and, it is said, succeeded.

Sept. 11, 1697, Father Lopez, with five other Friars carrying supplies of all kinds, sailed from Havana. After touching at Key West, they heard the old cacique was very ill and begged for baptism, which was administered. A house and chapel were erected for the Franciscans, but no attention was paid to their instructions, while a hut used for idolatrous purposes was thronged, and the Indians even called on them to give them food and clothing for their Gods. The priests were seized, robbed of their goods, and left at Matercombe. The vessel which had brought them over, rescued them.

In 1699, the Barkentine, "Reformation," was wrecked on the Coast of Florida, and Captain Jonathan wrote a journal of their adventures till they were rescued by a Spanish party, conveyed to St. Augustine, and sent northward along the coast from one mission to another. The shipwrecked men received the kindest treatement at St. Augustine, and, in September, set out with an escort.

At Santa Cruz, three leagues from St. Augustine, they found a large chapel with three bells, and a Franciscan in charge. The Indians were as constant to their devotions at all times and seasons as the

Spaniards. The party was lodged in a large warehouse, used as a general place of meeting. San Juan, on an island, thirteen leagues farther on, had its chapel and priests. At St. Mary's they found a Franciscan with his church, and a school of Indian boys. Near it was another mission, St. Philip, and, finally, St. Catherine's Island—a place called Santa Catalina, where there hath been a great settlement of Indians, for the land hath been cleared for planting for some miles distant." In fact, it was one of the old mission stations, where Church and Convent had been destroyed by the Carolina Indians. Yet Dickinson's narrative shows that these mission stations not only civilized the Indians, and reformed their savage character, but were a life saving organization along the coast, where the ship-wrecked found Christians welcome and aid. Yet the neighboring English colonies destroyed them.

The war of the Spanish succession gave South Carolina a pretext for hostility against its Catholic neighbor. Florida, Governor Moore was eager for the plunder of a Spanish town and for Indian Converts to enslave. The Apalache Indians had been forced to labor on the fortifications and sea wall. These saved Florida, for though the English from North Carolina, in 1702, took and fired the city, the fort resisted their efforts.

Governor Moore [1] instigated the Apalachicolas to

[1] Some of the Indians Moore employed in cultivating his own fields; others he sold for his pecuniary profit. Indian towns were destroyed, priests killed, and hundreds of converts hurried off as slaves to the West Indies. The war which the savage tyrant, Moore, made on the Christians of Florida, was really a religious war of the English on the Catholics. It extended also to Cuba, "the most beautiful land that human eyes ever beheld" said Columbus.

invade the Apalache country, where, under the guise of friendship, they burned the church, but the Catholic Indians saved vestments and pictures. A Spanish force pursuing the enemy was defeated and the commander slain. Moore fitted out an expedition, and coming in his vessels by sea spread devastation along the coast. The Christian Indians had in consequence of previous hostilities, retired to St. Mark's Island, where they formed three towns. These were burned, with their churches and Convents. Three Franciscans fell into the hands of the enemy. The Indian Converts fled to St. Augustine. Moore had effected a union with Colonel Daniel to capture the fort.

But the brave Governor, Zuñiga, having received a small re-inforcement, resisted all the efforts of the English. Some Spanish ships appeared in the harbor, and Moore raised the siege which had lasted over fifty days. Finding escape impossible by sea, he set fire to his ship, he retreated overland.

Before withdrawing, he committed the barbarity of burning the town. The Parish Church, the Church and Convent of the Franciscans perished, and plate to the value of a thousand dollars was carried off by Moore. " To show what friends some of them were —to learning and books," writes Rev. Edward Marsden,[1] a Protestant Clergyman, " when they were at St. Augustine they burned a library of books worth six hundred pounds, including a collection of the Greek and Latin Fathers. The Holy Bible itself did not escape, because it was in Latin. This outrage was done as soon as they arrived, by Colonel Daniel, a furious freebooter.

This was the fine Library in the Franciscan Convent

[1] Documentary History of the P. E. Church.

at St. Augustine. The Guardian of the Convent,
Father Martin de Aleano went to Spain to lay these
outrages before the king, who regarded the wanton
destruction of a defenceless town as a mark English
provincial hatred. The Spanish monarch ordered the
rebuilding of the Church and Convent, for which
funds were sent from Spain.

Governor Moore sought to carry off the Indian Converts of the Spanish priests to sell them as slaves, in
which he was, unfortunately, successful. Ruiz, Commander of the Spanish Garrison, twice repulsed the
assailants, but his ammunition failing, most of his
force were killed or taken prisoners. Many prisoners
were tied to stakes, tortured, and burned to death.
Father Miranda appealed to Moore to prevent such
horrible cruelties, but to no purpose.

Father Parga who had given absolution to the Indians before the skirmish, was burned at the stake,
beheaded, and his leg hacked off. Mexia, the brave
soldier, was held for ransom, Father Miranda and
others also, but the Spanish officers could not pay, and
all were burned at the stake. They bore their agonies
with heroic fortitude, praising and blessing God that
they had the honor to die for the Holy Name of Jesus.

Moore finally retired, carrying a thousand Indians
to sell as slaves. Several missionaries went through
the ruined towns. Scenes of indescribable horror met
their gaze everywhere. Parallel scenes might be
quoted of the priests massacred in the Huron Country.
But the butcheries perpetrated in Florida were enacted
before the eyes, and by the orders of a Christian
Governor of a Christian State.

CHAPTER LIII.

THE famous John Wesley desired to convert the Indians, but had small success in this direction, 1736. Charles Wesley went out as Secretary to Governor Oglethorpe. The more eloquent Whitfield devoted himself to establishing an Orphan House, in a place where children without means were few. He afterwards tried to turn this institution into a college. Wesley's reception in Savannah was not favorable, 1736. On his return to England he wrote: "I who went to America to convert others, had never been myself converted." Whitfield's design of establishing an Orphanage on lands obtained from trustees for that purpose, succeeded partially, for a while, but was abandoned after his death. George Whitfield is described as the founder of Calvinistic Methodists. None of these achieved any success in the work of Christianizing the Indian. They [1] failed in the South as a greater man failed in the North: George Berkley, afterwards Protestant Bishop of Cloyne in Ireland, who spent his time mostly in Rhode Island. None of them entered the Floridian territory.

Frobisher made three voyages to the New World,

[1] Of John and Charles Wesley, celebrated Methodists, Mr. Pickett says: History of Alabama, Vol. I. p. 311, "Among the colonists, with whom they resided many years, they became not only unpopular, but very obnoxious."

1576-1579, but his few discoveries were unimportant. The fictitious gold with which he loaded his vessels on two return voyages, proved to be worthless stones. The English instead of tilling the land, hunted for gold, and there was no English town on the American Continent at the close of the sixteenth century and but two of Spanish origin, St. Augustine and Santa Fe, within the present boundaries of the United States.

Sir Francis Drake, the first Englishman who circumnavigated the globe, or, as he said, "ploughed a furrow around the globe," was a daring pirate. He was also the first Englishman to see the Pacific, discovered by Balboa fifty years before. He pillaged the Spanish settlements in Chili and Peru and on the Spanish Main.[1] Meanwhile the Church was flourishing in many parts colonized by Spaniards and French, and, as time went on, the Catholic clergy even penetrated New England, although one of the blue laws ordained that "No priest shall abide in this dominion; he shall be banished, and suffer death on his return. Priests may be seized by any one, without a warrant."

Spain held Florida by right of conquest. The English divided it into East and West. Georgia the last of the thirteen States was settled by the English, in 1733. The people of Georgia and the Carolinas were, as we have seen, cruel enemies of the Catholics of St. Augustine. The Indian missions were destroyed by the English and their dusky allies, and it was long before Catholic priests and Religious again wended their way leading processions to the shrines and pilgrimages of the little city.

[1] The massacre of Father Azevedo and his seventy companions is given in Chapter 3rd of the second volume of F. Crétineau Joly—a scene of fiendish cruelty.

History, tradition, and even fiction, are eloquent of the terrors of the English pirates who scoured the Spanish main and descended on every place where booty was to be got, or Christian Congregations scattered. They sacked the most opulent towns and seized enormous treasures.

In 1589, to protect his treasure galleons from those dreaded "wolves of the sea," Drake and Hawkins, "who held the power and glory of Spain so cheap," Philip II. ordered two strong fortresses to be built to defend the Harbor of Havana, which are standing to-day. When the war broke out, Drake became more daring than ever. He ran unexpectedly into Spanish ports plundered the vessels, set fire to the shipping, and sailed off again. This he facetiously called: "Singing the Spanish King's beard. "He was for-ever trying to rob Spanish Galleons, and murder Catholics, Indian and Spanish. Among the treasures this freebooter seized was the great golden crucifix studded with emeralds as large as pigeon's eggs. On Drake's arrival in England, he gave a banquet at Plymouth, on board his vessel, the Pelican, to no less a personage than the famous or infamous Queen Elizabeth.[1] The food was served in silver dishes, the wine in golden goblets, all the fruit of plunder. The queen conferred on this ferocious pirate the honor of Knighthood. He had precious metals unlimited, on a land expedition he had seized a convoy of mules laden with gold and silver, and declared on his return to England that he had obtained his treasures by barter

---

[1] The depravity of public sentiment was such that the buccaneers boasted of their crimes. Says Bancroft: "when the sovereign of England, Queen Elizabeth, shared in its hazards, its profits, and its crimes, she became at once a smuggler and a slave merchant."

22

with the natives. Sir Francis Drake, on May 8, 1585, with a large fleet after plundering the Spanish Colonies in the West Indies sailed for the feeble settlements of Florida. . . . . The buccaneers plundered Fort St. John of fourteen pieces of brass cannon and two thousand pounds sterling. (Williams, Florida.)

This daring freebooter was not unlike the Queen who was, in some sense, in partnership with him, and always ready to share his ill-gotten goods. When the minister of the Pelican, in a moment of danger as the ship ran aground, bade the sailors think of their sins and their immortal souls, instead of urging them to busy themselves about the ship, the chaplain was summoned before Drake who was enthroned on a sea-chest. Drake judged him guilty of cowardice, and sentenced him to be put in irons. He further declared the poor chaplain excommunicated, cut off from the Church of God, and given over to the devil. While delivering these awful judgments Drake " sat aloft in awful state," and trumpets were sounded. He executed a deserter on board his pirate ship. He slept with sentries at his door. The Pelican which had seen such riotous times, and seized so many unoffending galleons was destined to become a Protestant relic, in which state it is preserved to-day in the University of Oxford, England. After being preserved for many years, it fell asunder, and parts of it were made into the chair preserved at Oxford. This cruel pirate attempted to " singe the Spanish King's head," once too often. He perished while on his way to attack the Spanish galleons at the West Indies. Others say he died of chagrin, 1596, for having failed in an attack on Panama.

CHAPTER LIV.

EARLY in the eighteenth century, Dr. John Chastang, lived on the Bluff named for him and there grew up about him the colored Creole Settlement which to this day represents his family.

Chastang is situated on the Mobile River, about fourteen miles above St. Philip, on the road to St. Stephen's, once the Spanish Capital of Alabama. It has an ancient Spanish cemetery, now in ruins.

At the close of the 18th century, three brothers from France cast their " tents upon a bluff which has since borne their name, Chastang's Bluff. A large tract was granted them by the Spanish Government, on part of which now stand St. Peter's Church and cemetery. The venerable Captain, Owen Finegan, who still walks among us though in the nineties, did much towards the building and decoration of this Church.

Jean, or Dr. Chastang, married a slave; the other brothers chose white wives, all were blessed with children. The descendants of Dr. Chastang are colored Creoles now in the fourth generation. The descendants of the other two brothers removed to different parts of the state and to other States, and sad to relate, many of them have lost the faith. There are more than two hundred Catholics at the Bluff, all more or less related. Recently on a visit of the Bishop, Right Rev. Dr. Allen, twenty-six made their First Communion and forty-six received the Sacrament of Confirmation, among whom was a woman of ninety.

There is a school attached to the Chastang Settlement (Mobile Co.) in charge of a Lay teacher. French is still spoken by the Creole Chastangs, but with a peculiar patois. The colony dates back to Dr. Chastang and his servants on the Bluff nearby. Before the war, the Afro-Latin Creoles were highly respectable freemen, often owning slaves, as did the rich negroes themselves, and, socially, keeping aloof from the negro population. They are much the same now, save that they cannot have slaves. The official Registers distinguish three classes: White, Creole, and negroes. Bishop Peñalvert entered the Creole class as Morenos or Browns.

Like its larger neighbor, New Orleans, Mobile has many races, but on a smaller scale. The sociability and hospitality of both cities are the same. French, Spanish, and Irish, with small contributions from other nations, have been the ancestors of the Mobilians of to-day, and the English language is heard in the ancient streets and flowery suburbs. The nomenclature of the streets throws light on the genealogy: Espejo, Esclaua, St. Emmanuel.—Conti, Dauphine, St. Louis, etc. The city tracts are mostly Spanish grants. Since the suppression of slavery there has been room for the working man in the ancient city. More than once we heard it said by those who prospered within our gates: " There is no better place in America for the industrious poor man than Mobile." Either in our streets or parks there is no memento of the Indian once so populous in Mobile. We have not a Chickasalogue Street or a Chocktaw Street. Naboth had a vineyard which the King coveted, and being the stronger he possesses it.   No doubt the Indians wept over their first home: "By the rivers of Babylon there we sat, and wept when we remembered Sion." And though a home was found for our expatriated Indians and some indemnification made them, they may not yet have learned to sing the song of the Lord in a strange land.   "If I forget thee, O Jerusalem, let my right hand forget its cunning." Many seem to have forgotten the true Jerusalem.   And now we can but pray and hope that they may find their real friend in the Black robe, and all the blessings of which he was the instrument to them, in the wilds to which their civilized brethren have banished them.

Many of the numerous settlers in Mobile dating back to Spanish times, and much of the immigration consequent on the religious wars in Ireland in Cromwell's revolutions or rather persecutions, and the English Revolution, 1688, made its way across the Atlantic, not a few settling in Alabama.

Many of the Acadians settled in the Attakapas country about the Teche, and some in Mount Vernon, Alabama.   Their sad story is immortalized in Evangeline.   The French language has remained the dominant tongue of those people.   There are many of Irish descent among them who do not speak or write English.   According to their Parish Register at St. Martinsville, their priests have been French, Spanish, Irish, Italian, and most of them labored in Mobile. Fort St. Stephen called after Governor Miro (Esteban) had a church, a priest, soldiers, settlers, traders. In this Fort, McClary first hoisted the American Flag, in 1799.

The Spaniards built a Church wherever they settled a colony.   Fathers, McKenna, Savage, Lamport, and

White, were among the first sent thither by the King
of Spain. These gentlemen were conversant with
several languages, and therefore able to exercise the
ministry in the languages spoken in their cosmopolitan
flocks.

.   .   .   .   .

In the pre-historic days of what is said to have been
the cemetery for nearly two hundred years, the
aborigines annually visited the spot. It was a favorite
camping place for the Indian tribes who peopled the
gulf coast contiguous. They came at intervals to
trade. Huge quantities of oyster shells are still found
a few inches below the surface. Ridges of shell de-
posits are covered with earth and overgrown with the
dank vegetation of this semi-tropical region.

The old Spanish method of burial was to lay a single
course of brick on the top of the ground rest the
coffin upon this, and brick in: Sometimes an arch
of brick was thrown over the casket. Again the brick
walls were carried up to a height above the level of
the coffin, and a slab of stone or marble laid on
the top.

A few old tombs were in fairly good preservation
and the inscriptions—some in Spanish,—could be
readily deciphered. It is over thirty years since we
first saw this venerable Campo Santo. Much of the
brick work was in good preservation. We were told
that when the tombs were built there was no brick
made in the neighborhood. All had to be imported
from Spain or the Islands: also that tombs had often
been rifled for the brick, when wanted for building.
The trees were then very beautiful, and like those
of the celebrated cemetery, BONAVENTURE, near
Savannah, heavily draped with silky moss.

Within a few years, a handsome new graveyard has been laid out near the old one, which is in a state of dilapidation. Many of the bodies of the military have been removed to the National Cemetery.

Tartar Point is now the Site of the Navy Yard. It was formerly called *Punta la Asta Bandera*—the Point of the Flagstaff. According to a treaty between the Creeks and the Seminoles,[1] represented by Mc-Gillinay, and Spain by Governor Miro, assisted by Count Arthur O'Neil, governor of West Florida, and Don Martin Navarro, Intendant General of Florida, entered into June 1, at Pensacola. The relations created by that treaty seem to have been observed up to the last day of Spanish rule in Florida.[1]

Anent the ancient cemetery, the following òdd incident seems like a step from the sublime to the ridiculous. A good industrious milliner of Pensacola died —a loss to her thrifty husband, financially, especially. He spoke of enlivening the gloomy Campo Santo by an elaborate monument to her cherished memory. Her trade was indicated by a very large board, oblong, painted in bright colors, and informing the public of her name and occupation. With some help, he removed this sign-board from its hinges, and tearfully carried it to the newly made grave, where he lovingly placed it at the head of her coffin. We saw him in the cemetery, apparently admiring the effect, though weeping copiously.

Visitors may still see the oak-shaded resting-place of many generations of Pensacolians, and, till recently,

[1] The Seminoles are seen at Miami and other trading parts. They are straight, keen-eyed. The women and children have not degenerated. They number about four hundred. Florida has about one thousand miles of sea-coast.

over numerous graves: " Died of yellow fever." The crumbling tombs, the mouldering head-stones, the ivy-wreathed graves of hundreds who have contributed to the up-building of the deep-water city of the Gulf, once called Santa Maria, are still to be seen.

CHAPTER LV.

GREAT were the sufferings of the Bishops at various epochs from the Trustees. Every pastor the Bishop proposed was usually rejected. It was six years before Bishop Portier could place in the desolated church of St. Augustine, Rev. Fathers Hackett and Rampon, who were finally received as its pastors. When the civil war broke out, it soon devastated the dioceses of the South. Bishop Quinlan's heart was almost broken by the sufferings of his people. The churches of Pensacola and Warrington were burned, and several congregations were scattered.

The Federal authorities were always friendly to the priests. Some, military men and civilians were old students of the Jesuits. General Banks sent a safe conduct to college and Convent, (Grand Coteau), and threatened with court martial any one who would interfere with their persons or property. Even the terrible General Butler gave leave repeatedly to export from New Orleans anything, not contraband, for the use of the college. At the close of the war, none were left in the country but women, children, old men and negroes.

The college which Father Portier opened in the old Ursuline Convent, New Orleans, soon had two hundred students. But when he became Bishop of Mobile, for lack of his powerful impulse and inspiring presence, the new college dwindled away, and soon ceased to be.   Before long many students followed him to Mobile and peopled Spring Hill College.

When a Bishop was placed in Florida, in our time, the Catholic property had been almost all swept away from the Church.   The " Casa Episcopal " the house and grounds owned by the auxiliar Bishops, had been given to the Episcopalians, and the Convent of the Franciscans which gave missionaries to the Indian tribes from Albemarle Sound to Pensacola, had become the barracks.   In 1857, Bishop Verot, became Vicar apostolic of Florida, and he announced the jubilee in 1858.   War and disease prevailed.   He endeavored to obtain Sisters of Mercy, and got a small colony from Providence, R. I. in the diocese of Hartford. They opened an Academy and instruction classes, April 1, 1859.   He had applied for Sisters immediately after his consecration, and Mother Warde, then in Providence, gave the zealous prelate Sister Liguori Major, a convert, and three companions.   These were re-inforced by two more whom the good Mother, hearing that their labors were ever on the increase, kindly sent to their aid.   They were cordially welcomed in the ancient city, and were well pleased with the courteous people of that land of Mañana, (to-morrow) where it seems to be always evening.   The soft speech and gentle apathy of the citizens contrasted with the sharp tones and stirring ways of their New England home.

Their first Convent was a small house on George's street, opposite the ancient Cathedral.   In August, 1860, the foundations of a new Convent were laid. In its construction, coquina was much used—a shell conglomerate formed in the waters about the city, and accumulated in the shell heaps or mounds so common throughout Florida.

The schools of the Sisters of Mercy were soon full, children came from the interior to be prepared for the sacraments. Special attention was given to the colored population, to whom the Bishop was greatly devoted. He valued much the zeal of the Sisters in instructing them. They soon learned to sing several hymns, and the Bishop delighted to hear them execute their favorite, with more vigor than beauty, in staccato movement :

> " I am a little Catholic,
> And Christian is my name,
> And I believe in the Holy Church
> In every age the same ! "

The Jesuit, Father Florencia, a native of St. Augustine born in 1720, is credited with writing " many works of renown," among them a History of New Spain. He died in Mexico, aged seventy-five years.

During the episcopate of Bishop Moore, the ancient Cathedral of St. Augustine was burned. He traveled over a great part of Europe and America soliciting funds for the restoration of that venerable edifice, which he rebuilt.

Bishop Verot after laboring incessantly for the good of religion, died suddenly, July 16, 1876. He was buried in the old Tolemato cemetery. The old cemeteries are not much used now. A new cemetery has been opened about two miles from the Cathedral. To this the remains of Bishop Verot will be removed with those of the late Bishop Moore. At San Lorenzo cemetery, St. Augustine, will soon be erected a mortuary chapel as a resting place for the departed clergy of the Diocese. It will also be a memorial to the late Bishop Moore. It will cost about fifteen thousand dollars.

A new Catholic Colony was founded at the town of San Antonio, under the presidency of Col. Edmund, Danne, in Hernando, now Pasco County. The Benedictines have been sent to this colony and placed in charge of the church and schools established in it. Colored congregations, churches, and societies, have greatly increased in Florida.

Bishop Verot made a brave struggle to recover the Church properties in the hands of the Federal Government, but without success. It has been said that " the United States Government is the richest government in the world, but sometimes the slowest to pay." But this is not always so.

At Chattanooga, the Catholics for some years labored to erect the church of SS. Peter and Paul, in fine Tennessee marble, much of the ornamental work being highly polished. When the work was about half done, the engineer officers of the U. S. army, demolished the Church, using the material to erect Fort Jones, for culverts, and even for macadamizing. A claim was made on the government. The authorities offered to return the broken and defaced stone. But when the matter came before Congress, a Committee reported that the church was entitled to $18,729.90 for the injury it had sustained.

Let us hope that justice may yet be done the rifled church of Florida.

CHAPTER LVI.

ALABAMA has its deserted villages. The ruins of old St. Stephen's once a formidable rival of Mobile, lie in a dense forest on the dark Tombigbee. It was once a city of several thousand souls. It had a newspaper called the *Halcyon*. It was settled by the French between 1697 and 1763, and was held by the Spaniards from 1763 to 1799. It became an important place, superior to Mobile. It had hotels, a bank, stores. Steamboats were built and launched there.

Now the bark of the squirrel, the hoot of the owl, the gobble of the wild turkey, are heard in its ruins. Fort St. Stephen, the highest point near the extinct capital, gives a magnificent view of Clarke Co., just across the river. The gateways of the fort are clearly marked. It was a haven of refuge from the Indians. Here white men braved the privations of the pioneers and smoked the calumet with Pushmataha, the friendly Indian chief who was wont to say: " Pushmataha love white man—the great Spirit take care of him."

The old earth-works of the fort remain. They would long since have been leveled with the earth but for the immense trees which have grown on them and held them together.

Tradition says that the original inhabitants utterly refused to allow the Name of God to be preached among them. A stranger who proposed it was driven from the town and told he would be decorated with tar and feathers if he again appeared within its inhospitable precincts. With uplifted hands, he prophesied that the day would come when only bats and owls would dwell there.

It is surely a bad thing to be " without God in the world."

Another dead town is Blakely, on the eastern shore of the bay. Little is to be seen on the site of this former rival of Mobile, but an avenue of live oaks and a few heaps of brick. The Confederate earth-works remaining are deeply ditched and covered with a dense pine forest. The old grave-yard has many head-stones, some erect, many prostrate.

The Blakely people seem to have been Christians. The following lines are on Dr. Stoddard's head-stone:

> " But all that the blast of destruction can blight,
>   And all that can fade in the tomb,
>   Shall spring from the grave of a brother all bright
>   In beauty immortal to bloom."

On Mrs. Stoddard's gravestone:

> " Lavinia's spirit firm and free,
>   Triumphant o'er the last dismay
>   Bright in its own eternity
>   Has passed away."

There is no record of any missionary residing in those vanished towns, or even visiting them.

High up on the Alabama, near Selma, is the beautiful ruin of Cahaba, once the capital of Alabama, now a deserted village. One must tread the tangled weed and the riotous vine, where the myrtle, the briar, and the thistle thrive, and bend beneath the cedar and the walnut to reach the ruins of what were once homes of wealth and refinement.

Among the green fields, and brown stubble, and tangled roots, and open prairie, and stretches of jungle, that diversify the site of this once prosperous city, there is no trace of bell or book or cross or sanctuary. No doubt, there were sometimes Catholics in its umbrageous streets who longed for the graces and blessings which only the true Church can give. No doubt, dying men and women coveted the Viaticum, and the last anointing. And we may well imagine the zealous priests of the neighboring Mobile, following to the couch the faithful servant who remembered the divine words: "Is any one sick among you. Let him bring in the priests of the church," to the bedside of the dying. Or the Catholic, Indian or European, longing to be shrived of his sins, and eager to feed on the bread of the strong. Such a Catholic could easily leave for a while the godless place and satisfy the wants of his conscience in the neighboring Catholic city of Mobile.

A school was established at St. Stephen's in 1811, the teachers being brought from New Orleans. They did not, however, remain long. A member of the Medici family is reported to have said, somewhat flippantly: "A state cannot be governed by Pater Nosters." If, by Pater Nosters, he meant Religion, we would vary the dictum: "A state would be badly governed without them."

Meanwhile, the Church progressed at Mobile though at one time, besides the Bishop and the Vicar-General, there was only one other priest in Mobile. The Vicar-General at that time was Father Chalon, nephew to Bishop Portier. The domestic concerns were managed chiefly by old Creole servants (slaves) who also nursed the children. These were much beloved in the families they served. An epitaph in Girod St. Cemetery, New Orleans, reads:

" Mammy, aged eighty-four; a faithful servant. She lived and died a Christian." Such servants made life easy for house-keepers everywhere.

One of the best priests that ever labored in Mobile and the founder of many works of benevolence there, was the Very Rev. James McGarahan, whose death in 1869 was hastened, if not caused, by the overthrow of The Confederacy.

CHAPTER LVII.

THE Ursuline ladies of New Orleans frequently came in contact with governors, magistrates, and other distinguished personages. And as the tone of the correspondence is the same now as it was in the beginning. We will give some specimens.

Extract from an address delivered by the French prefect, Laussat, when sent, in 1803, to take possession of Louisiana, to the Ursuline nuns:

"MESDAMES:—The French Government, having been informed of the need which the Colony has of you, the good which results from your labors, and the public esteem which you so justly enjoy, has decreed that you be maintained in the enjoyment of all your rights and privileges; and you may rely, MESDAMES, that I will protect you to the utmost of my power. You will assist the government in laboring for the preservation of morals, and the government will uphold you."

To the Sister Therese de St. Xavier Farjon, Superioress, and to the nuns of the Order of St. Ursula, at New Orleans, 1804:

"I have received, Holy Sisters, the letter you have written, wherein you express anxiety for the property invested in your Institution by the former government of Louisiana. The principles of the Constitution and

23

Government of the United States are a sure guarantee that it will be preserved to you, sacred and inviolate, and that your institution will be permitted to govern itself according to its own voluntary rules, without any interference from the civil authority.

Whatever diversity of shade may appear in the religious opinions of our fellow citizens, the charitable objects of your Institution cannot be indifferent to any; and its furtherance of the wholesome purposes of society, by training up its younger members in the way they should go, cannot fail to ensure it the patronage of the government it is under. Be assured it will meet with all the protection my office can give it.

I salute you, Holy Sisters, with friendship and respect.

THOMAS JEFFERSON.
Washington, May 15, 1804.

Washington, April 24, 1809.

Madame: I have received your letter of the 11th of March with the sentiments due for the respect and confidence which it expresses on the part of the pious Institution which you superintend.

In a country where all rights, religious as well as civil, are protected by the laws, and guaranteed by an enlightened public opinion, the best securities exist for the tranquility and esteem of those whose labors are devoted to the conscientious pursuit of laudable objects.

Therefore it only remains to assure you that however inferior to my predecessor in other merits, my dispositions are equally friendly to the task of training youth in the paths of virtue and useful knowledge, and that, with my thanks for the prayers for which I am indebted to the piety of your religious community, I offer mine for the happiness of the members, composing it.

JAMES MADISON.

MUCH RESPECTED LADIES:—

Your memorial to the Congress of the United States, having been referred to a select Committee, of which I had the honor to be chairman, I paid to it all the attention which it merited; and I have much pleasure in informing you that a law has been passed in compliance with your wishes, of which I enclose a copy to your friend, Governor Clairborne.

I sincerely hope that this change may promote the interest of that Seminary over which you, with so much propriety, preside; and that, while you continue to engraft on the youthful mind the principles of virtue, industry, and useful knowledge, you may receive not only the fostering care of your country, but the protection of that Divinity who is the author of all good.

Accept the assurance of my high respect and best wishes,

J. DAWSON.

Extract from Hon. H. M. Brackenridge's letter to PRESIDENT MONROE:

" The Convent in New Orleans is highly interesting to the old inhabitants of Louisiana, as the school where all the young ladies of the best families are educated; and I most confidently assert that it is a most valuable Institution.   The importance of the Institution in this respect, when we take into consid-

eration the habits and manners of the people of that
country, is much greater than might at first be supposed. All who are acquainted with the Ladies of
Louisiana, educated in this Seminary, speak in its
praise; and I assure you, Sir, that a deep interest is
felt in that country—among a class of people the least
presuming and inobtrusive—in whatever concern this
Alma Mater; and any indulgence which can be granted
to them, consistently with national interests, will be
received with a gratitude as sincere as it will be general.

I am, with high respect,
Your most obedient servant
H. M. BRACKENRIDGE.

The first American Governor, Clairborne, treated
the Ursuline Religious with perfect deference. A com-
edy being put on the stage in which the religious state
was held up to ridicule, the Lady Abbess invoked the
interference of his Excellency. A courteous letter in
which the Governor expresses great regret that the
feelings of these ladies should have been wounded,
concludes thus:

"The sacred objects of your Order, the amiable
characters which compose it, and the usefulness of
their temporal cares, cannot fail to commend the respect and confidence of the good and virtuous. I pray
you, Holy Sisters to receive the assurances of my
great respect and sincere friendship,
WILLIAM CLAIBORNE.

After the battle of New Orleans the Ursulines
turned their schools into infirmaries for the sick and
wounded soldiers, upon whom they lavished every

care. And when all was over, the general did not omit to pay his respects to the Ursuline Ladies, receive their congratulations, and thank them for their prayers and vows on his behalf. He also testified his high appreciation of the charity and devotedness with which they tended the sick and wounded. Andrew Jackson was the last great warrior who passed into the cloisters of the old Convent on Chartres-Street. Later, in 1828, he revisited his old friends. He is the only President of the United States who ever stood within the precincts of the new Convent.

Over two hundred Sisters have taught in this Institution since its commencement. They were from France, Spain, Ireland, Canada, and the United States. They labored to enrich the minds of their pupils with useful knowledge, and adorn their hearts with every virtue since the opening of this Institution, Aug. 7, 1727, and the work still goes on with fidelity and enthusiasm. Under such teaching and with such example, woman must become what she ought to be:— *the great moral force of society, the foundation upon which is built up the true greatness of states.* And so, our Religious have gone on, over two centuries, a blessing and a bulwark to the Church of God in this fair Southern City. And the Visitanidines, in the older, but, for many years, less important city of Mobile, have emulated the virtues of the New Orleans Ursulines, and, like them, founded an educational establishment which is the pride of Alabama, as the older establishment is the pride of Louisiana.

CHAPTER LVIII.

In 1833, Bishop Portier's flock was estimated at eight thousand souls in a population of three hundred and fifty thousand. In 1835, the Bishop convoked his clergy at Spring Hill College, in a diocesan synod, and many useful regulations were made. In 1842, the jubilee was proclaimed (granted by the Pope) and this became an occasion of missions and retreats throughout the diocese.

Priests came slowly to the Southern regions at first. In 1834, the New Orleans diocese contained twenty-two priests, but seven of the Parishes (counties) were vacant. A new re-inforcement, however, soon arrived, and all vacancies were filled. Now and then, there were trifling difficulties among some of the clergy. But the annalist to whom we are so much indebted writes: " I have never found in any letter, record, or manuscript, a word of censure on the conduct of Jesuits or Franciscans or other clergy."

The Territory of Orleans was formed in 1804, and the Territory of Louisiana, in 1805. Louisiana was admitted to the Union in 1812. The first church in New Orleans—a mere hovel—was dedicated to St. Ignatius, and was attended by the Capuchin, Father Anthony.

Bishop Dubourg was accompanied by Rev. Mr. Auduze when he was summoned, as we have said in a previous chapter, to give the last rites of the church to the granddaughter of the Duke of Orleans, Madame de Mezières at Natchitoches. He visited many of the country parishes of Louisiana, while on this mission of mercy. The church at Natchitoches had been destroyed by fire three years before; the people had not had any instruction for fifteen years. In early days, when the Venerable Father Margil was laboring among his Indians at Adayes, he heard of the spiritual destitution of the French at Natchitoches. The Venerable Father traveled fifty miles on foot to say mass for the French, preach to them, hear their confessions, and enable them to receive Holy Communion.

After the mission of Bishop Dubourg to Natchitoches, just before his lamented resignation of the See of New Orleans, the town of Natchitoches was put on a proper Catholic footing, and has so remained. It may be added that Natchitoches was established as a French post, 1717[1], and a priest stationed there, and has been an episcopal See since 1853.

---

[1] In 1776, Anthanase de Mezières was Lieutenant Governor of this post of Natchitoches.

There are a good many mulattoes by the name of de Mezieres living near Campti, in this part of Natchitoches. They are very light, almost white, and very respectable people, who claim to have descended from Philippe Egalité.[1]

---

[1] Letter from Natchitoches, March 12, 1908.

CHAPTER LIX.

Among the dear Ursulines who were specially beloved was Mother Seraphine Ray, who governed that holy community for nearly thirty years, and gained the love of all by her heroic charity. Bishop Dubourg presided at the profession of Sister Marie Tronard, June 21, 1825, the first to make her vows in the present Convent. This lady was sent, in 1851, to found the Ursuline Convent of San Antonio, Texas.

Bishop Portier often presided at elections and other ceremonies among the Ursulines. She was elected Superioress, Jan. 16, 1834. " It appears," says my informant, " that his Lordship was as glad as the community of the choice, for it is said that he confirmed the election with a voice of thunder—une voix de tounère!" We may mention here two of the Ursulines of Charleston, Mass., who, being left without a roof to shelter them by the burning of their Convent, on Monday night, August 11, 1834. Two Sisters made homeless accepted good Mother Seraphine's invitation to make the New Orleans' Ursuline Convent their home : one was Sister Mary Clare de Costa, the venerated aunt of the late Rev. Dr. de Costa, who attributed to her prayers his conversion to the true Faith. He was received into the Catholic Church, Dec. 3, 1899. Shortly before his holy death, he visited the spot where her remains repose, in the Convent cemetery, to pray beside her grave.

Mother Seraphine also received Mother Augustine, (Frances O'Keeffe) one of the most cultured women of her day. She became the worthy successor of the beloved Mother, Seraphine Ray, who was elected to the office of Superior ten times. Mother Augustine was one of the most accomplished superiors of her time. The writer had the pleasure of knowing her, and, on bidding her "good-by," left her poring over Rochbacher's Church history, preparing for her class. She wrote an account of the burning of the Convent at Charleston, Mass. She died on All Saints' Day, 1888, the anniversary of her profession at the Convent, Charleston, Mass., and died as she lived in faith, hope, and charity, revered and beloved by her dear Sisters. Like her beloved predecessor, Mother O'Keeffe was noted for her charity, within her Convent and outside of it. She was long remembered with reverent affection by her Sisters, her pupils, and the various objects of her charity in New Orleans.

CHAPTER LX.

DE LUNA, one of the explorers, who traveled most extensively over Alabama, and even as far as Tennessee, besides parts of Florida beyond the Bay of Pensacola, had the misfortune to have on his ship perpetual dissension, and the discontented were unhappily, in the majority. . . . In Holy Week, 1561, a reconciliation was effected by two monks so creditable to all concerned. . . . that its insertion here will be forgiven.

Both Brothers Salaçar and Annunciation had labored incessantly, in the spirit of their Divine Master to secure peace, with but small result. At last, on Palm Sunday, Brother Annunciation, having confessed himself and the general, the camp-master, and the army, being assembled to celebrate the solemnity of so great a Day, Father Annunciation began to say mass.

Having reached that place in the service where he was about to consume the most Blessed Sacrament, he turned toward the people, with the Holy Host in his hands, holding it upright above the postess. All were surprised at the novelty, waiting for what was to follow. The Blessed Father paused a little, while, gazing devoutly at his God, his eyes shedding copious tears. In the midst of his tears, he lifted up his voice with the authority which God knows how to grant to him who serves Him, and called, by His own name, the governor who was kneeling, in the place to which his rank entitled him.   He rose at once, and went in front of the altar, where he remained kneeling, in expectation of what the holy priest required of him. Again, the blessed Father paused a little, as if waiting to receive from God that which he was to say; and it was thus that God spoke through him:

He said to the Governor with a celestial grace: "Do you believe that this, which I hold in my unworthy hands, is the Body of Our Lord Jesus Christ, son of the living God, who came from heaven to earth to redeem us all?" The Governor answered: "Yes, I believe it, sir." Again the monk said: "Do you believe that this same Lord is to come to judge the living and the dead, and that upon the good He will bestow glory, and upon the wicked eternal suffering in hell." He answered: "Yes, sir."

At the second answer, the Governor began to fear greatly, and his eyes filled with tears.   For, of a truth, God had touched his heart; then the blessed Father said to him: "If, then, you believe this, which every faithful Christian must believe, how is it that you are the cause of so many soils and sins which we have suffered for five months, because you will not reconcile yourself with your captains, to treat of a remedy for all this people who for your sake have perished, and are perishing, as I have often warned and implored you? If, until now, you have not hearkened unto men, listen to the Son of the Virgin, who speaks to you; and fear that same Son of God who shall judge you.   By this Lord, whom I hold here in my hands, I warn, I beseech, I command you, that you now do that which until now you have not wished to do, and if you do it, by command of the same Lord, I promise you succor for all, before three days have passed; and if you do it not, chastisement as by His hand."

Having thus spoken, he turned to the altar, and having finished the mass, went in and removed the sacred vestments. The Governor rose from the place he had taken at the foot of the altar, when the Blessed Father called him, for he had remained there kneeling, up to this point; and, turning to the people, he said to them with all feeling and gentleness: " Gentlemen, you have seen what Fray Domingo has done, and have heard the strange words he spoke to me. I declare that, if the fault is on my side, God has never willed that I should follow it, nor be the cause of so many evils. Until now, and for the future, for the love of God, I forgive you all, gentlemen, from the bottom of my heart, and I beg you for the love of God that you forgive me the injuries I have done you, and the evils you have suffered for my sake.

" I know that, because of my sins, God has chastised you all, and so, I ask you all, forgiveness, as the aggressor and the guilty one. When he came to these words he could no longer contain his tears.

* * * * *

When Fray Domingo de la Annunciation related this event, thirty years after its occurrence, so fresh had he preserved those tears of the general and his captains, that the blessed old man shed them in abundance, giving thanks to God for His mercies, and moving even my heart, when I heard him. . . .

A number of Friars soon came to convert the natives. With them came gifts for the two courageous monks. Frays Salaçar and Annunciation, in whose hands the small quantity of flour left by the Provincial vicar had not failed for the service of mass, and the comfort of the sick and dying, through all this time—not the least of several miraculous occurrences during De Luna's expedition.

*   *   *   *   *

Brother Domingo (Annunciation) accompanied De Luna in his Florida expedition and exercised the dangerous office of peacemaker. He died at the age of 91. He never failed to observe the fasts of his Order, and, though blind, would rise at midnight to say matins.

CHAPTER LXI.

EVERY Bishop of Mobile was a devoted friend of the
Visitation Order in Mobile. From its superiority in
numbers, Bishop Portier selected Mobile as his residence. He also selected it as the site of the Visitation
Convent, which a good Irish priest of Florida gave
him some means to begin. Bishop Portier was a
gentleman of high culture and fine social qualities.

He had known the Visitandines in Lyons in his
early days. There being a dearth of Catholic schools
for girls in his diocese, he resolved to apply to the
Holy See for full powers to erect a Convent and Academy of the Visitation in his episcopal city, there being
then but one establishment of that Order in America.

Rome accorded him an indult, and he at once wrote
to Most Rev. Archbishop Whitfield, of Baltimore, for
a colony of nuns from the Georgetown Convent. This
worthy prelate promised his co-operation in the good
work. He informed Bishop Portier that there was
then at the Georgetown Visitation a member of the
Order from Fribourg, Switzerland, a lady of much
ability and great experience, Sister Madeleine Augustine D'Arréger, whom he would request to take charge
of the Mobile foundation.

This lady was originally a professed nun of Annecy.
Having consulted her Superiors in Europe, Madame

D'Arréger was left free to accept the Archbishop's offer. Archbishop Whitfield made known his wishes to the community at Georgetown, D. C. All was speedily arranged, and, with Sister Ignatia Miles and Sister Paulina Millard, Choir Sisters, and one Lay Sister and one out-Sister (Tourrière), the little band set out from Georgetown, Nov. 27, 1832, and reached Mobile, Dec. 31, same year. Very soon, Bishop Portier finding his colony too small for the work before them, went to Georgetown for a reinforcement. He obtained several, among them Sister M. Austin Barber, a member of a celebrated family of converts. This lady was gifted with extraordinary ability as a teacher, much of which, as Directress of the Academy, she communicated to those associated with her in the schools, which from the first have been eminently successful.

The early buildings soon became too small for the numbers who flocked to their seminary for no training was deemed so elegant as the exquisite culture given by the Visitation nuns. They are now teaching the children, the grandchildren and even the great-grandchildren of their earlier pupils.

The splendid sites of the College and the Visitation Convent are in the country. The site of the Cathedral, the Orphan girls' Asylum, and, till lately, the Bishop's residence, were on an old Indian graveyard. This with some adjoining property was deeded by the Spanish crown during the administration of Governor Galvez. The Cathedral is an elegant structure among the finest Church buildings in the South.

We shall merely glance at the chief pastors who have ruled the Mobile Church since Bishop Portier's day.

Bishop Quinlan was called the kindest of men. Unfortunately he came in evil days, with the Civil war. When the war was over he wore himself out at the work of restoration. Visiting the Eternal city in the interest of his suffering diocese he caught the Roman fever on the Campagna. He returned to Mobile with spirit broken and health shattered, hoping to be benefited by a sojourn in New Orleans. But he rapidly grew worse, and died a holy death, March 9, 1883. Very Rev. Father O'Callaghan, his V. G., came to New Orleans to return to Mobile with his holy remains. His body lies at the entrance of the Mobile Cathedral according to his dying request. "John, second Bishop of Mobile. Pray for his immortal soul," are his epitaph.

Bishop Manucy of Texas was appointed to succeed him. But his health was wretched and he asked Rome to relieve him of the burden, and closed a holy life by a happy death, Dec. 4, 1885.

After an apostolic life in Maryland, Dr. Jeremiah O'Sullivan was consecrated Bishop of Mobile, Sept. 20, 1885, in Baltimore, where he had been a priest for eighteen years. He was full of zeal and piety, and a marvel of financial ability. He paid off a heavy debt, built churches, established schools, and literally wore himself out in the service of God, dying rather suddenly, August 10, 1896.

The fifth Bishop of Mobile, happily reigning, is Right Rev. Edward Patrick Allen, consecrated in Baltimore, May 16th, 1897. During his episcopate, Religion has made extraordinary progress. The number of priests has greatly increased. Many churches have been built. New schools, hospitals, and charitable institutions have been founded, and several new mis-

sions and parishes established. Right Rev. Dr. Allen
was consecrated by H. E. Cardinal Gibbons, May 16,
1897.

*   *   *   *   *

The Visitation nuns of Mobile found many kind
friends in their troubles of fire and storm, as Messrs.
Beroujon, Walker, Parker, etc. Nor should we omit
the honored name of Major H. C. Semple. Very
Rev. C. T. O'Callaghan has been connected with the
Monastery for thirty years, and the Rev. Fathers of
Spring Hill College have been its warm friends since
its foundation.

24

CHAPTER LXII.

*   *   *   *   *

THE extraordinary indulgence of the Portinucula has been attached to the New Orleans Ursuline chapel since the time of the Capuchine Fathers in the 18th century.

The chapel of Our Lady of Prompt Succor, the seat of an arch-Confraternity, has from early days promoted devotion to Our dear Blessed Mother. Many of the first navigators and explorers were singularly devoted to the Holy Virgin—as Ojeda, the warrior protege of Mary, who, as we have related, carried her picture in his knap-sack. He would often take it out, place it against a tree, kneel before it, and pour forth his devotions to his heavenly Patroness. Associated with him was Coronado, Lord of the golden House. Like his friend, Las Casas, his practice of his religion was his strongest shield in life, and his only comfort in death.

The ladies of Louisiana, mostly pupils of the Ursuline Convent, determined to crown the statue of Our Lady of Prompt Succor and the Divine Child with jewels rich and rare, which they themselves presented to the Mother and the Child. These crowns were made by the Feely Co., gold and silver smiths, Providence R. I., for the statue of Our Lady of Prompt Succor, Ursuline Convent, New Orleans.

Our Blessed Mother's Crown.

The bracelet forming the front of the band, consists of seven alternate rows of solid pure gold beads and turquoises of equal size encased in gold, with a rosette-shaped ornament in the middle, which is also made of gold beads and turquoises. The rest of the band is of solid gold ornamented with large amethysts and opals.

Over this band are two sections of exquisite design and workmanship, each having a star in front and tapering towards the back. The star of the lower section is about two and a quarter inches in diameter, and in each of its six points are three diamonds. The centre is composed of a rosette-shaped ornament consisting of a large diamond, surrounded by eight smaller ones. Between each point are alternate rows of diamonds and rubies to the number of thirty-six. The centre contains nine diamonds.

The rest of the upper section is ornamented with still larger diamonds, amethysts, topazes, rubies, and emeralds, the last mentioned being arranged in shamrock-form, and surmounting all, the star excepted.

CROWN OF THE DIVINE CHILD.

The band is ornamented with diamonds, emeralds, amethysts, topazes, pearls, opals, rubies, sapphires : the second part with rows of diamonds and rubies, and the third, with diamonds, emeralds, rubies, amethysts, sapphires, topazes, pearls, and opals.

The globe and cross form the centre of this section. The globe is ornamented with three rubies and pearls. The cross is ornamented with eight large dia-

monds, and about thirty small rubies and four larger
ones. In the centre is an amethyst surrounded by
eleven small sapphires and one ruby, which, I imagine,
are emblematic of St. Ursula and her eleven thousand
companions, martyrs. The emeralds are done in Sham-
rock form.

As to commercial value, the crowns of the miraculous statue have been estimated at from ten to twelve
thousand dollars. But Our Blessed Mother and her
Divine Son alone can form a just estimate of their real
value, for they alone know the extent of the sacrifices
made by their grateful clients in Louisiana and other
states, in giving up precious family jewels, some of
which were so exquisitely set in the purest gold, that
the makers of the crowns embodied them therein,
without undoing the setting. Some of the jewels were
given by the Sisters, by whom they had been cast
aside on the day of their religious reception.
The small statue of Our Lady of Prompt Succor
venerated in an oratory near the dormitory, is also
adorned with exquisite crowns made of gold and gems.

The Very Rev. Napoleon Joseph Perché who lived
at the Ursuline Convent for many years, as aumonier,
or chaplain, was greatly devoted to Our Lady of
Prompt Succor. His charity knew no bonds. He
went out every day mostly towards evening laden with
medicines and food for the poor. The good nuns who
would do anything for their aumonier, prepared all
he needed for his poor, and slaves were relieved as well
as the free. And while relieving their bodily neces-
sities, he instructed them in the truths of our holy
Faith.

He had a special zeal for attracting infidels and atheists to our holy religion. Many of this class, then so common, he brought into the holy Catholic Church. He once asked a penitent, a rabid infidel and an atheist, to tell him if he ever really believed there is no God. "Never," said the *soi-disant* atheist emphatically. "At times when I was worst I knew in my heart that there was a God, who would one day judge me."

Most Rev. Napoleon Joseph Perché became Archbishop of New Orleans, in 1870, in succession to Archbishop Odin, and died December, 1883.